Manoj Kumar Jena is professor and Chairperson at the Centre for the Study of Social Systems, School of Social Sciences, Jawaharlal Nehru University, New Delhi. His areas of research include sociology of science and technology, digital technology studies, media and cultural studies, social theory, ritual and marginal Studies. Prof. Jena has multiple publications in the form of books, chapters, and articles in Scopus, Web Science and multiple UGC approved peer-reviewed journals. Recently, he has edited a volume titled *Sociology of Covid 19 Pandemic in India: Education, Digital Divide, Work and Wellbeing.* His interviews and lectures have been broadcasted on NPR (National Public Radio) USA, and the CEC- UGC audio-visual live lecture programme.

WAYS OF BEING INDIAN

Essays on Religion, Gender and Culture

Edited by

Manoj Kumar Jena

SPEAKING TIGER

SPEAKING TIGER BOOKS LLP
125A, Ground Floor, Shahpur Jat, near Asiad Village,
New Delhi 110049

First published by Speaking Tiger Books 2024

ISBN: 978-93-5447-836-9
eISBN: 978-93-5447-935-9

10 9 8 7 6 5 4 3 2 1

Typeset in Arno Pro by SÜRYA, New Delhi
Printed at HT Media Ltd, Greater Noida

This book is dedicated to our teacher, Professor Renuka Singh, who is an inspiration for all of us.

CONTENTS

FOREWORD

I am happy to learn that doctoral students of Professor Renuka Singh from the Centre for the Study of Social Systems at JNU, have contributed to a volume being published in her honour. Prof. Singh has been associated with me since the days of her Masters, M.Phil and Ph.D Programmes at the Centre for the Study of Social Systems, Jawaharlal Nehru University, New Delhi. She was also my colleague at the CSSS. All the contributors were Prof. Singh's doctoral students at the CSSS. Singh has been keenly interested in understanding of religion, gender and culture with regard to the inner voice of subjectivity and consciousness.

With a view to quench her quest for the spiritual dimension of the cherished fields of knowledge, Prof. Singh has focused on understanding of the role of myth, ritual, cross-cultural marriage, diaspora etc. in the context of subjugation and oppression of women. Her works, *The Womb of Mind* and *Women Reborn* reflect 'subjectivities' of women, their real and inner thought systems. To understand such deep-seated ways of thinking, Singh has explored a new method and discourse, quite different from the conventional methodological pathways. This, in Singh's view, is a new feminist social praxis. Such an approach is not only interdisciplinary, but is also rooted in phenomenological and ethnomethodological moorings. Singh emphasises on the semblance between theory and ground reality.

The contributors have focused on themes which further reiterate her unconventional but radical departure in sociological imagination. The volume incorporates culturally resonant themes such as status of widows, death rituals, ritualistic practices, spirituality, mythology, women's land rights, violence against women, cross-cultural marriages, masculinities, diaspora, and so on.

I am sure that bringing back culture, subjectivity and consciousness in sociological discourse would inspire the new generation of students and researchers. This volume is an apt testimony of Prof. Renuka Singh's commitment to a 'new form of culturology'. The contributors of this endeavour have further advanced her approach to sociological knowledge and praxis.

K.L. SHARMA
Formerly, Professor of Sociology,
Centre for the Study of Social Systems and Rector, JNU,
Vice Chancellor, Rajasthan University, Jaipur

INTRODUCTION

MANOJ KUMAR JENA

This volume has been conceived as a collection of essays in honour of our teacher and mentor, Professor Renuka Singh, who retired from the Centre for the Study of Social Systems, School of Social Sciences, Jawaharlal Nehru University, New Delhi, where she was part of the faculty for over two decades, and has also been associated with several non-governmental organizations, University of Delhi and University of Oxford. All the contributors here are her former students writing about their major academic concerns, namely, gender, religion, diaspora and culture. Needless to say, that her expertise and poised presence has been an inspiration and beacon of hope for them.

During her academic career, Renuka Singh did pioneering research in understanding the oppression, roles, position and nature of women. In particular, her books *The Womb of Mind* and *Women Reborn* shine a light on the hidden and subterranean levels of women's subjectivity, contrary to conventional ways of only emphasizing the external determinants and dimensions, like economy, polity, education and society. By exploring the subjective dimension in her studies and by developing an appropriate feminist methodology through this, Prof. Singh has discoursed about the internal reality of the mind as reflected in the consciousness of individual social actors, and the meaning they attach to it. Her work has attempted to reduce the gap between social sciences and its practitioners.

In the classroom, she consistently professed the application of self-examination to the creation of a fine balance between culture, personality and society, thus highlighting the fact that humanism should suffuse our criticality. Generation of knowledge, she emphasizes, is fluid and always an ongoing process related to ones' positionality, historicity, and multiplicity of voices/identities. Her courses on gender studies, culture and personality, and youth and identity nurtured her students' mind, instilling in them a passion for freedom, creativity, knowledge and wisdom. She has guided over 25 doctoral students and 45 M.Phil. students during her tenure.

The daunting task of exploring borders, expanding and crossing them in terms of interdisciplinarity and making a clear-cut distinction between religion and spirituality may have invited some criticism from her contemporaries, nevertheless, she did not ever give up her emotional and intellectual commitment to ways of seeing and understanding reality phenomenologically.

Her wide oeuvre spans a variety of genres consisting of empirical works in sociology, Buddhist studies, diaspora, poetry and edited/compiled philosophic works of His Holiness the 14th Dalai Lama. Prof. Singh's works also reveal her engagement with the hegemony of modernity, with its positivism, essentialism, dualism and humanism, and that old fault line in the social sciences, namely, Objectivism vs. Subjectivism, in understanding cultural reality. Through her entire body of work, and through her engagement with science and spirituality, Prof. Singh has tried to develop approaches to emerge out of the post-modernist trap.

By accepting plurality and rejecting the grand narrative of explanation, her work reflects a non-foundationalism as both, an aesthetic and a critical intervention in the discourse about modernity at the micro level. It is not over-determination that counts but multiple modes of meaning-making.

Prof. Singh did not just inculcate her knowledge into the minds of her students, but endeared herself to them with a capacity to always respond to their needs in a sensitive manner. For us, she epitomized the goal of maintaining a transcendental self in human experience without ignoring the world.

About the Book

This volume broadly deals with the themes of religion, gender and culture in the contemporary social order. It further tries to understand the key concerns related to self, myth, caste, ritual, cross-cultural marriage, violence, migration, diaspora, and the COVID crisis, in the context of socio-cultural reality and cultural contradictions. The essays in this volume draw on theory, experiential practice, and research, as well as multidisciplinary approaches. This book presents historical shifts as well as a contemporary overview of the discourses related to culture, gender, and religion. Furthermore, all the essays focus on various new dimensions in the sociologies of religion, gender, and culture.

Nilajana Goswami, in her essay titled *Disciplined Body of the Widows: A Sociological Analysis,* argues that widows are expected to devote their lives to the memory of their husbands and are therefore abandoned. They are expected to renounce luxuries and are expected to withdraw from society. The range of social marginalization consists of changes in diet and attire, restrictions imposed on a widow's remarriage, and strict surveillance of her behaviour. The principal method for the social marginalization of a widow is through turning her body docile through the processes of 'external regulation', 'subjection', and 'transformation'. To determine the status of a widow, society finds it necessary to strip her of her attributes as a woman and to transform her into an asexual being. The present essay explains how society creates docile bodies of the widows of Nabadwip through the propagation of dominant societal norms.

Manoj Kumar Jena, in the essay titled *Death Rituals Rites Among Odia Hindus: An Ethnographic Account,* tries to understand the practice of death ritual rites among Odia Hindus. The first segment of the essay minutely analyzes the socio-anthropological analysis of the death ritual. It argues that death rituals constitute an important component of the socio-religious life of the Odia Hindu community. Death is considered as one of the crucial elements of their belief system—the notion of gift *(pinddaan)* and worshipping the *preta (soul)* and *prita (ancestor)* is very much part of the ancestor worship. The essay provides an ethnographic account of the death ritual rites of Odia Hindus while enquiring on the processes of its integration of everyday life.

In the essay titled *Menstruation and Ritual Symbolism,* Himashree Sarma argues that even though the process of menstruation and associated taboos are considered as constituting a private affair for a woman, the very essence of the process becomes cultural as well as social once there is an external influence exerted for control and conduct. Considering that menstruation is largely understood as polluting, the Kamakhya temple, located in the state of Assam, seems to defy this universal premise by celebrating the process of menstruation of the presiding deity of the temple, who is believed to menstruate every year. This essay describes how the festival *(Ambubachi Mela)* presents a paradox when one tries to understand its processes of legitimation while also considering menstrual taboos as cultural universals in an Assamese society. The essay presents a case study of the festival to understand the sociological meaning of menstruation and how cultural and religious norms govern the production of a social narrative that is highly hegemonic and regulated.

In the essay titled *Building and Sustaining a Spiritual Organisation: A Case Study of Sri Aurobindo,* Ipsita Mitra articulates spirituality from a theoretical perspective as well as 'in practice'. The essay addresses the following questions: What are the characteristics of a spiritual organization? How does a spiritual ideology get translated into socially effective practices to sustain a spiritual idea of development?

The author seeks to describe forms of identity, membership and commitment which exist in the subjective realms of emotions and meanings of its members. Along with this, the objective manifestation of spirituality provides an analytical framework to study how these meanings are produced and infused in the community of believers, and how political, economic, and ideological factors contribute to the formation, functioning, and sustenance of organizations based on spiritual values.

In the essay titled *Exploring the 'Other' in Hindu Mytho-epic Imagination: A Gendered Rereading,* Kamalini Mukherjee engages with popular mythologies from the Indian subcontinent, to establish a gendered analysis of mythological stories that defy modern perceptions of gender, sexuality, and queerness. It argues that the cultural memory of India is deeply entrenched in its Hindu mythological ancestry, it is indeed an imagined connection to the divine, but in its manifest form, the same shared, collective unconscious brings forth an array of cultural behaviours. The everyday experience of morality and acceptability of personhood in Indian society is regulated by its interpretations of mythological texts. The consequence of such interpretative imagination, which percolates through generations, is that the derived or imagined symbols and meanings in society have, over time, projected 'otherness' as an archetype—in gendered contexts, this would indicate the abstract yet marginalized location of the 'queer' folk.

Geetanjali Atri, in the essay titled *Debating Caste and Dera Association in Punjab: Introducing an Alternative Narrative,* posits that Sikhism, theologically, is a religion founded on the promise of egalitarianism. The foundation of Sikhism was thus, laid with a vision of social justice. However, owing to various factors, Nanak's vision of a casteless religious order was compromised. Today, one can find caste-specific cremation grounds, Gurdwaras, marriage venues, etc. in Punjab. Thus, there is a scholarly consensus that the fissures in the promise of social justice have paved the way for the emergence and consolidation of multiple religious subsects in modern-day Punjab. With them is identified the historicity of the modern-day guru-led religious organizations in Punjab, known as the 'deras'. In this context, the essay addresses the debates concerning the historicity of deras and their contemporary forms, with insights from primary observations at a guru-led organization in Punjab.

Anindita Tagore, in the essay titled *Urban Women and Matters of Land: An Analysis of Land Politics in Urban India through Gendered Lens,* tries to map first, the history of land rights within India and how it has addressed the aspect of gender. Second, the essay focuses on mapping the similarities as well as the differences in land ownership in urban and rural contexts. Finally, it highlights the formal and informal barriers for women concerning land ownership in urban India. Given the imperative of securing women's rights to land as India grows and develops, the essay intends to expand the knowledge base within this area, specifically in the context of urban women.

Ellina Samantroy, in the essay titled *Women and Violence in Workplace: Socio-legal Perspective in the Indian Context,* tries to understand the operation of violence and harassment at the workplace. It tries to examine the existing legislative framework tailored for addressing these issues, its alignment with the international labour standards, and finally, the state of its implementation. The essay is largely based on desk review of literature drawn from secondary sources, including review of legislations and international labour standards and also data drawn from labour force surveys (NSSO, PLFS) for estimations on labour market and discussions with various stakeholders.

In the essay titled *Marrying Out: Why Khasi Women Marry non-Khasi Men?* Sarah Sawkmie posits that owing to forces of change (urbanisation, migration, globalisation, and economic development), livelihood issues and illegal influx from across the border, cultural contact between the Khasis and non-Khasis has been increasing rapidly. This is perceived as posing a threat to the Khasi way of life, especially when manifested in cross-cultural marriages between Khasis and non-Khasis, which are deemed as threats to Khasi identity itself. The essay features the narratives of common Khasis on intermarriages. It further tries to understand the contemporary trend of cross-cultural marriages among the Khasis, and also appraise various regional differences in patterns of cross-cultural marriages.

Koyal Verma, in the essay titled *African Diaspora in India: Hybridity, Memory and Human Ecology*, presents a study of the early-century migrations from Africa to India through the Indian Ocean, following permanent human settlements of people of African origin on Indian shores. The essay develops on this definition and particularly focuses on the African diaspora, with regard to religion, culture, identity, and dispersion of community in India. First, it outlines the African identity from a historical perspective, and changes incurred within it. Second, it analyses the migration patterns from Africa to India. Finally, it engages with the discourses and debates concerning religion, migration, and cultural adaptation.

In the essay on *COVID-19 and Its Impact on Women,* Elizabeth Imti tries to understand how the pandemic has not only had catastrophic effects on human development, but at the same time, has led to increase in domestic violence and contributed significantly to the marginalization of women in their homes and communities. It is argued that the COVID-19 pandemic has intensified and increased risks for women and girls. Inadequate health services, weak government programs, along with gender-related violence, have compounded difficulties that women face in their everyday lives, to harrowing degrees.

In the essay titled *Negotiating Masculinities: A Case of Male Sex Workers in Mumbai,* Reenu Ram presents a critical understanding of institutionalized, compulsory heterosexuality while locating male sex workers within this structure. Though male sex workers are male (outer social reality), they cater to male clients and in that capacity, take on the roles as desired by clients in same-sex sexual intercourse. She argues that the lives of male sex workers are characterised by the dialectic of transgression and conformity resulting from conflict, and deriving out of both, masculine and feminine self-representations. It addresses the issue of how male sex workers contest, reproduce and modify masculinity in their everyday interaction with clients, partners, wives, and significant others. There are multiple hierarchies in their expression and negotiation of masculinity.

Mahalingam M., in the essay titled *Juxtaposing the Status and Experience of Indian Women in Colonial and Post-Colonial Malaysia,* captures and compares the status of Indian women in colonial and post-colonial periods in Malaysia. The composition of women of the Indian diaspora in Malaysia draws from diverse backgrounds such as caste, class, religion, and region. During the colonial period they lived in rural as well as urban social milieus, and were subjected to traditional patriarchy under the guise of 'Indian culture'. They were perceived as embodiments of Indian culture and reproducers of Indian ethnicity. Nevertheless, they used their 'agency' and proved themselves in an alien environment and under hostile circumstances. In the post-colonial period, while women of Indian descent have been increasingly participating in various walks of life; this essay addresses the numerous challenges and issues they encounter, principally due to intersectional factors such as race, ethnicity, and gender.

Altogether, this collection of essays presents critical analyses of a wide range of subjects from a sociological perspective. These critical reviews include multiple perspectives consolidating scholarly works pertaining to diverse fields and professions. It reflects on emerging research issues, trends, and contemporary concerns. This volume thus, is an attempt at moving beyond disciplinary boundaries while addressing various contested, contradictory, negated and negotiated questions.

DISCIPLINED BODY OF WIDOWS
A Sociological Analysis

Nilanjana Goswami

Introduction

The widow has always been considered a potentially disruptive element, and this implicit fear has very often been mediated through injunctions regarding their ominous nature. To understand the marginalisation of Hindu widows, it is crucial to understand the way widows are perceived as 'burden', 'inauspicious', and 'sexually dangerous' (Leslie, 1989). Marginalisation of Hindu widows occurs broadly at two levels—social and economic. Social marginalisation takes place in terms of poverty, mortality, and sexual inauspiciousness. The economic marginalisation takes place in terms of property and social security (Giri, 2016; Prasad Eswara, 1995). In this essay I shall discuss social marginalisation of widows and how it transforms them into docile bodies. To understand docility we shall look at the narratives of the widows of Nabadwip.

In contemporary times, with the decline of the Hindu joint family, an increasing number of elderly widows are forced into abject dependence (Vatuk, 1990; Chinnappan, 2015). Widowhood among older people is significant everywhere, from

40 percent in the developed countries and Latin America to 50 percent in Africa and Asia. According to the 1984 Government of India report, widowhood is experienced primarily by older women above sixty years of age, in developing countries, although it affects younger women as well as those with children (Chen, 2000; Chinnapan, 2015). Most societies in India have various rules and norms that regulate the lives of women. These norms have dire impact on the lives of Hindu widows. To understand the vulnerability of Hindu widows in the rural belts of India, I decided to study the discourse around devout elderly widows of the temple town of Nabadwip, West Bengal. Nabadwip is home to Radha and Krishna as well as to disciples of Chaitanya. The place carries historical significance, being the birthplace of Chaitanya and the centre of Vaishnavism in Bengal. The aim of my work is to explore processes which, through religious codes of conduct, discipline and transform widows into docile bodies.

Social marginalisation of Hindu widows in India is determined by social order where the ideal wife is described as 'pativrata'—a wife who has vowed fidelity to her husband in three ways- by serving food, and providing care and children; by observing ritual fasts for his well-being; and by remaining devoted towards her husband for life (Sahoo, 2013; Staal, 1996). The abuse and ill-treatment experienced by widows are inexorably tied to gender inequality in a society where women are produced as dependent subjects. Of her natal house, the woman is a temporary member, a 'burden' till she is married off. Post-marriage, she devolves into secondary membership of her in-law's family. With the death of her husband, her position in the family deteriorates as she often loses out on property rights and in some cases, is subject to sexual harassment (Young, 2006).

The Hindu marriage and kinship rules impinge heavily on the relationship between men and women, with particular focus on the conduct of women. The relationship is based on the idea of purity and an imperative to preserve the purity of women. The virtue of a woman is crucial for maintaining the blood purity of lineages and also the position of the family within the social hierarchy. The idea of purity is closely associated with a perception of honour or prestige (*'izzat'*) (Leslie, 1992). Women, by virtue of being daughters, wives and mothers, are compelled to function as keepers of family honour. Honour aligns the behaviour of an individual woman to the idealized norms of the community. To maintain family honour, the woman is required to exhibit proper conduct (dharma) by following her *'stridharma'* (Patel, 2006). In doing so, she attains the virtues of goodness and truthfulness (*satitva/ sativrat*a) thereby, preserving the honour of her family (Beek, 1988; Bean, 1981). Further, she is expected to perform various rituals and *vrats* (ritual fasting) to ensure her husband's long life. If a woman outlives her husband, she is generally regarded as unprotected and uncontrolled. A widow is hence, expected to lead an ascetic life out of devotion and loyalty to her dead husband. She is expected to acquire this identity through self-control and disciplining (Gilbert, 2001). There are various mechanisms at work to control or restrain her. It includes multiple rules aimed at regulating her sexuality, most of these pertaining to her dress, diet, and general demeanour. Such rules are prescribed to further marginalize a widow and turn her body docile (Lamb, 1997).

Thus, at the very inception of widowhood, many women are rendered socially handicapped. As a widow, the woman is a running threat to the honour of her family and the society at large, and as such, necessitates monitoring. Her husband is no longer around to control her, and there is no acceptable way for her to satisfy her sexual desire (Lamb, 1993). Sexuality of a widow is generally seen as unleashed and unfettered (Chen,

2000:118). Suspicion is not limited to her sexual life: the fact that she outlives her husband produces greater anxiety. The logic that works behind this is 'karmic'. Per karmic philosophy, widows are potentially harmful to others. In some parts of India, especially in certain communities in both, the north and the south, widows are considered to be the 'devourers' of their husbands (Lamb, 2001; Khanna and Price, 1969). Many widows are accused of witchcraft and threatened with death. Widows are thus associated with power, awe, and dread of dying and the dead.

Now, why do villagers associate widows with destructive powers? According to cultural anthropologists, there are two explanations: first, society attributes dangerous powers to widows as a way of labelling them and demarcating their social role and identity. Second, communities often offset guilt felt towards widows or persons of low social standing in society, by arrogating innate destructive qualities to them (Chen, 2000; Thapan, 1995). Some people use these local superstitions against widows to serve their own interest. For instance, they would accuse certain widows of possessing dangerous powers, or accuse them of committing harmful acts in order to ostracise them. Tactics as such often force the widow to leave the village and thus, forfeit rights to her ancestral property.

Therefore, a widower holds a privileged position than a widow. As a widow, a woman not only undergoes pain, but is considered as highly inauspicious. After attaining widowhood, she is expected to perform specific rites and practices. She is laden with the responsibility of preserving the good repute of her late husband's family. In the following section, I shall review some literatures on the idea of the docile body, and how widows of Nabadwip encounter social marginalisation.

Understanding Docility

Imposition of strict dietary rules and fasting is a fundamental step towards marginalisation of widows (Mackenzie, 1996). From this point on, a widow's quotidian life is ruled by various religious rituals. The two most important aspects of these rituals are restrictions on diet and controls on behaviour. These rituals are culturally mediated and aimed at reinforcing patriarchy (Talukdar, 2014; Bell, 1992). The rationale behind the restrictions is disciplining the body of the widow, keeping the body 'cool,' and turning it docile (Anzia, 2007). Foucault's 'panopticon' provides a framework for understanding the ways in which the docile body is produced. Disciplining is effected through rules we agree to live by in communities (Foucault, 1995). In *Discipline and Punish* (1995), Foucault enunciates how social norms work to produce docility. Foucault's innovative work describes how the body is disciplined in 'correctional institute' (Dolezal, 2010: 361). Referring to Bentham's 'panopticon', Foucault describes the organisation of prison cells around a central watchtower, the latter structure being the node of individuated surveillance and psychological control (Foucault, 1995). With surveillance emanating from the watchtower, prisoners' conduct is aligned to institutional parameters, 'as they are conscious of the possible gaze of a judgmental and punishing overseer' (Dolezal, 2010:362). As Foucault writes, 'There is no need for arms, physical violence, material constraints. What is required is just a gaze. An inspecting gaze, a gaze which each individual under its weight will end by interiorizing to the point that he or she is his overseer, each individual thus exercise their surveillance over and against themself' (Foucault, 1995:55). Constant surveillance fosters fear of punishment within the subject, inspiring it to self-regulate.

In an analogous manner, social control, in its various codes of conduct, is 'manifestation of punishment' (Dolzal, 2010: 362) which uses multiple mechanisms to render the social body docile. McNay posits that social control in modern societies substitutes direct repression with more visible strategies of normalization thus, motivating individuals to regulate themselves (McNay, 1994: 97). Foucault describes the body as political. It is through the body, specifically through its disciplining, surveillance, and punishment, in all its microscopic physical actions, that a political order is maintained (Foucault, 1995.) Foucault (1977) identifies this self/body relationship as the foundation of social power. This power is inscribed on individual bodies and is controlled, regulated and disciplined (Davis, 1997). Panoptical surveillance operates through self-discipline where a body becomes docile through various means of control in their gestures, desires and habits (Fraser, 1989 In Shilling, 2016) that are useful for continual reproduction of the system. The body is continuously regulated by social norms and cultural value (Mathur, 2008). For instance, the value of Hindu religious codes of conduct is closely related to disempowerment of women, and widows in particular. Women's plight in the private sphere, and especially of widows, is fundamentally related to traditional notions of femininity. The body of women is considered as 'body of others' (Thapan, 1995: 72). 'Docile bodies' refers to a self-policing collective that has internalised the surveilling gaze (Foucault, 1995). The body of the widow thus becomes docile through external control and internalisation of the constant social gaze. To mark the status of the widow is to reduce her attractiveness as a woman, and transform her into an asexual being (Chen, 2000). Docile bodies are produced as continuation and reproduction of dominant societal systems. Stringent codes of conduct within the household gives elaborate emotive descriptions of the subjection, humiliation and powerlessness of a widow (Giri, 2012).

Tradition dictates that the widow's body must operate within rigid boundaries of supervision and control, that a widow should renunciate worldly desires, and that these conditions need to be produced through constant disciplining. For instance, white cloth and strict dietary restrictions represent socially sanctioned appropriate standards for widows. They make it possible for the body to be self-contained (Patil, 2000; Chen, 2000), and prepares the self of the widow to enter into ties with God (Lamb, 1999). Widows' experiences and their normalised plight provides for empirical knowledge production. These methods of social control and knowledge production have acquired universal dimensions, and exceed spatial particularities. As Bartky argues, 'In a contemporary patriarchal culture, a panoptical male connoisseur resides within the consciousness of most women, they stand perpetually before his gaze and under his judgment' (Bartky, 1984: 34).These standards manifest in the ways that a widow's body functions in the society.

Objectification of women is achieved by turning their desires against an embodied self. This is doubly true for widows who are reproduced as normalised subjects in a way that induces them to externalize their sexuality while at the same time, assuming an embodied identity. The restriction and constraint, the enforced passivity, pain and humiliation, define the context of sex for women. It is undoubtedly true that sexuality, gender and body are at the roots of women's oppression in contemporary India (Mathur, 2008).

From the outset, girls are trained in ways of becoming 'normal' and inculcating that quality as part of their evolving sexual identities. Feminist scholars work with theories of the body to demarcate the difference between a female body and a woman. The notion of a 'real body', reflecting biological determinism, differentiates men and women, and is employed in all societies. These biological units provide basis for production of the culturally mediated category of gender (Das, 1985; Moore, 1998). Cultural production of women's embodied identities deploys the narrative of 'destiny' as a powerful tool for normalization (Heenan, 2002). For widows, their conditions are normalized through the language of 'destiny' and/or 'inevitability.'

The pain experienced by a widow has a positive effect in that, it produces a power that is particular to a marginal identity, and specifically, to a practice that sustains a constant state of self-alienation (Davis, 1997; Myers et al., 1987). It relates to, what is described in Focauldian terminology as the 'pain-pleasure' complex. The emotional violence that women encounter in everyday lives lacks a register pending objective evidence. In any case, prospects of stigmatisation and disruption of family life compels women to keep mum about their emotional plight. Variously, narratives of shame, honour and inevitability enforce a rule of silence on women, especially in matters pertaining to their sexual and emotional lives. Thus, they are subjected to a power that is not only internal, but one that specifically discerns redemption in pain to the extent that it creates a desire for auto-administration of such pain. Power is not always imposed but rather, it 'Seeps into the very grain of individuals, reaches right into their bodies, permeates their gestures, their posture, what they say, how they learn to live and work with other people' (Foucault, 1995: 217).

Data and Method

I am focusing on the bhajan ashrams and various temples and ghats of Nabadwip, West Bengal, where widows find shelter. Nabadwip's identity as the final abode for many widows is most ostensibly determined by its religious profile. The city, now dubbed the 'city of widows,' provides not only spiritual solace, but also offers free food and shelter, addressing the denial of these basic rights to widows within their own homes. Historically renowned as the epicentre of Sanskrit learning, Nabadwip gained prominence during the life and times of Chaitanya Mahaprabhu, who propagated Vaishnavism across the region.

In present times, beyond the temples, Nabadwip is marked by the presence of widows of all ages, populating the streets, ashrams, and temple corridors. Each widow, yearning to follow her husband (to the afterlife), sustains herself by singing hymns and collecting alms in the temple precincts. Some reside in the bhajan ashrams, engaging in prolonged hymn-singing in exchange for three meals a day. Unlike Vrindavan, Nabadwip hosts a single bhajan ashram run by Marwaris, providing widows with rice and lentils for survival in return for their devotional singing.

For these widows, the temple and the bhajan ashram are more than just shelters; they transform into homes. Blunt and Dowling's (2006) perspective on the home as a continual process of creating and understanding dwelling and belonging resonates as widows, abandoned by their families, found new homes in these sacred spaces. Leaving behind their previous lives, they form a collective identity as 'mais' (sisters), sharing their everyday joys, sorrows, dreams, and fears with others of similar fate.

Through shared experiences and emotions, widows in Nabadwip find strength and confidence, crafting their identity within the cultural context of the temple town. They exhibit a 'sense of responsibility' toward one another, reinterpreting their individual selves as a 'cultural production.' Actively participating in the temple town's culture, they visit temples, engage in *sankirtan* (prolonged chanting/singing to the glory of god), perform rituals in ashrams, observe fasts, and collectively cook food. In this shared journey, widows in Nabadwip build connections, finding solace and support in the unique space they create within a scared milieu.

Evidence from the place is illustrative, but not necessarily representative of the whole country's scenario. It ought to be pointed out that while there are stout bodies of research compiled on social marginalisation of widows, the temple towns of West Bengal figure very minimally in those studies. Extant research on temple towns mostly focuses on Vrindavan and Benaras as fields.

With regard to method, in the study I have used observation and in-depth interview method to collect data. I have conducted in-depth interviews of 10 widows for comprehensive analysis of their real life experiences. Analysis is based on the narratives given by the widows of the ashram and those living in the temple corridors. Cases from the ashram and temples were chosen using purposive and snow ball sampling method.

Widows of Nabadwip: Narratives

A long-standing tradition of commencing the ascetic life apropos to widowhood, is by embarking on pilgrimage (Chen, 2000; Bhattacharya, 2008). Widows are found in the bhajan ashram, in the corridors of temples, and on flights of steps leading down to the river (these structures are called 'ghat' in local parlance), often reduced to begging. Most of these widows are ostracized, these places becoming their refuge after the fact (Guha, 1987 In Chen, 2000).

Destitute widows flock to bhajan ashrams and temple corridors because such spaces provide both, material and religious sustenance, and give these women a vocation while redeeming them to marginally respectable standings. I found two bhajan ashrams in Nabadwip called, 'Kangaler Thakurer Annachhatra' and 'Nabadwip Bhajan Ashram'. There used to be one more by the name of 'Manipuri Bhajan Ashram', shut down long time back. Compared to Vrindavan where there are around fifty bhajan ashrams, here there are only two. So a large number of widows and destitute women seek refuge in the temple corridors. Along with the widows, there are also women who live in these spaces because they were either deserted by their husbands or had abandoned homes under various oppressive circumstances.

Kangaler Thakurer Annachatra is run by a monk (popularly called baba) who, while initially a 'shakto' (literally, worshippers of power in a feminine form, focusing on the notion of an original power/Shakti/Devi), later took to the Vaishnav faith. On my maiden visit to the ashram, I found him cooking 'khichuri' (a common subcontinental dish consisting of rice and lentils, prepared in one pot style) in a large wok. On my entry, he greeted me with '*Hare Krishna*' (Krishna be praised) and showed me to a chair, right by his cooking space. Another person present in the room, who I learnt was from Bangladesh, introduced himself as Basudev Bhattacharya. He had been staying in the ashram for a week by the time, along with his wife, two married daughters and their children. Basudev is a retired bank official from Bangladesh, presently committed to religious services for solace. He keeps returning to Kangaler Thakurer Ashram, making monetary contributions each time. This time of the month, he has come to perform 'seva' during 'Kartik' month of the Bengali calendar (in English calendar, October to the first week of November). 'Seva' denotes selfless service. On that day, 'kangalbhojan' (feeding the destitute) was organised at the Ashram with Basudeb's donation. The feast is an entirely vegetarian affair. While interacting with me, the 'babaji' (monk) of Kangaler Thakurer Ashram said, 'We are poor, not as rich as Nabadwip Bhajan Ashram that is run by Marwaris, but we try to provide food to the destitute and widows living in street.' He adds that he cooks one pot of 'khichuri' every day, and survives on alms (popularly known as 'bhikka' in Bengali). It was disheartening to know that despite being government registered, Kangaler Thakurer Annachatra no longer receives any support from the government. It is solely through charity and largesse of patrons and devotees like Basudeb Bhattacharya that this ashram is able to sustain its mass-feeding operations. One late-middle-aged widow, Malati, assists babaji with his daily chores. One day I met her at a ghat where she was buying vegetables. She came up to me and we chatted for a while. During our interaction, Malati said that she is babaji's 'everything.' She does all the work for babaji including handling of finances. Unprompted, she added, 'We occupy separate beds in two different rooms, babaji loves me like a sister and takes care of everything'.

Facing the Kangaler Thakurer Annachatra is the Nabadwip Bhajan Ashram. The latter also runs a tourist inn. However during my visits, I took up lodging in one of the roadside hotels for commuting convenience. The most convenient way for me to visit the ghats, temples and Ashrams was by 'toto' (a three-wheeled passenger plying vehicle). Later, on my extended stay, I hired one of these for exploring the lanes of the city.

On my first visit to Nabadwip Bhajan Ashram, I detected suspicion and veiled hostility from the ashram folks and the few widows who were doing kirtan (they called it '*Radhar naam*').This was a response not entirely unexpected. After sitting there for half an hour simply observing, I met a man who introduced himself as the son of the owner. His name is Arabinda Jha. He asked me what I wanted to know about the widows, definitely presuming that I do not belong to the ranks of the devout. His conviction and curt manner of speaking threw me off but I persisted in trying to impart a more informal air to our interaction, to erase any hostility. Jha reiterated that the institution critically depends on donations from Marwari patrons. He added that Bengalis are not too forthcoming with such donations. The ashram is run by a board of trustees. However, it is not entirely dependent on its Marwari patrons as donations from them account for roughly ten days of operations while the rest of the month is sustained with the ashram's own resources. It also has a branch in Vrindavan. I got the impression of a well oiled corporate machinery striving to fulfil its aim of raking profits. The ashram's political anchoring was apparent from the framed photographs of ministers and some local MLAs adorning the wall of the small office. I had no doubt from my very first visit that this is a place where religion and politics candidly go hand in hand. By the time our interaction was about to chart two hours, Jha's demeanour started getting friendlier. He revealed that his lineage is from Rajasthan, but that his family's residence in Nabadwip traces back to three generations prior. With my regular visits, Jha started opening up and one day, invited me to join the feast. I politely declined as I needed to leave for the day, but promised to return. My visit to Nabadwip Bhajan Aashram twice a day, in the morning and the evening, during the kirtan hours, became a daily affair. Along with bhajan ashrams, some temples also organise daily '*bhajan mandalis*' (singing circles) during the hours of prayers and worship. The service of the 'mais' is entirely ancillary; the principal rituals are performed by male priests with the help of their male assistant. The 'mais' receive a small payment, sometimes in kind, for their basic sustenance. But the little work they do in the temples brings them joy of active participation. Their participation also ensures smooth operation of the temple on a daily basis. They do not consider themselves wage workers but participants in an epiphanic discourse. However, the widows are not allowed to stay in the temple complex after 8 pm. They have to find their place on the streets and sometimes, under the awnings of shops.

On my first visit to the bhajan ashram, I was informed that the *bhajan mandali* would start session at 6 pm. I returned around 5.30 pm and stood beside the door of the *mais'* quarter where they had started assembling. Next morning I returned to find between two hundred to two fifty women gathered in the hall. I had never come across so many widows at a single spot; the enormity of the collection disconcerted me. In the morning, I used to arrive at around 5 am; from about 6 am, the *mais* started queuing outside the gate for their daily alms. Their day starts with a dip in the Ganges, followed by offerings to the deities accompanied by hymns of '*Radheyy Radheyy.*' Some married women join the ranks of kirtan singers in order to supplement their family income, while yet others do so on account of being ousted from their marital homes. In some cases, bitter rivalries emerge between them and the widows.

As the widows gather in the hall, standing in rows, they engage in the rhythmic chanting of Radha Krishna's names for nearly an hour. Some play small cymbals known as 'khanjanis,' while others swing the 'chowri', a fan made from tail hair of *chamri gai* (yak), traditionally used in rituals. Their heads are modestly covered, with some older women sporting shaved heads adorned with 'tulsimala,' a sacred tulsi wood collar, and patterns of white clay on their foreheads, indicative of the Vaishnav way. Some move with a slight stoop due to advanced age, relying on improvised walking sticks for support.

In the temple town, where no stigma is attached to alms seeking, these devout patrons, including widows, actively contribute to the upkeep of the sanctum. They participate in activities such as cleaning, making garlands, grinding sandal blocks, and stitching the deities' attire. Among them is Hemlata, a member of the cleaning staff, who shared that she earns a monthly stipend of a hundred rupees for her services at the Bhajan Ashram. Hemlata diligently saves most of her income, occasionally treating herself to betel leaves and tea from a nearby roadside shop. Additionally, she participates in Radheynaam in exchange for food, and resides in a rented home in Nabadwip.

Two other dedicated workers at the ashram, Sharala Das and Dipa Roy, contribute to its upkeep. Sharala, involved in cleaning, also receives a monthly stipend of a hundred rupees and occasionally, a sari. Despite having her own house nearby, Sharala prefers staying in the ashram. She values the companionship of her fellow worker Dipa, cherishing shared meals and times spent together.

During our conversation, Sharala's granddaughters visit, offering sustenance and urging her to return home. She gently refuses. Despite her family's love, Sharala explains that she prefers staying on at the ashram, emphasizing that she has no issues at home and simply loves the work there.

Dipa, responsible for floral arrangements, hails from Bardhaman and has resided in Nabadwip for long. Having lost her husband and children five years ago, Dipa joined the bhajan ashram for employment. Despite numerous attempts to secure a widows pension, she has not received any support. Remaining reticent about her life, Dipa lives in constant anxiety about the prospect of being expelled by the ashram manager, as the ashram has become her sole refuge.

Some, not many, avail of shelter facilities within the ashram; six rooms are shared by sixteen heads. However, these widows suffer from abject poverty and subsist entirely on alms, and with no other amenities like toilet facilities, electric light, and running water. Most, if not all visiting devotees make some bit of monetary offerings to the deities, sometimes sparing a few coins for the widows to render a particular bhajan. For the elderly widows, these services represent the only way of eking out an existence. During my fieldwork, I found that many of them have been staying in these ashrams for a decade or so. Each of the widows living in the bhajan ashrams renders kirtan twice everyday in four hour shifts. The 'Radheynaam sankirtan' is a round-the-clock undertaking, running for nearly twenty four hour per day. If any of the widows fail to show up, they are denied food and shelter. So they pour in consistently. Widows who do not stay at the ashram do not escape surveillance on that account as their names are regularly registered in daily rolls. The resident mais que up for coupons against which they receive uncooked rice and dal, sometimes topped off with two rupees by the temple assistant. Non-resident widows who participate in the bhajan receive 200 gms of uncooked rice and occasionally, some raw vegetables like potatoes. These coupons are handed out only to those who figure in the temple rolls.

Most resident widows confess that they do not like the quality of the ration received from the ashram. They hence prefer to sell the uncooked rice, consolidate their alms and purchase vegetables collectively with their colleagues, and cook the entire lot together. Some of the widows living in the ashram are not fortunate enough to have lodgings with dedicated cooking facilities. Those who share rooms, pool in their daily sustenance to cook together in a communal pot. Rakhi, Anjali and Urmila share their room in the ashram. According to them, the cooked food in the ashram is near-inedible as it is routinely half-cooked ('*kacha kacha thake, khawa jay na*'). During my visit, I saw them preparing their shared meal. Mukti Das, another resident of the bhajan ashram, elaborates that the widows accumulate the uncooked rice for a couple of weeks before selling it in the market. For lunch, they receive half-cooked rice and vegetable which they further boil and eat.

The owner of the ashram told me that apart from food, the widows and other destitute women are given a sari twice a year. When asked about it in a group discussion, the widows refrained from being too candid in presence of the owner but it seemed to me that they might not be entirely satisfied with two saris a year.

In this context, I would like to recount an incident during one of my visits during the morning arati. I used to observe a woman who from her attire, seemed to be a widow, standing at a distance, watching me, every day. She never joins the widows in the prayer. One day, she comes up to me just as the arati has concluded. Without prompting, she introduces herself as the wife of the co-owner of the bhajan ashram. When asked about her husband, she informs of his demise two years prior. She also adds that she has a daughter studying in Kolkata. I introduce myself as a research scholar, and tell her about my interest in the lives of the widows staying in Nabadwip. From her facial expression I gather that this revelation does not make her happy. Nevertheless, she suggests that I go to Ranaghat, a place near Nabadwip, to witness how widows are brutally oppressed. She further adds, quite confidently, that widows living in this bhajan ashram are all liars. 'They are lobhi (greedy)'. When asked why she feels that way, she says, 'We give the widows rice, but the greedy women living here sell it in the market. We give them ten saris per year and they either sell them in the market or pass them to their family. So to check that, we have made a rule that every one of them should wear the saris they receive, on the very next day'. She adds that the widows are not diligent in their prayers and fuss incessantly.

The banter of the woman shook me. It was a stark realization of how abjectly dependent these widows are on the largesse of the bhajan ashrams and the temple employees. I realize that these apparently philanthropic activities are bereft of any genuine sense of benevolence. A brute, coercive religious structure continues to dominate and guide their existence. The resident widows are under constant surveillance. Even a few minutes of delay in turning up for their kirtan duties earns them strict rebuke from the manager of the ashram. Neither are the non-resident widows, who are otherwise dependent on the ashram for sustenance, exempt from surveillance. The manager denies coupons for food to the widows whose names are not in the list. So there is constant surveillance and control of widows and destitute women for 300 grams of rice that they receive in lieu of their services. I will recount another incident: one day while I was conversing with the manger, a woman came and asked for fifty rupees that she could not receive two days back on account of being absent. The manager retorted harshly, 'Has your husband left anything for you?'At this, the widow silently turned away to take her place among the singers. On being asked, the manager explained, 'We have received some monetary donation, and we decided to distribute it among the widows who are enlisted in the ashram list. But this widow is showing up after two days, for the money, is it possible to give it to her now?' But where are her fifty rupees, I asked. Without hesitation the manager replied, 'We have used it on their food'. I gathered that this was not an exception but a norm. Unfortunately, the widows keep silent, blaming their own sins for their suffering. Their sin is evidenced by the loss of a husband.

The infrastructure of the temple town makes no provision for the homeless. Mostly, the non-resident widows jointly rent a small dwelling near the ghat or the market thereafter, sharing their utensils and an oven. Begging fetches around fifteen hundred rupees a month, which they feel is enough to survive. Kerosene for the oven comes for five hundred, fan usage costs a hundred and fifty rupees, and rent takes away another eight hundred. These expenses are shared among three or four widows staying together. Shefali, who once used to beg near Sevasadan says, 'I used to earn enough for my living.' Her house rent is three hundred rupees, and she purchases cooking gas at the rate of two fifty rupees per four litres. However, after sustaining a leg injury which left the limb deformed, she started staying at the ashram. Gunjari, a beggar near the ghat, narrated a similar story, about how she subsists by begging near the ghat and for survival, depends on the ashram.

Thus, the bhajan ashram emerges as a space of garnering *punya* (spiritual credit), manifested in the practice of charity by the wealthy. Along with bhajan ashrams, temple corridors are the common refuge for those who have nowhere else to go. People living in temple corridors earn their livelihood through 'madhukari' or alm seeking. The essence of madhukari lies in staying content with basic necessities.

Each of these widows that I met at the ashram, the temple and the ghats, had individual tales to narrate. Some are victims of the partition. Others, unable to withstand neglect from their children and other members of their families, have either left home or has been pushed out. Some eloped to Nabadwip during their youth, only to be abandoned by their partners. Some, upon losing their life savings which they had deposited with their *gurus* in trust, were pushed into poverty. Thus, financial uncertainty adds substantially to their plight. Most of them receive not even a hint of medical care from the ashram and temples. They are not even sure who might perform the last rites should any of them die.

Each of the widows suppressed a profound sense of having been wronged by their husbands, sons and daughters-in-law.

Most of them maintain a dignified silence about the hurt they carry along. Quite often, they express the sense that it is better to be on one's own than to endure insults and neglect. It seems that the widows are completely absorbed and assimilated into the system, but their individual stories indicate rupture as well continuity. However, widows do not always succumb to oppression. Instead, they devise coping strategies to deal with the situation and emerge on top of it. As Foucault posits, power and resistance go hand in hand. Whenever there is a power relationship, there is a possibility of resistance (Foucault, 1995).

Conclusion

The examination of resistance amid social oppression, particularly experienced by widows, reveals the nuanced nature of individual responses. While such resistance marks the initial steps toward transformative practices for overall societal change, it is imperative to recognize that individual efforts are not enough to effectively counter the disciplining power ingrained in pervasive oppression. Instead, these acts of resistance foster micro-empowerment by weakening processes of victimization. As highlighted by Moore (1998), the dynamics of women's resistance are shaped by subjective factors, including caste, region/spatiality, socio-economic status, and education. The fluid and diverse nature of these determinants emphasize the need for a nuanced understanding of resistance, as women navigate different subject positions, either accepting them, denying them outright, or manipulating situations through apparent acceptance while concurrently offering resistance (Thapan, 1995).

Acknowldegment: I would like to thank Prof. Ulrich Oberdiek, Prof. Renuka Singh and Prof. Mans Broo for their valuable comments and detailed discussions on the topic.

References

Anzia, L. (2007, November Monday). Nothing to go back to: The fate of the widows of Vrindavan, India. *Times of India*, 1-4.

Bean, S. S. (1981). Towards a semiotics of purity and pollution in India. *American Ethnologist*, 575-95.

Beek, W. E. A. van (Ed.). (1988). *The quest for purity: Dynamics of Puritan movements*. (Religion and Society No. 26). Berlin.

Bhattacharya, M. (2008). *In Radha's name: Widows and other women in Brindaban*. New Delhi: Tulika Books.

Bell, C. (1992). *Ritual theory, ritual practice*. New York.

Blunt, A., & Dowling, R. (2006). *Home*. London: Routledge.

Chen, M. A. (2000). *Perpetual mourning: Widowhood in rural India*. New Delhi: Oxford University.

Chinnappan, A. (2015). Elderly widows living alone: Is it a case of desertion, retraction, or locating space? *Indian Journal of Gerontology*, 294-306.

Davis, K. (1997). *Embodied Practices: Feminist perspectives on the body*. London: Sage.

Das, V. (1985). Paradigms of body symbolism. In: *Indian religion*, 180-207.

Dubois, J. A. (2000). *Hindu manners, customs and ceremonies* (3rd ed.). New Delhi.

Dolezal, L. (2010). The (In)visible body: Feminism, Phenomenology, and the case of cosmetic surgery. *Hypatia*, 25(2), 357-375.

Foucault, M. (1995). Docile Bodies. In *Discipline and Punish: The birth of the Prison* (pp. 135-169). United States of America: Second Vintage books edition.

Gilbert, S. (2001). Widow. *Critical Inquiry*, 27(4), 559-579.

Giri, D. V. (2012). *Living Death: Trauma of widowhood in India*. New Delhi: Gyan.

Giri, D. V., Khanna, M., & Bhandari, D. M. (2016). Status of widows of Vrindavan and Varanasi. New Delhi: The Guild of Service, Supported by National Commission for Women.

Khanna, R., & Price, J. (1994). Female Sexuality, Regulation and Resistance. *Focus on Gender*, 2(2), 29-34.

Lamb, S. (1997). *White Saris and Sweet Mangoes: Aging Gender and body in North India.* London: University of California.

Lamb, S. (2001). Being a widow and other life stories: The interplay between the lives and the words. *Anthropology and Humanism, 26*(1), 16-34.

Lamb, S. (1999). Ageing, gender and widowhood: Perspectives from rural West Bengal. *Contribution to Indian Sociology, 33*(3), 541-570.

Leslie, J. (Ed.). (1992). *Roles and rituals for Hindu women.* Delhi.

Mathur, K. (2008). Body as Space, Body as Site: Bodily Integrity and Women's Empowerment in India. *Economic and Political Weekly, 43*(17), 54-63.

McNay, (2004). Agency and experience: Gender as a lived relation. In Adkins, L., & Skeggs, B. (Eds.), *Feminism after Bourdieu.* Delhi.

Moore, H. (1998). 'IS FEMALE TO MALE AS NATURE IS TO CULTURE?': Thoughts on 'Making Gender'. *Social Analysis,* 42(3), 159-163.

Myers, D. A., Burkhauser, R. V., & Holden, K. C. (1987). The transition from wife to widow: The importance of survivor benefits to widows. *The Journal of Risk and Insurance, 752-759.*

Patil, G. D. (2000). *Hindu Widows: A study in deprivation.* New Delhi: Gyan.

Pearson, A. M. (1996). 'Because it gives me peace of mind' Ritual fasts in the religious lives of Hindu women. New York.

Patel, R. (2006). Hindu property Rights in India. *Third World Quarterly, 1255-68.*

Prasad Eswara, K. V. (1995). Social security for destitute widows in Tamilnadu. *Economic and Political Weekly, 794-796.*

Sahoo, D. M. (2013). An Analysis of widowhood in India: A global perspective. *International Journal of Multidisciplinary and Current Research, 2321-3124.*

Schildkrout, E. (2004). Inscribing the Body. *Annual Review of Anthropology,* 33, 319-44.

Shilling, C. (2016). *The Body: A Very Short Introduction.* United Kingdom: Oxford University Press.

Staal, F. (1996). *Ritual and mantras: Rules without meaning.* Delhi.

Talukdar, J. (2014). Rituals and Embodiment: Class Differences in Religious Fasting Practices of Bengali Hindu Women. *Sociological Focus, 47*(3), 141-162.

Thapan, M. (1995). Gender, Body and Everyday Life. *Social Scientist, 23*(7/9), 32-58.

Vatuk, S. (1990). To be a burden on others: Dependency anxiety among the elderly in India. In: Lynch, O. M. (Ed.), *Divine passions: The social construction of emotion in India.* Berkeley, 64-88.

Young, K. (2006). Widows without right: Challenging marginalization and disposition. *Gender and Development, 199-205.*

DEATH RITUALS AMONG ODIA HINDUS
An Ethnographic Account

Manoj Kumar Jena

Introduction

Death and birth constitute the rhythm of our life cycle. Death can be described as the heralding of life; it revitalizes, dis/integrates the social system. Death is deeply embedded within our social, cultural and ritual practices. Rituals of death can have many uses in life and the study of these rites can illuminate much about a culture and a society (Mendelbaum, 1959). Death is an important event and occurrence in everyone's life. As per Hindu belief system, death and birth are integrated in a recurring and revolving process. Death initiates a new beginning and is not an end in itself. Death ritual has always been a vibrant topic for sociologists and anthropologists alike, the world over. Scholars of various fields attempt recovering the embedded meaning attached with death rituals including, the process of grief, mourning ritual and purification among different communities. Death rituals among Hindus are elaborate and incorporate various rituals, rites, gifts and sacrifices. Communities fashion unique responses to death and bereavement. It is an undeniable fact that death rituals have considerable social, psychological and religious significance in human life. Therefore, it is necessary to understand the function, symbolism and significance of ritual in our everyday religious lives.

Death rituals are observed both, privately and publicly, in forms of mourning and *pretakriyas*[1] (soul rituals) among Hindus. The Odia Hindu(OH) community believes in the principle of rebirth and concepts of *karma*[2] and *mukti*[3]. Odisha is a vibrant state replete with cultural and religious diversities. Religious ritual among the Odia Hindu communities is an embedded aspect of their lives. Odisha was established on the basis of linguistic re-organization. The diverse linguistic landscape of the state is represented by the Odia language which is the official language of the state and one of the classical languages of India. In this essay, I have attempted to appraise ritual practices among Odia Hindus through a composite lens of language and religion. Odisha has been home to various faiths, languages and ethnicities since pre-historical times. Each such community has evolved with its distinct legacies, legends and myths. This essay seeks to provide an ethnographic and observational account, to understand death rituals among Odia Hindus. Avoiding any generalisation of practices followed in Odisha, I focus on communities that reside in the coastal parts of Odisha and particularly, in the districts of Bhadrak, Cuttack, Jajpur, and Puri. As per Census 2011, Hindus constitute 93.63% of the population in Odisha. The districts selected for the present study represent dense populations of Odia speaking Hindu populations (Puri 96.83%, Jajpur: 94.44%, Cuttack: 93.65%, Bhadrak: 92.84%[4], except marginal percentage of migrants from other states).

Death Ritual from Sociological and Anthropological Lenses

Death is one of the longest-standing topics of extensive research among various fields of studies. Anthropologists and Sociologists have variously studied and explicated bereavement, death rituals, and their relevance in community lives. According to Sociologist John W. Riley, Jr., 'Death is both inevitable and irreversible. Throughout history death has been universally regarded as an event of social significance, and every known culture had rules and norms for defining death as the ultimate rite de passage, and for dealing with its consequences. Yet during the twentieth century, the phenomenon of death and its social meanings have been transformed, creating unprecedented opportunities for sociological inquiry'[5]. Death rituals are widely considered fundamental practices that ordain and sustain religio-cultural discourses. Anthropologist Edward Tylor, in his celebrated work *Primitive Culture* (1871), describes the emergence of ancestor worship in context of the idea of death and the afterlife as marking a successive phase along an unbroken continuum. Emile Durkheim, in his work, *The Elementary Forms of the Religious Life* (1912), propounds that funeral rites, and other death rituals, strengthen social ties and reinforce the social structure of a group by fostering feelings of togetherness and social solidarity (Durkheim, 1912). For Durkheim, 'spiritual beings' must be understood to mean conscious subjects that have capacities superior to those of ordinary men, which therefore, rightly includes the soul of the dead, genies, and demons as well as deities, properly so-called (Durkheim, 1995: 27). According to Tylor, 'Even waking men in broad daylight sometimes see these human phantoms, in what are called visions or hallucinations. They are further led to believe that the soul does not die with the body, but lives on after quitting it, for although a man may be dead and buried, his phantom-figure continues to appear to the survivors in dreams and visions[6].' Robert Hertz expands on Durkheim's ideas on death and ritual conducts. According to Hertz (2004), 'With the occurrence of death a dismal period begins for the living during which special duties are imposed upon them. Whatever their personal feelings may be, they have to show sorrow for a certain period, change the colour of their clothes and modify the pattern of their usual life. Thus death has a specific meaning for the social consciousness; it is the object of a collective representation'[7]. Hertz (2004) further argues that death is not felt as an instantaneous destruction of an individual's life. It is rather to be seen as a social event, the starting point of a ceremonial process whereby the dead person becomes an ancestor. Death is like an initiation into a social afterlife, making it a kind of rebirth[8]. In death, the soul is supposed to have entered into a realm which while ethereal, is nevertheless marked by distinctions and stations identical to the temporal plane. These diversities hence, invariably reflect in various forms and denominations of ritual practices. Radcliff Brown posits that 'Death rituals are collective expressions of feeling appropriate to the situation. In the common display of emotion, individuals signal their commitment to each other and to the society itself. Ritual functions to affirm the social bond'[9]. Ritual not only reveals social relationships but their very enactment mediates the dynamics of group relations, allowing members to define and redefine their allegiances within the group (Kiong & Schiller).

Death Ritual Among Hindus: A Case of Odia Hindus

Death rituals among Hindus constitute an integral part of socio-religious habitat and settings. These elaborate rituals are embedded in religious principles and reflect Hindu religious imaginations. They involve cosmological interpretations in articulating a socio-cosmic framework of comprehension. They also employ a rich system of symbols in construction of symbolic spaces and the use of symbolically rich libations (Clothey, 2006).

Intricate explanations of death and life are constant fixtures in Hindu scriptures. According to the Bhagavat Gita, 'Birth is sure to happen to that which is dead; death is sure to happen to that which is born. Birth and death are certainly unavoidable. Therefore, you should not grieve over an inevitable matter.'[10] The Gita also includes a rounded description of the human body in life and death, 'The physical body is a combination of the five elements. It is seen by the physical eyes only after the five elements have entered into such combination. After death, the body disintegrates and the five elements go back to their source; it cannot be seen. Therefore, the body can be seen only in the middle state.'[11]

Hindus believe in the notion of *Moksha* that is, liberation from the cycle of rebirth. According to the Bhagvat Gita, *Moksha* is liberation from the bondage of *Samsara,* or the tautology of life and death. *Karma* is the basic principle animating an individual within the cycle of *samsara. Moksha* or escape from this cycle can be achieved through absorption of *Aatmic Gyan* (knowledge of soul/about soul). Veena Das writes, 'Hindu belief and ritual, the lateral and spatial categories provide important symbols for dividing the sacred, cosmic world into two parts: the sacred associated with life and the sacred associated with death. The state of purity is considered appropriate for dealing with the cosmic when it is experienced as integrated with the social. On the other hand, the symbolism of impurity marks off those liminal situations where the paradigm is provided by birth and death, when an individual experiences his social world as separated from the cosmic and has to be brought back to an earlier reality, enabling him to see society and cosmos as an integrated whole' (Das, 1976).

Odia Hindus posit faith in all the routine dualities held in a Hindu way of life such as *papa* (sin)/*punya* (virtue), *atma* (individual soul)/*paramatma* (universal soul) and so on. Lord Jagannatha, who is an avatar of Vishnu/Krishna, is worshipped as the community's principal and representative deity. Heaven is referred to as *Baikunthapura* or the dwelling of *Baikunth* (Vishnu). It is the belief among Odias that liberation from *samasara* would be achieved after attaining *Baikunthapura.*

Death Ritual of Odia Hindus: Practice of *Sudhi Kriyas*

Sudhi Kriya or purification rites among Odias involve extensive activities spread out over twelve days. It includes the *pind dana, preta* and *pitru puja.* It is believed that posthumously, the *atma*(soul) sheds the physical body, moving towards the *Yampura* (city of death) and then onto *Baikunthapura/ Bishnupuri* (abode of Vishnu). The *daana(gift) and pinda dana* (offerings of rice and wheat balls) are fundamental aspects of these rituals. *Daana* (Gift) is considered a significant aspect of everyone's socio-religious life. There is a popular adage among Odias which goes, '*dei thele pai n dei thele padiare godhana charai*' meaning, if you have given something in form of a gift, you will get the return out of it or else, you won't get anything. Upon reaching the *Yampura,* each soul is judged according to its conduct on the temporal plane. It is after this penultimate reckoning that the soul gains a pass to attain the *Baikunthpura.* Practices focussed on penance and spiritual purification include fasting and performance of various *pujas.* Death rituals among Odia Hindus vary on the basis of age, gender and marital status. It has been observed that simple burial is followed in case of death of child. If a child dies six months before the appearance of milk teeth, or more than ten days after the same, then only the parents can perform *sudhikriya (purification rites),* within one day. If a child dies after developing of milk teeth and before attaining the age of six years, then the parents are to observe the rites over a period of three days. If the child dies after attaining six years of age then ten days of *sudhikriya* is mandatory for family members and extended kins. Married women are exempted from initial death rituals when someone in their maiden families pass away, as women are considered absorbed within their in-laws' families post-marriage and therefore, inheriting the obligations of those families. The daughters however, gather at their maiden homes on the ninth night to partake in the consumption of the *kasabhata* (ritually cooked rice) and hence, observe the following day as the penultimate day of ascetic diets.

Death is qualitatively bifurcated into *sadharan mrutyu* (natural death) and *akalamrutyu* (unnatural death). The latter kind is largely considered inauspicious, as reflecting some major sin in this life or past, and as a conspicuous impediment to attaining salvation. The *preta (soul)* of one so departed is believed to be lingering on in the temporal plane on account of its unfinished or unsatisfied wills. Specifically, death by accident and suicide are considered ominous for both, the deceased and his/her family. People of Odisha believe that this kind of death brings multiple consequences for the *preta*. These liminal entities, straddling the line between the temporal and the ethereal, are often observed as possessing the living in order to guide their unfulfilled desires to conclusion. Magicians and tantriks are often brought in to perform exorcising rituals. In Odisha, tantriks and medicine men (locally known as *gunia*) have traditional followings mainly as ghost and spirit repellers.

Mourning and Funeral Rites

Funeral rites are important part of the ritual process and represent a kind of communication with the living, the dead and the cosmos. As Van Gennep (1960) posits, 'Funeral rites which incorporate the deceased into the world of the dead are most extensively elaborated and assigned the greatest importance'. The period between the demise of a person and the completion of purification ritual for the soul, constitutes a liminal phase. It is believed to have considerable significance for the entire family, the village, and people who are closely associated with the dead person. The entire family of the departed, those who come in contact of the corpse, are considered as existing in an impure state, and this impurity lingers till the *maarjana* (penultimate purification ritual on the tenth day). Immediately upon the death of a member, the family sends message through the *barika* (messenger) to all their relatives so the rest of the family may enter the mourning phase. Due to ease of communications in current times, the traditional practice of sending a *barika* is on the wane. The *barika* however, is present and assists in performance of various other rituals and rites as per prescribed norms. Traditionally, mourning among Odia Hindus assumes a public dimension. Public outpouring of emotions, crying, weeping and wailing often continues for periods extending up to twelve days. Relatives and friends who join at the time of mourning also manifest public grief. On the matter of display of grief, Radcliff Brown (1964) explains weeping and embracing as collective expressions of sorrow or happiness. He enumerates seven kinds of ceremonial weeping related to initiations, marriages, deaths, friendships, and peace-making. Traditional mourning often gives way to melancholy; as Sigmund Freud propounds in *Mourning and Melancholia*, 'Mourning is regularly the reaction to the loss of a loved person, or to the loss of some abstraction which has taken the place of one, such as one's country, liberty, and ideal, and so on. In some people the same influences produce melancholia instead of mourning and we consequently suspect them of a pathological disposition' (Freud,(1917e [1915]). Gennep posits that 'During the mourning, the living mourners and the deceased constitute a special group, situated between the world of the living and the world of the dead, and how soon living individuals leave that group depends on the closeness of their relationship with the dead person'(Gennep, 1960). Collective mourning also reflects a fundamental aspect of community support. Across civilizations, the culture of collective mourning at the time of death and after death, is an intrinsic aspect of socio-cultural life. Collective as well as individual mourning may, on instances, extend up to a year. Death in a family also affects kinship: consanguineal kin and affinal kin. Death of the head of a house (*murabi*) presents an immediate lacuna and a crisis; somebody from the next of kin has to take up his position as the next *murabi* of the household, taking the final call in matters of decision-making in familial as well as community matters. Odia Hindus are patrilineal communities wherein the *karta* is the male head who leads all rituals and socio-religious undertakings. Men are always the preferred choice for the *murabi* over women. On the eleventh day, in the presence of the village community, the priest ordains the eldest surviving male as the succeeding *murabi* of a household. Analogous practices are followed in most Hindu communities. For instance, the *pagri* ceremony practiced in Punjab, Rajasthan and some parts of UP involve the transfer of responsibilities from a predecessor (deceased) to a successor (living person), in the male lineage.

Astrological Calculation and Its Consequences: *Puskar Kriya*

Discerning the exact time of demise both, on the clock and the calendar, or the closest approximation of the same, is a fundamental requirement for organisation and performance of death rites. Therefore, immediately following a death, astrologers are consulted to pinpoint and record the time of death so as to take out predictions on the future of the family going ahead. Astrological calculations identify a *puskar* (a stage and condition of the deceased as well as family members) within a cosmological framework. It is traditional belief that errors in such calculations may lead to flawed observances and hence, to prolonged periods of plight and misfortune for the family.

A *puskar* has three constituents: *naxetra* (star), *tithi* (cosmological bracket), and *baara* (days). Accordingly, a *puskar* may be *ekpadi* (one leg), *duipadi* (two leg), *and tinipadi* (three leg).

Categories	
1.	Naxetra: Purnabasu, Utarsadah, Krutiaka, Utarphalguni, Purbabhadra and Bisahkah
2.	Tithi: Twuitya, Saptami and Dwadasitithi
3.	Baara: Sanibar (Saturday), Rabibar (Sunday) and Mangalbar (Tuesday).

In *Ekpadi puskar*, there is occurrence of one factor (either naxatra, thithi or days), *dwipadi* is caused by combination of two events, and *thinpadi*, by a combination of all three. Each kind is characterised by different entailing lucks: *naxatrapuskar* will have adverse impact on the *vansa* (family); *tithipuskar* will bear adverse impact on *godhan* (cow wealth); *baarapuskar* will impact agriculture. *Nibaranprakriya,* part of the *puskar shanti karma,* is guided by the priest, and is considered essential for averting possible misfortunes that may have befallen the family from the death of a member.

There are separate prescriptions as well as rituals to offer *dana,* particularly to Brahmins. For *bara puskar,* consisting of Sani, Rabi or Mangalbar (Saturday, Sunday and Tuesday, respectively), the *karta/murabi* has to gift a piece of land to a Brahmin. If it is *thithi puskar* then a cow is to be gifted. For *naxatra puskar*, the *karta* is obliged to offer gold. Rites likes these may also be seen as reflecting the redistribution of wealth in a community. Fear of further loss on the temporal plane inspires such ritual practices. No one barring the *purohit*, *karta* and the *barik*, and on occasions, one person from the village, is allowed to be present at the *puskar shanti* ritual.

Funeral Rites Among Odia Hindus

Ritual practices are guided and differentiated for different gender, age, and relation. The body of the departed is clad in new clothes and food and *gangajal* (water of Holy Ganges) offered to the departed soul. *Gangajal* is considered the eternal source of quenching one's thirst, even after death. As part of collective mourning, the entire village refrains from eating and drinking till the body of the deceased is enroute its final journey. It is believed that if a person consumes any food and water in that particular period, food will turn into raw meat and water into blood. These narratives work to enforce proscription of certain practices during a particular phase of the mourning. During this period, worship of any deity or any other auspicious activities is put on hold. Similar instances are found in Malinowski's study of Trobiander Islanders where 'Even in and around the village where a death has occurred there is the greatest fear of the *mulukuausi* (The mulukuausi are objects of real terror), and at night the natives refuse to go about the village or to enter the surrounding grove and gardens' (Malinowski, 1948).

Saba Yatra: Funeral Procession

After completion of basic rites at home, all family members head towards the cremation grounds. The journey is undertaken under the *Sabayatara bidhi* (rules concerning funeral procession). The corpse is carried on a*kokai* (platform/bedmade of six pieces of bamboo) to the ground which is traditionally situated on river banks. The journey entails scattering of coins, *koudi* (seashells) and *khoi* (parched paddy/fried rice/puffed rice) on the way. The body is covered and adorned with white cloth and flowers and accompanied by constant chants of *'hari nama satya he, ram nam satya he'* (true are the names of Hari and Ram).

Funeral Rituals

Upon reaching the *samashan* (cremation grounds) the *karta* initiates the rites with the selection of a spot for laying down the body. The body is laid along a north-south axis with the head towards the north. This is followed by the *pretasagaya* or the worship of the *preta*(deceased person). The soul headed for the *yamalok* (purgatory) is called *preta*. The third stage involves preparing the pyre (*chitagni*) with specific materials (*samagri*) like sandal wood, basil, and flowers like *palas* and *aswagandha*. Unavailable materials are substituted with prescribed alternatives. Often, those with limited means resort to alternatives and more cost-friendly options. The *chitagni* is an important part of the rite as fire is considered as a consecrating element. Clothey writes, 'Socio-cosmic contract between the realm of the gods and that of human was thought to be maintained through sacrificial ritual system centred on fire. Fire and *agni* are the most important Gods in Vedic ritual principles' (Clothey, 2006). This is succeeded by the *pind dan prakariya* or the ritual feeding/offering of rice to the *preta*. This is followed by the *Mukhagisampanam*, a ritual in which, before dedicating the body to fire, the *karta* calls upon the deceased thrice by their name, and with *Indra*, the *dasadigapal*, *Chandra (Moon)*, *Surya (Sun)*, and ancestors as witness, declares the deceased person as primed for the journey to the next world, and ready for the pyre. After the declaration, the *karta* or the son recites the name and *gotra* (ancient lineage identity) of the deceased, finally offering *mukhagni* or the leading touch of fire to the face. All accompanying individuals pile wood upon the pyre as mark of last tribute. Hindus of all denominations firmly believe the body as constituted by the five elements or the *panchabhuta*: *prithivi* (earth), *akash* (sky), *jal* (water), *vayu* (air) and *agni* (fire). Post-cremation, the remains are placed in an urn and floated in the water, for finally merging with the earth. Some Odia Hindu communities also follow the practice of burial. This is however, the only difference marking these rites, everything else is observed commonly at large. Often, the burial takes place in personal land and near home locations. According to Fred W Clothey, burial is still practiced by certain indigenous communities in India. It probably has roots in an agricultural imaginary in so far as the body, like a seed, is placed in a grave, and eventually, in an urn, possibly awaiting rebirth (Clothey, 2006: 19).

David G Mandelbaum, in his study of the Kotas of the Nilgiri Hills found that the community observes two funeral ceremonies: green funeral and dry funeral. 'Green funeral' takes place shortly after the body is cremated while the 'dry funeral' is held once a year or once in two years, for all deaths that have occurred since celebration of the last dry funeral. The terms are analogy to a cut plant, the memories of which are still green and fresh in mind; at the second instance it is dried out. Mandelbaum further posits that the dual ceremony of the Kotas serve religious as well as social purposes. The religious logic spells that the spirit of the dead person is not ready to depart for the 'Motherland,' the Kota afterworld, until the second funeral has been completed. Only then is the sprit purified enough to reach God. The social reason is that the dead person retains certain attributes of social personality until his second funeral (Mandelbaum,1959). In fact, Taylor also posits that, 'The funeral sacrifices, which in one shape or other are remembered or carried on still in every part of the globe, give us the clearest idea how barbaric religion takes in together the souls of men, animals, and things'[12].

Beginning of Final Rituals: Preta to Pitra

On completion of the funeral rites, the funeral party bathes and returns home where food, usually *dahichuda* (curd and beaten rice) and *chudamudi* (combination of beaten and puffed rice), are served to all before they take leave of the mourning family. Thus begins the first day of the ritual period. Within this period, immediate family members and relatives are considered to be in an impure (*asudhi*) state. As such, they are required not to touch anyone outside the family, or participate in auspicious or religious proceedings. They can neither enter temples nor touch any deity present therein. The *karta* performs *dasaka puja* everyday for the satisfaction of the *preta. Udakasnanatonitakhyar dana vidhi* (beginning rites to every day gift ritual) begins from the first day, continuing to the twelfth. Within that period, the *karta* goes to the cremation grounds to collect the ashes for further ritual purposes. From the fifth to the ninth day, there is continuous performance of the *karmavidhi*. Traditional narrative speaks of this period as one within which the *preta* attains wholeness (from feet to mind). Maurice Bloch and Jonathan Parry (1982) write, 'The Hindu concept of the body (*sharira*) does not entirely correspond with our own, and the real aim of mortuary rites is more specifically the radical destruction of the 'gross' physical body (*sthula sharira*). The limb by limb creation of the new body for the deceased is the central purpose of the ritual sequence of the first ten days after cremation. But the new container for the soul is a 'subtle or ghostly body' (*pretasharira*) of a more refined and less elemental form. What is more, the *pretasharira* appears to be a transitory form which will soon be dissolved or transformed, with the assimilation of the deceased into the category of the ancestors'[13].

Tenth day marks the most complex and rigorous part of the rites. The *karta* wakes before sunrise, cleans the dwelling, and sets off to the river ghat accompanied by a pundit. While performing the ritual, it is essential that the *karta* focuses on the deceased.

Dagdhabhanda/Dagdhahandikarma is a specific kind of ritual performed on the tenth day at the *ghat.* The *karta* prepares this *dagdhahandi* (literally, 'burnt pot', laced with ghee and then burnt). With the flaming pot, he enters into the water while chanting the name of deceased, and then proceeds to the break the pot (dagdhahandi) followed by a dip in the water. This is followed by the barber tending to everyone participating in the ritual. *Karta* and all family members offer *tilotoaanjali* to the *preta.* On returning home, the pundit performs the last purification ceremony followed by distribution of purified water, ghee and honey among all present.

On the eleventh day the *karta* performs the *sraddha* and *preta puja.* These rites are followed by a feast, invitees including relatives, friends, neighbours, and other associates. Late at night, they embark on the *preta bisarjan* or the seeing off of the *preta.* Departure of the departed soul is known as *pretagaman* and is an important part of the ritual.

After this, the *karta,* accompanied by few relatives and friends, carries a *mala handi* (container/pot with food/edibles) and few sundry items like brooms and such, and walks to the end of the village where the contents of the container and the other objects are spread out in the open, and dedicated to the *preta.* The offerings are all dedicated to the name of the *preta.* While the *karta* is away, at home a spot is prepared with sand, a lamp is kept in the middle and covered. Upon return, he cleans up, taps the ceiling, and starts a kind of dialogue. He asks if anybody is up there. In reply, a family member declares that *Brahma, Vishnu* and *Mahesh* are awake. His wife asks where he had been, to which the *Karta* replies, 'pilgrimage'. He is further asked what he has got (from said pilgrimage). 'Happiness in exchange for unhappiness', he replies. At this, the door of the house is opened for him. Upon entry, the *karta* removes the lid upon the lamp and identifies the symbols of animal to confirm the departure of the *preta*.

Jonathan Parry propounds, 'At death the soul becomes a disembodied ghost or *preta,* a marginal state dangerous both to itself and to the survivors. The purpose of the first ten days of ritual is to reconstruct a physical form for this ethereal sprit, though this new form is of less gross kind than the one the deceased had formerly inhabited. Each day a *pinda* (rice ball) is offered in the name of the deceased, each offering reconstituting a specific limb of the body. By the end of the tenth day the body is complete, and on the eleventh day life is breathed into it and it is fed. On the next day a ritual is performed which enables the deceased to rejoin his ancestors. The wandering *preta* becomes an incorporated ancestor (*Pitr*)'[14]. If there is *puskar,* then between the eleventh late night and the twelfth early morning, the priest performs the complex *puskar shanti puja*. It is advised that no one other than the *karta* and the priest stays up during these hours.

Finally, on the twelfth day, the *karta* worships all Gods and ancestors, followed by *pinda daan*. This ritual is called *swapindkarn*. On this day the *preta* becomes *pitr* (ancestor). Ancestors are worshipped for the well-being of the entire family. It can be seen as ritual reciprocity between son and father, *putra* and *pitr*.

Conclusion

Death ritual, including mourning and funeral ceremony, is considered intrinsic to the Hindu belief system, and particularly among Odia Hindus. It is symbolic as well as manifest. Further, it is an expression of collective grief and continuity of a religious tradition. Death inevitably triggers considerations of *karma* (work/remit) and *punya* (virtue). Socio-cultural and religious activities associated with death encompass the family and the community as a whole. Death ceremonies, like other cultural forms, evolve through time and reflect changes in societal, cultural, and psychological environments. Yet, the fundamental psychological and social purposes that are accomplished through funeral rites remain quite similar (Mandelbaum. 1959: 215). Odia Hindu death rituals bear testimony to this fact. Death rituals still occupy an important position in the Odia cultural and religious landscape. For Odia Hindus, the ultimate goal is to attain or reach the *baikunthapura.* In *Baloma; The Spirits of the dead in the Trobriand Islands* (1948), Malinowski posits that among the natives of Kiriwana, death is the starting point of two series of events which run almost independently of each other. The soul (baloma or balom) leaves the body and goes to another world, there to lead a shadowy existence. The members of the community mourn for the deceased, but also celebrate the passing of the soul to the afterworld with community feasts. Worshiping the dead is common phenomena among Odia Hindus. Annual worship and offerings to the soul of the father and other ancestors, on the death anniversary of the former, is still practiced widely among Odia Hindus. These rites include performance of *dana* (gift) and *pinda* (offerings to the dead).

References

Blochm M & Parry J. (ed). (1982). *Death and the regeneration of life.* New York: Cambridge University Press.

ClotheyF,W.(2006). *Religion in India: A Historical Introduction.* London: Routledge

Das, V. (1976). The uses of liminality: society and cosmos in Hinduism, *Contribution to Indian Sociology,* Vol.10, No 2.

Freud, S. (1917e [1915]). Mourning and melancholia, On freud's 'Mourning and Melancholia' Edited by Leticia GlocerFiorini, Thierry Bokanowski, Sergio Lewkowicz (2009) Karnac Books London.

Gennep A.V. (1960). *The Rites of Passage.* London: Routledge.

Hertz, R. (2004). *Death and the right hand.* Oxon :Routledge.

Hubert, H & Mauss, M. (1964). *Sacrifice: Its Nature and Functions.* Chicago: University of Chicago Press,

Levi Strauss, C. (1963). *Structural Anthropology*: Volume I and II. USA: Basic Book,

Levi-Strauss, C. (1978). *Myth and Meaning.* London: Routledge.

Malinowski, B. (1948), *Magic, Science and Religion and Other Essays.* Glencoe, Ilunois: The Free Pres.,

Mandelbaum, David. G. (1959). Social Uses of Funeral Rites, Feifel, Herman (ed). *The Meaning of Death,* New York: The Blakiston Division, McGraw Hill Book Company.

Mauss, M. (2001). *A General Theory of Magic.* London: Routledge

Turner, V. (2017). *The Ritual Process: Structure and Anti-Structure.* New York: Routledge

MENSTRUATION AND RITUAL SYMBOLISM

Himashree Sarma

Introduction

Religion has always presented us with the idea of duality, the most prominent being that of *sacred* and *profane*. This opposition has become a yardstick for a society where religion sets prescribed rules of conduct in terms of what is allowed and what is not. One such process which has a seemingly dual nature, but taboo being the dominant view with respect to religion and society, is menstruation. The female body has been political for a long time. And this is predominantly true for what is popularly known as *periods.* Even though menstrual taboos have constructed menstruation as a private affair, it acquires a political dimension once there is an outside influence exerted for control and conduct. Menstruation is not to be understood simply as a biological phenomenon, but rather as an experiential process that women feel within a social context. In a society where heterosexuality is the prescribed standard for women, a girl's first periods mark her as a sexual object capable of reproducing, differentiating her from boys. Many girls report feeling sexualized and ambivalent about their bodies after their first periods, often evoking a sense of disgust in both men and women and considering it a stigma that should be hidden[1].

Menstruation is a biological function of the female body. But interestingly, a lot of socio-cultural ideologies of pollution and social stigma are associated with this regular physiological process which bears a fundamental impact on the health of a woman. This stigma has developed not only due to traditional beliefs and ideas of impurity, but also because of the conditioning in girls to refrain from publicly discussing the topic. Although there is no concrete history of how stigmatization has developed over centuries, mythology presents us with several narratives which allow exploration of possible meanings behind the prevailing attitude towards this phenomenon. Even though we are aware that menstruation is a natural phenomenon, what counts as menstruation is a social construct, where the biological and cultural interpretations of the process have become inseparable.

Despite menstruation being closely related to and identified as a polluting process, a temple located in the state of Assam seems to defy this universal premise by celebrating the process of menstruation of the presiding deity of the temple who is believed to menstruate every year. Considered as one of the fifty-one *sāktipitha*[2], and located in the city of Guwahati, the Kamakhya temple celebrates a *bleeding goddess* in one of its annual festivals known as *Ambubachi Mela*.

The term *Ambubachi* is Japanese in origin, tracing its meaning to an old agricultural idea. The word *Ambu* means water, and *vācī* means flow. *Ambubachi* or *Ambuvācī*, or the Assamese term *Ambubosi*, literally means issuing forth of water, referring to the rains expected during this month that is the monsoon season that makes the earth fertile and ready for procreation[3].

The festival seems to contradict the pre-dominant ideology of purity and pollution when observed at a superficial level, and is one of the main festivals of the temple celebrating the annual menstrual cycle of Goddess Sākti who is the consort of Lord Shiva. It presents a paradox when one tries to understand its processes of legitimation while also considering menstrual taboos as culturally universal in an Assamese society.

Any popular narrative of a menstruating Assamese woman will reveal her status as an isolated being on whom social control is asserted in the names of beliefs and traditions. The festival of Ambubachi Mela speaks volumes about the dual nature of this process where centuries of reverence and devotional energy of the spiritual shrine of Kamakhya and its festival have been nurtured by its devotees through faith and inner power. To understand this better, a case study was conducted to bring to light the sociological meaning of menstruation in the form of celebration and taboo in the life of an Assamese woman, and the strategies employed by them to identify themselves in two distinct spaces. Menstruation in Assamese culture is highly hegemonic and its expression in everyday space has gained momentum through the use of euphemisms.

Context of the Temple

The Kamakhya Temple is located in the Nilachal hills, in the city of Guwahati, between 91°42'20'E and 26°10'0'N, approximately at an altitude of 293m from the sea level. The temple witnesses lakhs of devotees throughout the year and even more around the month of June. It is a renowned pilgrimage site for people. One of the interesting facts about the temple is that it does not have an idol or image of a deity. Ma Kamakhya is worshipped in the form of a *yoni*[4] (womb) which is located in the *garbhagriha*[5] (sanctum sanctorum) of the temple. This is also one of the reasons why Kamakhya temple is considered to be one of the most sacred *sāktipītha* (seat of power) in the world. The yoni which is placed inside the inner cave of the temple known as *Manobhaba Guha*, is understood as a symbol of pleasure and reproduction from where life originates, indicating the sexually attractive form of the Goddess (Deka, 2004). While there are several narratives and legends related to the temple, one of the most popular one states that it was Sati's yoni[6] which fell in this particular place giving rise to the birth of this yoni temple. Kamakhya is also believed to be present here in her ten manifestations which are collectively known as *Dus Mahavidyas*[7]. All the ten forms exist within the temple premises with their individual significance and respective practices. Together, they are considered to be the ten great Mother Goddesses of Wisdom, a template integral to Tantric practices.

The celebration of Ambubachi Mela in the temple is an event of harmony between the reproductive female body and the cycles of nature[8]. During the initial three days of the cycle, the temple, which is open to all devotees throughout the year prohibits their entry into its premises. This phase implies that the goddess should be resting and hence, should avoid any contact with her devotees since she is believed to be ritually unclean. Only the local priests are allowed entry inside the temple premises to perform a small daily ritual of lighting a clay lamp and incense sticks. Although the temple forbids entry inside the main *pithasthana* and the premises, devotees and visitors are allowed to assemble in the outside complex of the main temple so that they can stay within the vicinity of the menstruating goddess as this proximity is considered to be auspicious. Reading of any religious scriptures is also forbidden during this time. Devotees and followers who partake in the celebration of fertility and menstruation also abide by the prohibitions on temple entry and performance of any religious activities in their respective households. This marks the beginning of *Amoti Suwa*[9].

During these initial three days when the temple doors are closed, most ascetics who come to be near the bleeding goddess are variously found in states of trance, channelling her great power, conducting ritualistic *yagna* outside the temple, singing songs/hymns, or sitting in a state of meditation until it is time for the doors to open for public. The devotees seek Ma Kamakhya in her purest and truest form during this phase. Interestingly, even though the temple celebrates the goddess's menstrual cycle representing fertility, no menstruating woman is allowed inside the temple throughout the year. While sadhus and sannyasins visit the place to connect with transcendental reality, devotees arrive to seek the blessings of the caring mother Kamakhya[10]. Upon reopening the temple, the cloth that covers the deity during the three days of sequester, is distributed as *prasad* among the devotees. Known as *angavastra,* this article is believed to be the blood-stained cloth of the goddess which ushers fertility into every household, and even a tiny piece of the cloth or a thread, is considered to be imbued with her blessings.

Theoretical Understanding

From an anthropological perspective, the starting premise of religion concerning human cultures is the absence of a single word that can designate a set including a host of elements such as moral imperatives, rituals, prescribed forms of behaviour, supernatural agents, taboos and a gradual building of a community around all of this. Some assume that people develop categories and define them in their world to create a reality that enables manifestations of specific norms and transactions to occur. Thus, the concept of 'religion' becomes a coherent term that is similar to 'economy' which places certain key features within its ambit (Boyer, 2013).

- The acceptance and display of behaviour and thoughts of imagined agents such as mythical heroes, fictional characters, deceased beings, and superhuman agents with standard mental processes such as spirits, gods, ancestors, etc., as universal and evolved cognitive dispositions (Boyer, 1992, 2001)
- Such thoughts and behaviour are communicated and transmitted through 'attractors' of cultural transmission (Sperber, 1996)
- Fostering of such transmission through institutions that standardize, codify and 'brand' a particular version of tradition and promote ideas of being exclusive and unique.

Thus, religion becomes a special domain that is ideological, and creates large, corporation-like establishments which promote a special service corresponding to a special institution. From the perspectives of various scholars across disciplines, it appears as a central force that mobilizes and motivates individuals through the idea of faith that has been embedded in its understanding. Sociology of religion discusses sacredness as presented in the functionalist perspective, and processes that influence spiritual beliefs and rituals through the process of social construction. It is a systematic and scientific study of ways in which culture, society, and personality influence religion, its origin, practices, doctrines, leadership, and the groups that express it. It is also a study of ways in which religion affects society, personality, and culture, as well as the various social processes of change and conservation that comes into play along with normative structures and personality[11]. Analysis of culture in context of religion and society attaches critical value to rituals. This is apparent throughout the works of cultural anthropologists like

Marshal Sahlins, Edmund Leach, Clifford Geertz, and Victor Turner, all presenting cross-disciplinary analyses of rituals. Functionalism emphasizes the idea of religion as part of a complex social system and not as something irrational that has developed to connect aspects of society for survival and maintaining its equilibrium.

Works of the three classical theorists of religion- Marx, Weber, and Durkheim- are the ones that have optimally influenced the interpretation of religion in sociology. Although neither of them was particularly religious, they were nevertheless interested in the influence of religion and spirituality on people and society. In most societies, such beliefs are associated with the subjective well-being of an individual wherein life satisfaction, happiness, and protection from the fear of the unknown feed the minds of those seeking existential security. Spirituality is an experiential and subjective state that overlaps theology and belongs to the area of religion in terms of reproducing, guiding, and incorporating forms of rules and regulations, making it an indispensable part of human life.

The concepts of sacred and profane (Durkheim, 1912) represent a system of binary opposites that lays down the procedures for what is culturally allowed and what is not. This is not limited to a particular sphere of life, but extends to the overall organization of various elements that constitute society. For Durkheim, the understanding of sacred and profane is not to state that something is good or bad, for anything which is considered sacred can either be good or evil. And that which is considered profane, can also be in the same parameter. In context of societal prohibitions, a menstruating woman presents the inherent profanity of her physical and social self during her phase of menstruation. Her representation shifts from her everyday identity for these few days, and her presence or participation in any auspicious event spells taboo.

By the nineteenth century, most primitive religions were characterized by two peculiar features which separated them from the great religions of the world. One, being propelled by fear, and the other, an inextricable confusion between defilement and hygiene (Douglas, 1966). Even though there is no definite timeline to trace the origins of the concepts of purity and impurity, these are sensitive to change. The impulse which established the rules remains responsible for their continued existence and imposition. While the idea of sacred has a very particular meaning, in some primitive cultures, it also carries a general meaning which extends beyond prohibition, thus dividing the universe into two distinct dichotomies- things, ideas, and actions that are restrictive and non-restrictive. Sacred rules are therefore, merely rules that are hedging off divinity, and impurity signifies danger due to contact with divinity (Douglas, 1966). The Hindu ideas of pollution can sometimes be quite relative and vary according to context due to the fluidity of a social milieu that is dynamic and complex. Hence, the ideas of purity and impurity cannot be strictly understood as opposites. What is considered to be clean in one context may be considered unclean in a different one and vice-versa. Thus, pollution itself becomes a complex algebra that defines its significance according to the variables in each context, and menstruation represents one such variable. Even though menstrual blood is viewed as being inherently polluting, the process of menstruation is considered to be a celebration in certain cultures, symbolizing an inherent characteristic of the female form. While *menarche*[12] marks a sacred 'rite of passage' (Turner, 1969) for a woman, the social and religious construction of the process makes it appear profane and polluting. Menstrual rituals in Assam are quite predominant in nature and vary amongst a wide range of communities and ethnic groups present in the state. The starting point of understanding menstruation in an Assamese society is through euphemisms that are hegemonic and patriarchal, and perpetuate the process of constructing women as carriers of something impure, and ones who are responsible for maintaining its modesty.

It is interesting to note that menstruation related taboos are not considered negative or discriminatory in an Assamese society. They are rather seen as general rules of conduct as is applicable for any other social process existing in their culture like marriage, pregnancy, family, kinship, etc. The menstrual rules are however quite detailed and restrictive, which not only restrict movement, but also extend to other activities of eating, dressing, cooking, sleeping etc. It is also believed that a shadow cast by a menstruating woman on a tulsi plant leads to the death of that plant. Puberty, in the life of an Assamese woman, is marked as a celebration. Thus, menarche becomes a rite of passage for an Assamese girl whose transition to a woman marks an important stage of her life.

The understanding of menstruation and menstrual fluid plays a crucial role in the everyday life of an Assamese woman. It is not just the menstrual blood that is considered to be polluting, but also the body of a menstruating woman, which leads to social exclusion. Sacredness implies reverence as well as fear and mystery. In the context of the temple, its sanctity reflects in the celebration of the menstrual cycle of the goddess and menarche of an Assamese woman who has reached puberty. It is appropriate to assume that the period of seclusion observed during the annual menstrual cycle of the goddess is imposed on her believers and devotees in the form of prohibition on entering the temple premises. Hence, the restrictions enforced are not on the goddess but on the external environment, preventing any outside contact with her. Menstruation is thus seen as a process that is valued and celebrated as divine while at the same time, imparting a symbolic ambiguity to the position of a woman in this discourse of purity and pollution (Deka, 2020).

The discourse of menstruation, although largely debated and contested in various anthropological and women's study circles (Buckley, Gottlieb, Strassman, Douglas, Bobel, Foster), has not received due attention in academic discourse. Menstruation has been treated as a conventional stigma developed through the ages by social conditioning. Despite being a routine biological process of the female body, it has extraordinary significance for various cultures and societies. It is a process which is as old as the human race itself, and has received cross-functional attention from various disciplines. According to Buckley and Gottlieb (1988), 'The symbolic power so often attributed to menstrual blood and the exotic stringency of rules applied to menstruating women have placed it in the foreground of anthropological studies of taboo and more recently symbolic pollution'[13]. Menstruation and the meaning of menstrual taboos as a topic, have mostly focused on the attitudes of mainstream culture in the popular domain. These taboos are transcultural in nature, represented along a continuum ranging from mild uneasiness and distrust of menstrual fluid and menstruating women, to elaborate complexes of restrictions, and ultimately, to complete seclusion during the menstrual period. However, the restrictions are not universal; some societies are observed as completely casual about menstruation and impose no taboos (Montgomery, 1974). There have been various attempts to explain and understand the origin of taboos associated with menstruation, which are not mythological. Even though most studies focus on the biological and observe the potentially harmful effects of menstrual fluid as precipitator of taboos, some focus on the shared psychological experiences that have developed through various childhood experiences.

Menstruation is not just a subject for discussion in sociology or anthropology, but the additional impact on the health of women has made it an issue of burning concern for many theorists who are largely influenced by the age-old beliefs and customs that the process represents. Hence, social constructionism is an important perspective that emerges in any discussion of this biological process. Cultural dominance of menstruation, in most societies, is largely sustained through folklore, contemporary legends, mythologies, etc., all of which carry narratives of cultures from the past to the present. The shift of folklore studies from antiquities and curiosities to its presence in everyday life adds value to the belief systems of the society. Although the field of critical menstrual studies has started gaining momentum, years of inadequate attention on the topic has not only led to a knowledge gap, but also augmented the powers of misogyny and stigma in suppressing production of knowledge on the topic. For most feminist theorists, the body is a unit that is shaped socially and colonized (Brown & Gershon, 2017). The dominant impression of an individual's body labels it either as valuable (heterosexuality) or abject (homosexuality). Butler argues that gender is not a cultural overlay or construct imposed on given sex (or body). Such a view is problematic since gender so conceived absorbs and displaces sex. In contrast, Butler maintains that the concept of sex is itself problematic. Sex is not a pre-given object but an ideal construct that is forcibly materialized over time. It is a regulatory/cultural norm governing the materialization of bodies over time (Butler, 1993, p. 1). Turner (1984) argues that since governing the body is basically regulating one's sexuality, therefore, this regulation is mostly directed at female sexuality within a patriarchal structure.

Across histories and cultures, menstrual blood has always been considered to be poisonous as well as imbued with magical powers. Therefore, menstrual rules were invented to regulate a woman's body and her movement. Her bodily discharge during this phase has been culturally constructed as disgusting, which is a feeling inculcated and internalized by women themselves, who are compelled to acquiesce to the fear and shame attached with menstruation. Interpreting the female body as ritually unclean, contaminated and corrupted, as opposed to a male body which is not symbolically marked with such attributes, eventually leads to a fragmentation of the self and the body for a woman. Since the 1980s, there has been a steady rise in interest and attention towards the 'body' as a subject, and its cultural politics in a post-industrial society. Women's bodies are given meaning within misogynist societies, where everyday experience is negotiated and lived concretely to sustain such a discourse. Their bodies are synonymous with the earth and nature and hence, particular adjectives such as 'flashy', 'earthy', and 'smelly' are used to mark their identity in the society. Men's bodies are associated with the power of knowledge and reason, leading them to imagine their bodies as exempt from such attributes.

Methodology

To capture data and understand the inherent paradox of this process, a field study was conducted using case study method as primary fieldwork tool. A total of 47 case studies were collected comprising of devotees from different age groups, sex, and across geographies, including priests who are associated with the temple, female members from the priests' households, members from the temple management committee, and government officials from the tourism department of the state. For data collection, the study involved face-to-face interviews, one focused group discussion, online interviews, and collected field notes and visual images along with voice recordings. The study was compiled while being mindful of establishing a rapport with each participant who would become a consenting contributor to the study, and share their personal and collective experiences according to respective cultural frame of reference. While participants from the Kamakhya temple and the government officials were chosen through a snowball sampling method, the rest were chosen through random purposive sampling. Since historical narratives of cosmologies and symbols render the cosmos intelligible, the study has used oral narratives shared by participants from the temple to make sense of the existential reality of their space. Story-telling becomes a more practical method of research as well, since it provides a glimpse of the internal dynamics of a particular culture or community, and how such narratives influence the reflexive life-choices of the people of that community, ensuring that the legacies and relevance borne of such narratives are carried across generations.

The case study method helped analyse the complex interactions within daily discourses of menstruation and understand how euphemisms are cemented as cultural norms. It also helps comprehend the processes through which religious symbolism dictates one's personal feelings of shame while reinforcing the mythology of a sacred space. Affirmation by influential religious leaders, whose narratives are absorbed into everyday life, ensures that certain beliefs and practices are normalised in the guise of faith. Faith in any religious belief or practice has to be understood through the perspective of the people in whom the same is deeply embedded and who, in turn, encourage others to equally invest in such beliefs.

Analysis and Conclusion

There is an existential and intentional element in the understanding of religious symbolism that connects ultimate social reality with the quest for salvation. This is a salient feature of all religions. The biological, social, and psychological limitations of life become embodied in religious forms and symbols that give meaning to the chaotic reality of human lives. Following Feuerbach, Marx presents a reductionist and compensatory theory postulating religious symbols as projections of unfulfilled material needs borne by the socio-economic conditions of the society. Menstrual norms in Assam are protected through the various mythological cosmologies related to the process. Since there are no written narratives on the origins of these norms, it is popularly held that Assam being the house of the goddess's yoni makes it binding upon women in that region to abide by menstrual norms. Another possible explanation is that, since the Ambubachi celebrates the menstrual seclusion of the goddess, women of the region are expected to emulate the tradition of isolation during their own menstrual cycles.

Totemism, according to Durkheim (1912), is the most primitive and simple form of religious life. It is a system where individuals of a society are believed to have mystical or kinship ties with a spiritual being represented in the form of an animal, a plant, or an object that serves as the symbol of unity for the group. The yoni at the Kamakhya temple can be viewed as nothing short of a totem in a concrete complex, epitomizing its characteristic of fertility, and uniting its believers, practitioners, and devotees into a single religious life. Its sanctity represents the external form of a totemic principle or God. Since the sanctity derives out of its symbolism, its relationship in society stands at the centre of supremacy, power, and spiritual beliefs.

Bhattacharya (1977) notes that in Hindu culture, the colour red signifies auspiciousness and growth. In the case of menstrual blood, it communicates the positive value of fertility. Religious beliefs have always allied with this power of female potency, maintaining that women are related to the earth and hence, are fundamentally motivated, assertive, and vigilant in their religious practices. In her study of Karimpur village in Uttar Pradesh, Wadley (1975) observes that the concept of *Sākti* (literally, power) is central to an understanding of the sacred as manifested in the form of female energy, irrespective of the deities' status as good or bad. She also suggests that human beings and Hindu deities are bonded together in a mutual relationship of give and take wherein the granting of boons and mercy is conditional to 'appropriate' ritual conduct and services. Hence, she asserts that gods are necessary for humans as humans are necessary to gods. Both Babb and Wadley connect religious symbols to human interaction and ritual conducts, bringing about a sense of essential cohesion. Spirituality and belief in a goddess 'reflect the self-affirmation of the strength of women and encompasses the holistic understanding of nature as the earth or sometimes being the earth itself which is perceived as the body of the goddess'[14]. Such images give spiritual feminists, what is called, a 'model of empowered selfhood,'[15] reinforcing Kakati's (1989) assertion that every woman in Kamarupa[16] is a 'miniature incarnation of the Goddess.'

The power of the goddess comes from her devotees and hence, its current attention can be attributed to a 'feminist spiritual experience' which connects with the energy of the goddess as a source of power. The case of the Ambubachi mela in Kamakhya reiterates this sense for every devotee—male and female alike. The power of fertility drawn from the menstruating goddess is considered sacred and this period is considered to be the most appropriate time to seek her blessings. Since it is believed that her menstrual phase is the time when she is in her nurturing best, as a 'mother,' and as a warrior in defence of her children, blessings obtained during this period are certain to end all sufferings and negativity. A deeper understanding of goddess worship will throw light on its meaning which does not rest on the rejection of the world or replacement of a male god with a female but rather, provides deep affirmation and profound emotional satisfaction and sustenance for believers (both, male and female). Although the myth of Sati critically hinges on the saga of the mutilation of her corpse, the prominence of all the sites representing her divine identity as Sākti lies not just in worshipping the relics, but revering her as a living goddess whose lived experiences become a part of the religious lives of devotees (Ramos, 2017).

Empirically, Ambubachi is understood as a festival. But its usual employment of the word 'mela', meaning 'a fair,' hinders a thorough assessment of the symbols and meanings deriving out of this event. It is important to realize that although the terms 'Ambubachi' and 'mela' are used synonymously, they imply different contexts. Whereas 'Ambubachi' denotes celebration of fertility, 'mela' stands for the external festivities and commercialization (of religion) that capitalize on the increased footfalls at the temple during this time. Appraising the terms festival[17] and fair (mela)[18] from a sociological perspective, it is to be noted that at any point, a festival can be converted into a fair, or merged with the idea of a fair. The opposite however, may not necessarily be possible. It is an accepted fact that the festival of Ambubachi is the celebration of Goddess Kamakhya's menstruation. However, it is also seen as the menstruation of Mother Earth herself, and since Kamakhya is considered to be the seat of creation it has been the focal point for related festivities since ancient times. Ritually, Ambubachi indicates the phase in which the goddess is in her impure state and daily services at the temple stand suspended. When one uses the term Ambubachi Mela, it signifies a longer period which includes the days of both, her pure and impure states.

It is to be noted that Ambubachi marks the ambivalent power of blood as both impure as well as life-giving. As Marglin (1985) states, menstrual blood is both sacred and accursed and can be seen as the epitome of auspiciousness that renders it dangerously impure and tremendously powerful with its characteristics of fertility and creation of new life[19]. Carrying forward Durkheim's understanding, it is important to take note of the shared attention and affirmation of solidarity generated through this festival. Thus, the festival of Ambubachi presents a mood of collective effervescence which creates a shared ecstasy through symbols and rituals. Barthes (1957) articulates the ideological impact of myths which have become embedded in mass communication and popular culture. One of the most important aspects of his analysis is the development of myths through the discourse of dominant bourgeois ideology that eventually leads to their acceptance in a larger group thus, reproducing them as cultural universals.

Durkheim (1912) describes how rituals generate a sense of emotional arousal leading to collective effervescence which is experienced as a heightened awareness of group membership as well as the consciousness of an external force with sacred significance[20]. Since this sacred sentiment is at the centre of a group's ritual attention, these groups are required to come together periodically to engage in rituals and renew a sense of belonging through reaffirmation of the sacred symbols and practices that bind them. Thus, Durkheim's analysis reveals the various mechanisms that help generate the intense collective emotions observed during the festival of Ambubachi.

Menstruation on the other hand, is seen as a fact of life which starts unexpectedly for most, and eventually gets adapted into a series of menstrual management techniques which are devised by women themselves, as per their respective contingencies.

The process is not to be understood as a strict opposition of the sacred and the profane, but as one which manifests in the public-private dichotomous framework. Simply put, what is expressed, is 'public', and what is hidden, constitutes the 'private'. On closer observation however, the Ambubachi Mela portrays a scenario where features of both, public and private manifest simultaneously on a horizontal scale. The process of menstruation of the goddess, which is supposed to be 'secret,' is concealed, hidden, and made 'private' by keeping devotees at bay, along with imposition of similar measures in individual households. The celebration and promotion of the festival which brings all the devotees near the goddess, where they keep waiting outside till the day the temple doors reopen, can be seen as bringing out the 'public' dimension simultaneously. A similar process can be discerned in the context of a menstruating woman, on a vertical scale. Puberty rituals mark a girl's transition into womanhood, which is made public and announced during the celebration of menarche. Once the transition is complete, the monthly cycle becomes a 'private' affair whereby the girl is expected to follow customs and norms appropriate to a menstruating woman, and carefully conceal the process and attending activities under the guise of dignity, fear, shame, and honour. The discomfort surrounding menstrual experiences exists in both, public and private spheres, leading to a social situation where discomfort seems natural, rendering it (menstruation), invisible and subsequently normalising this attitude. The menstrual experience of Assamese women presents a complex interaction of religion and culture, and neither element can be appraised in isolation. Hence, it can be affirmed that menstrual taboos have been established in ways that turn them into a celebration of the Assamese culture itself (Patar, 2019).

Thus, religion and traditional beliefs are embodied in an individual's outlook, attitudes, and emotions, and everyday behaviour is shaped by myriad external constraints which manifest after being internalised by the subjective consciousness of the individual. The social fact of beliefs that venerate the temple of Kamakhya, and the festival of Ambubachi, are therefore, based on social activities commissioned by the collective consciousness of the people and the Assamese community in which it exists.

References

Barthes, R. (1972). *Mythologies* (A. Lavers, Trans.). New York: Hill and Wang.

Beteille, A. (1992). Religion as a Subject for Sociology. *Economic and Political Weekly.* 27(35), 1865-1870

Boyer P (2013) Explaining religious concepts. Lévi- Strauss the brilliant and problematic ancestor, in D Xygalatas & L McCorkle (Eds.) *Mental Culture, Classical Social Theory and the Cognitive Science of Religion.* Durham, UK: Acumen, 164-75

Buckley, Thomas. (1982). Menstruation and the Power of Yurok Women: Methods in Cultural Reconstruction. *American Ethnologist.* 9(1), 47-60.

Buckley, T., & Gottlieb, A. (1988). *Blood Magic: The Anthropology of Menstruation.* University of California Press: Berkeley

Burgess, R.G. (1984). In the Field: An Introduction to Field Research (1st ed.). Routledge: London

Butler, Judith. (1988). Performative Acts and Gender Constitution: An Essay in Phenomenology and Feminist Theory. *Theatre Journal, 40*(4), 519-531.

Butler, Judith. (1999). *Gender Trouble: Feminism and the Subversion of Identity.* New York: Routledge

Deka, A. (2020). Women and Their Bodies: Menstrual Celebrations and Construction of Sexuality in Assam. In R. Kumaramkandath& S. Srivastava (Eds.), *(Hi)Stories of Desire: Sexualities and Culture in Modern India.* Cambridge: Cambridge University Press, 152-170

Dobia, B. (2007). Approaching the Hindu Goddess of Desire. *Feminist Theology. 16*(1), 61–78.

Douglas. Mary. (1966) *Purity and Danger- An Analysis of The Concepts of Pollution and Taboo*. Routledge: London & New York.

Durkheim, Emile (1898). Incest: The nature and origin of the taboo. Stuart, New York: 48-70.

Durkheim, Emile. (1912). *The Elementary Forms of Religious Life*. London: George Allen & Unwin.

Eller, C. (2000). Divine Objectification: The Representation of Goddesses and Women in Feminist Spirituality. *Journal of Feminist Studies in Religion, 16*(1), 23-44.

Kakati, B.K. (1948). *The Mother Goddess Kamakhya*. Assam Publishing Corporation: Guwahati

Lee, Janet. (1994). Menarche and the (Hetero) Sexualization of the Female Body. *Gender & Society* 8(3), 343-362

Mahalaxmi. R. (2011). *The Making of the Goddess: Korravai-Durgā in the Tamil Traditions*. Penguin Books: Delhi

Marglin, Frederique Apffel. (1985). Female Secuality in the Hindu World. *In Imaculate and Powerful: The Female Sacred Image and Social Reality*, eds., by Clarrisa W. Atkinson, Constance H. Buchanan, and Margaret R. Miles. Beacon Press: Boston, 39-60

Montgomery, R. E. (1974). A Cross-Cultural Study of Menstruation, Menstrual Taboos, and Related Social Variables. *Ethos*, 2(2), 137–170

Muthukumar S., David. (2019). *Goddess Spirituality in Feminism*. Pre-printed, 1-11

Ortner, S. B. (1972). Is Female to Male as Nature Is to Culture? *Feminist Studies, 1*(2), 5–31.

Patar, Maitrayee. (2019). Tuloni: Experiences and Negotiations around Womanhood in Assamese Society. *Explorations*. 3(1): 65-88.

Ramos. Imma. (2018*). The Visual Politics of Menstruation, Birth, and Devotion at Kamakhya Temple in Assam* in Motrescu-Mayes, A., and Banks, M. (eds), Visual Histories of South Asia. Primus Books, 52-68

Segal, Robert A. (1988). Interpreting and Explaining Religion: Geertz and Durkheim.

Soundings: An Interdisciplinary Journal: Geertz, Religion, and Cultural Systems. 71(1): 29-52

Singh, Renuka. (1990). *Womb of the Mind: A sociological exploration of the status-experience of women in Delhi.* Vikas Publishing house: Delhi

Singh, Renuka. (1997). *Women Reborn: An exploration of the spirituality of Urban Indian Women.* Penguin books

Summers-Effler, E. (2006). Ritual Theory. In: Stets, J.E., Turner, J.H. (eds) *Handbook of the Sociology of Emotions. Handbooks of Sociology and Social Research.* Springer, Boston, MA, 135-154

Urban, Hugh. (2019). 'The Cradle of Tantra': Modern Transformations of a Tantric Centre in Northeast India from Nationalist Symbol to Tourist Destination. *South Asia: Journal of South Asian Studies.* 42(2). 1-22.

Valk, Ulo. (2020). Goddess temples in North Eastern India: Overcoming Narrative Distance in place-lore. In: M Mani Meitei, R.K. Dhawan (eds). *Folklore Studies: Local and Global.* Prestige books International: New Delhi, 125-128

Wels, Harry, et al. (2011) Victor Turner and liminality: An introduction, *Anthropology Southern Africa.* 34(1-2), 1-4

Yinger, J. (1958). The Influence of Anthropology on Sociological Theories of Religion. *American Anthropologist, 60*(3), new series, 487-496

Internet Links

- https://directortourism.assam.gov.in/frontimpotentdata/ambubachi-festival, accessed on 25-05-2021, time 9:00 hours
- https://directortourism.assam.gov.in/portlet-sub-innerpage/temples-pilgrimages accessed on 22-10-2020 at 16:45 hours
- https://www.tourmyindia.com/blog/ambubachi-mela-kamakhya-temple/ assessed on 16-10-2022, time 20:00 hours

BUILDING AND SUSTAINING A SPIRITUAL ORGANISATION

A Case Study of Sri Aurobindo Society

Ipsita Mitra

Introduction

Significance of spirituality in public life, especially in institutional structures through which spirituality operates within the society, has been generating renewed interest of late. Although spirituality is defined as a personal experience of faith, it finds collective expression through the formation of spiritual organisations. Most spiritual organisations work within the community and engage in developmental activities for the betterment of its people. Spiritual organisations can thus be located at the intersection of the sacred and the secular, and have a unique position by virtue of which they become important institutional actors in the social welfare sector in India.

Spiritual Organisations: Context, Meaning and Definition

In social science research, the study of spiritual organisations is situated within the ambit of faith-based organisations (FBOs). One of the earliest works on faith-based organisations is by Gerard Clarke (2008), who deploys faith as an analytical lens through which marginalized communities rationalize poverty and suffering.[1] He presents a typology capturing the most significant dimensions of FBOs:

- Faith-based representative organisations or apex bodies that rule on doctrinal matters. These organisations govern the faithful and represent them at state and global levels.
- Faith-based charitable or development organisations that mobilize the faithful in support of the poor and other social groups, and fund or manage programmes which aim to remove poverty or social exclusion.
- Faith-based political organisations that deploy faith as a political construct and mobilize social groups on the basis of faith identities to pursue broader political objectives.
- Faith-based missionary organisations that seek to convert non-believers.
- Faith-based radical, illegal or terrorist organisations that promote radical or militant forms of faith-based identity and justify the use of violence on the grounds of faith.

Close examination of this typology reveals that FBOs are characterized on the basis of how religious doctrines shape the interaction of the FBO with the wider community. This analysis indicates that FBOs are not only engaged in social welfare activities, but are also enmeshed in a complex network of social and political relations.

Bradley (2011) notes that such a broad definition digresses from the issue of development per se since several FBOs are not guided by explicit developmental guidelines. In her study, Bradley proposes adding another dimension to Clarke's typology. She defines the sixth category as,

> 'Local or grass-roots organisations that seek to support and enable their individual adherents to reach a better understanding of their faith and openly share their spirituality with others. Examples of this type of group are Bible or Scriptural study groups or prayer meetings, meditation and/or yoga classes.' (Bradley, 2011:108) Bradley's addition of a sixth category incorporated local community level engagement with FBOs and can be seen as crucial for understanding the functioning of FBOs. Practices of community engagement prepare grounds for larger societal engagement with development and also form the basis for local understandings of economic, cultural and political constructs of FBOs. FBOs have always been identified in reference with religious doctrines, however, in some cases, spiritual ethics alone guide the work ethics and vision of such organisations.[2]

The spiritually defined FBO acts, not just as an intermediary between non-local donors and the community, but also establishes a deeper connection with local beneficiaries on the basis of spiritual and religious capital. Collective identity coalesces around a shared cosmology on the basis of the commonly held values of compassion, service and morality, generating an enabling environment for FBOs to work with faith communities in times of crises and suffering.

Spiritual values, which recognise the multi-dimensional character of human nature, focus not just on materially dispossessed groups, but also take into account social, cultural and moral well-being of vulnerable groups in society. Spiritual ethics therefore, contribute in a unique way to arrive at a holistic understanding of community members, and seek to transform their lives in totality.

From a sociological point of view, analysis of the role of spiritual values in the successful implementation of social welfare programmes helps us assess spiritual organisations as important actors in the social welfare sector. At the core of any social welfare programme, is the recognition of the essential values of dignity, liberty, equality and pursuit of happiness, which must be granted to all members of society regardless of gender, caste, class, region and religion. Thus, the codification of these values can be traced back to spiritual and religious thought.

In the context of development, faith, spirituality and charitable values produce an energy that seems able to sustain itself as a lasting commitment to the service of the disadvantaged. This component of spirituality, aligned with social welfare principles, can contribute to expand our understanding of spiritual organisations.

Case Study of Sri Aurobindo Society

This essay looks at Sri Aurobindo Society in Delhi and Noida as a Faith-based Organisation, and analyzes its community welfare programmes which are part of the organisation's social welfare objectives. The mission statement of the Society gives an insight into how spiritual development of the self is linked to social welfare of the community. The organisation 'Seeks to bring a dynamic spirituality into material life and all its activities, so that the global problems can find a true solution, and the dreams of humanity, through the ages, can be realized.'

Named after Sri Aurobindo, Sri Aurobindo Society (SAS) was founded by the Mother in 1960. An international spiritual, educational, cultural, not-for-profit NGO, Sri Aurobindo Society is recognized by the Government of India as a charitable organisation, a research institute, and an institution of national importance. Sri Aurobindo Society works throughout the world for individual perfection, social transformation, and for garnering human unity in diversity. It invites participation of all who want to work together for a better tomorrow irrespective of nationality, religion, caste, or gender.

Membership of the Society is open to any individual, institution or organisation that is influenced by the philosophy of Sri Aurobindo and The Mother. A group of twelve or more members can start a centre in their area and can grow to become a full-fledged branch of the Society. Centres and branches of the Society are primarily meant to be centres of *sadhana* (meditation/contemplation). Service to the divine takes the form of programmes, workshops, seminars, youth camps and other group activities. The aim of the Society is to work towards individual perfection, social transformation and human unity. It has several ongoing projects in health, education, business, village development, and the youth and media.

The organisational structure is flat, as described by many respondents. There are three levels: top-level management, which looks into administrative and financial details and is the main decision making body; middle-level management, which manages the various programmes, and grass-roots workers comprising of members and volunteers. A distinction needs to be drawn between volunteers and members. Volunteers of the organisation are active workers who are engaged in running various programmes at the ground level. Members of the organisation on the other hand, may or may not be engaged in social welfare activities.

A) The Spiritual Leader: Discourse and Ethics

Sri Aurobindo Society draws its objective from the works of Sri Aurobindo and The Mother. The Society's aim is to facilitate social transformation through individual sadhana. It is imperative to begin by analysing the philosophy of Sri Aurobindo and The Mother, and comprehend the way in which they linked spiritual growth to activism and philanthropy.

The central tenet of Sri Aurobindo's work is that the greatest service to humanity includes in devising a way to connect individual salvation to collective salvation. Religion and spirituality of the future has to consider whether spiritual fulfilment can be extended beyond the individual and into the collective. This highest vision of collective humanity is a kind of internationalism or globalism.

Sri Aurobindo envisaged an inner universal brotherhood which would be a product of progressive moral, psychological and spiritual evolution, possessing the capacity to recognise the inner spiritual fraternity of all of mankind. His dream for the future was an all embracing spiritual synthesis of the ideals of religion, humanism and secularism. He hoped that this new ideal of the future would lead to a spiritual religion of humanity.

Sri Aurobindo's views on philanthropy and responsibility towards the community can be derived from his writings on the meaning of charity. According to Sri Aurobindo, inner consciousness can maintain a close union with the divine. This personal realisation however, is not complete in itself. Pending an awareness of the wider self, it would remain in the confines of narrow egoism and personal salvation alone, which should not be the goal of humanity. For Sri Aurobindo, salvation in the truest sense, is attainable through the transformation of one's surrounding world, by expanding one's own consciousness to the collective self. According to him, the individual should seek to help other members of society as part of his own salvation. An individual who has achieved personal transformation must now bring light and bliss to those around him, modestly accepting the gift of grace from the divine.

Sri Aurobindo, on observing the tribulations of workmen, stated that the poor and the dispossessed are far more charitable than those who are economically strong. He believed that it is fatal to subscribe to the notion of accumulating riches before distributing them. A spiritual member of society is empowered by means other than material aid, to bring a difference to the world around him. Sri Aurobindo instructed his followers to turn themselves into channels of divine grace, channels which must let the grace flow and pour out, rather than keeping it within oneself. The flood of vital, intellectual and spiritual forces must flow abundantly from the individual and join a greater universal current, and this must be the key defining principle of any form of charity.

According to Sri Aurobindo, when service is linked to material possessions, the idea of possession itself must be challenged. Every item in the universe belongs to all of humanity, and to say that something belongs to one individual, creates a separation that does not exist in reality. Every aspect of human life and its creations, ultimately belongs to everyone.

The spiritual discourse by Sri Aurobindo and The Mother referred to altruism as a form of the ego, of those who are not connected with the divine. There is serious fallacy in the claim that altruism is devoid of self-interest. In fact, 'It is the sublimest form of selfishness'. Human pity is a slave to emotional impulses. For every individual to contribute fully to the development of humankind, it is essential that he/she channels divine grace and compassion, rather than pity. There is a distinct quality that spirituality and the teachings of Sri Aurobindo bring to the members of the organisation. Every member is deeply connected to his/her community and accepts work for the community as a moral duty, without being imprisoned by the same. Work, especially through structured welfare programmes, has the idea of service to humanity embedded within it. Further, members do not perform service in pursuit of personal ambition rather, seeing themselves and functioning as instruments of the divine grace.

B) Sri Aurobiondo Society as a Spiritual Organisation

Five important factors are involved in an analysis of spiritual organisation. These are, ideological, material or economic, power relations, institutional advocacy, and activism and its position in aid networks. We will look at how each of these factors qualifies Sri Aurobindo Society as a spiritual organisation.

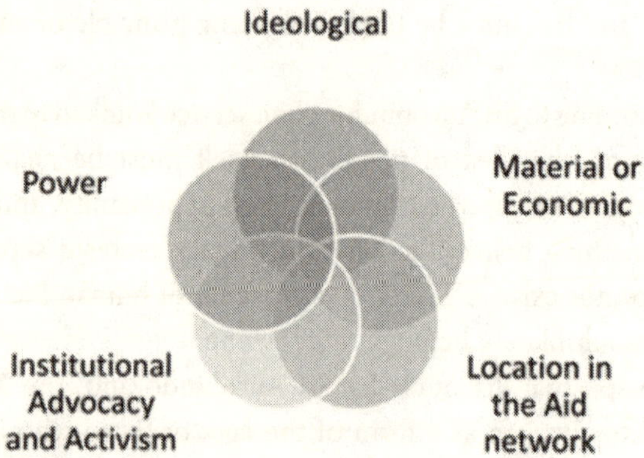

Ideological

Every spiritual organisation is founded on the basis of ideas and principles derived from a spiritual discourse. Sri Aurobindo Society is based on the spiritual teachings of Sri Aurobindo and The Mother. All members interviewed during the course of the fieldwork believe that following the practical guide laid down by the spiritual leaders would enhance their quality of life. Further, transformation of self is considered the first step toward transforming the community. All respondents agreed that the organisation was not a religious organisation or a Hindu organisation even though Sri Aurobindo was deeply influenced by Hindu scriptures, especially the *Gita.* All members also believe that the Society does not 'preach' or 'spread propaganda' as both were strictly forbidden by The Mother. One of the respondents in Puducherry, very aptly described the principle philosophy as *'humanistic, rather than religious.'* In fact, another respondent made an interesting point in this regard. She said that far from being Hindu, the teachings of Sri Aurobindo helped in '*debrahmanising*' the scriptures, making them accessible to all.

Material/Economic Aspect

Sri Aurobindo Society economically sustains itself through three main sources: guest house tariffs, funds from the school run by the Ashram, and devotee funds. Money obtained from these sources is used to pay salaries of the payroll employees of the organisation. Apart from this, the organisation funds its several programmes from resources that are provided by corporate organisations and NGOs. Besides economic resources, the organisation sustains itself on spiritual capital.

Spiritual capital functions as an independent sub-system, integrating all members into a spiritual community. The network of relationships based on a shared cultural belief system helps maintain the integrity of Sri Aurobindo Society. Spiritual capital is also instrumental in increasing membership of the organisation through link membership, and like any other form of capital, has been passed on from one generation to another. Spiritual capital opened up avenues for material resources by acting as a bridging capital between members of the organisation and followers of Sri Aurobindo and The Mother, outside the organisational structure. These networks are important in garnering civil participation, donation, and membership strength. Thus, apart from material resources, Sri Aurobindo Society is strengthened by spiritual capital that flows within and outside the organisation.

Institutional Advocacy and Activism

All members of the organisation firmly believe in social transformation and improvement of the overall well-being of the community. The organisation runs several programmes to increase awareness amongst the uninitiated, through workshops, study circles, yoga camps, seminars and talks. These events are organised by all branches and centres across the country, and are closely monitored by the head office in Puducherry. The idea of activism is deeply ingrained in the consciousness of all members of the organisation. This is partly due to the teachings of the spiritual leaders and partly because the organisation identifies as an NGO. According to the Chairperson of the organisation, even though the primary identity of the organisation is a spiritual one, the organisation needed to be registered as an NGO in order to exist as a legal entity in India. He said that due to the legal requirements of the same, the spiritual goals aligned perfectly with the goals of an NGO engaged in community services and social welfare programmes.

Power

Analysis of Sri Aurobindo Society from a political economy perspective adds a critical dimension to the study by taking into account the power relations embedded within the organisational structure. Power, hegemony and domination have been analysed in relation to the work environment, authority structure, chain of command and hierarchy. It was found that Sri Aurobindo Society is a flat organisation where roles and hierarchy are not clearly defined. There is freedom to work according to one's potential and commitment. It was also observed that there was no attachment to (higher) positions as The Mother is (still) regarded as the Executive President. Members occupying positions of power believe that they are working as instruments of divine grace.

Further, study of the social welfare programmes allowed for close analysis of the sites and dynamics of power marking the relationship between the organisation and beneficiary communities. It was found that the organisation does not disregard local knowledge but rather, adopts a collaborative approach to welfare by including the community members in the decision-making process. The perspective of community members is not thoroughly explored in this research but only briefly touched upon. Mutual reciprocity was discerned when observed from grassroots perspective.

Organisation members perceive no difference between the beneficiary and the benefactor, believing that through work, they were contributing to the larger goal of collective sadhana. This insight is a critique of several development projects, which viewed the aid relationship as an unequal relationship, hierarchically structured between those who give aid, on one hand, and recipients of aid, on the other.

Although the work ethos of sadhana went by the open, collaborative and participative logic of Sri Aurobindo Society, it was observed that some of the programmes aimed at standardising their procedures and streamlining work, which stands in contrast to the ideal work ethic followed in the organisation. The power component in Sri Aurobindo Society is not destructive and exists where it contributes to better functioning of the organisation.

Location in the Aid Network

In order to understand the relationship between FBOs and other development actors, including the state and secular donor organisations in the Aid Network, we refer to the 'Aid Pyramid' which is based on the flow of economic resources.

Location of FBOs in Relation to Other Actors in the Development Sector

As shared by the chairman of the Noida branch of the Society, the branch has over the last year, partnered with the Government of Uttar Pradesh for an education programme called 'Rupantar', where teachers are trained to focus on holistic development of students. Some of the collaborations with the government failed because of the rigid structure of government programmes. The management as well as the members believe that the organisation is under no obligation to work with the government and would collaborate in so far as it did not alter the spiritual objective of Sri Aurobindo Society.

The organisation actively collaborates with corporate organisations and accesses corporate responsibility funds that are set aside for social welfare programmes (this is due to the mandatory CSR legislation that directs corporations to spend a certain percentage of their profits on social programmes). Over time, the organisation has evolved to fit the requirements of corporate organisations while remaining true to its spiritual core. Corporate partnerships are seen as result of the credibility and proven effectiveness of the Society in social welfare programmes.

Even though Sri Aurobindo Society can be positioned at the base of the Aid Pyramid, as it receives grants and funds from the government as well as corporate donors, it does not depend on these external sources for implementing its spiritual objectives in the community.

Any spiritual organisation, thus classified, may run the risk of institutionalisation of values, routinization of individual charisma (of the leader), and progressive 'NGOisation'. To understand the translation of spiritual ideals into practice by the members of the organisation, we must therefore take into account questions of legitimacy, sustenance and opposition from other agencies working in the same space. The findings suggest that the organisation is able to avoid routinization of charisma, avert stark NGOisation, and continues to serve the community according to the ethics of sadhana. We will now look at each one of these briefly.

a) Routinisation of Charisma

The positive role of spiritual values in social welfare programmes conducted by Sri Aurobindo Society is a consequence of the charismatic authority of Sri Aurobindo and The Mother. The charisma and grace of the spiritual leaders is so strong that the organisation still recognises and reveres The Mother as the executive president of the Society. Most members believe that The Mother's blessings continue to guide them even in her absence. Some however, are of the view that the physical absence of a spiritual guru poses a challenge to the organisation. There are several spiritual organisations in India whose leaders are physically present to guide, inspire and direct the members of the organisations. In the case of Sri Aurobindo Society, spiritual guidance comes from the works, letters and discourses from the lives and times of Sri Aurobindo and The Mother.

The absence of a spiritual leader (in physical body) can pose a serious challenge to charismatic authority, which Weber termed as 'routinisation of charisma'. For Weber, charismatic authority must necessarily move in one of three directions: toward dissolution, toward traditional authority, or toward rational-legal authority. Charisma thus, faces a dilemma: it must change in order to survive, but in changing, it threatens its definitive, essentially charismatic qualities. This is the problem of routinisation of charisma, the solution to which may be central to better understanding of the successful transition of collective behaviour into institutionalized or quasi-institutionalized movements or organisations. Routinisation of charisma, although referring to a critical phenomenon, is largely undefined in sociological literature. In particular, the mechanisms through which routinisation proceeds remain problematic. The following components and sequence comprise an approximation to an ideal-type of the theory of charisma. First, there is the sudden appearance of a dramatic, unconventional charismatic leader with his 'gift of grace'. This leads to the gathering of an inner circle of disciples, persons who themselves are believed to possess special qualities or share the charisma of the leader. With time, there is the equally sudden, dramatic, and unexpected martyrdom of the charismatic leader, leaving an initial, temporary void of leadership which is partially filled by the inner circle of disciples as a collective body. This is followed by a rise, from within the discipleship, of a new leader, also charismatic, who then consolidates and organises the group. It is observed that the process of institutionalization follows, in some concrete and/or symbolic form, the now martyred, original charismatic leader and the treatment of this by the second charismatic leader and the followers.

In this description of the ideal-type, there are a number

of factors to note: although the charisma of Sri Aurobindo and The Mother corresponds more closely to Weber's original definition and to traditional usage, what distinguishes the two leaders is not so much a difference of charisma as the direction in which their leadership efforts are focused. The first leader was fascinating, unusual, and unearthly. The second was more conventional, mundane, and practical. The first leader brought the elect together, the second created an organisation to contain them. The first leader was inspired by a vision while the second elaborated and translated that vision into a plan.

The partnership of Sri Aurobindo and The Mother resulted in The Mother being accepted as the spiritual successor of the organisation. Once she took over the organisation, she too was greatly respected and revered, so much so that even today, all meetings, seminars and workshops are dedicated to her for her blessings.

Further, since the martyrdom of Sri Aurobindo as the first charismatic leader was figurative, that is, real, physical death did not occur, there was only the cancellation of a role when Sri Aurobindo handed over the organisation to The Mother. The Mother symbolically took over as the leader even before the demise of Sri Aurobindo.

Institutionalization of the spiritual leader is especially important in solving the problem of the routinisation of charisma. Even before Sri Aurobindo could experience the transitory nature of charismatic authority and the elusive quality of charisma, he was able to transfer all his power to The Mother who was then recognised as sacred and exclusive.

Thus, in context of Sri Aurobindo Society, routinisation of charisma was substituted by a transfer of charisma. This charisma has sustained even in the physical absence of the spiritual leader. One of the factors contributing to this was that organisationally, even though the structure was bureaucratised to a great extent, there was a democratic and fair election to positions of authority. The highest position, that of executive president, continues to be symbolically occupied by The Mother, effectively foreclosing all possibilities of power struggle.

b) Process of NGOisation

The anthropology of NGOs is a developing field and is based on foundational critiques of development as opposed to its functional critiques. Research in this domain has found that NGOs tend to neutralize the position of the community they work with, robbing them of their class, caste and other social properties. The communities are depoliticized in ways so as to turn them into technical problems that could have easy solutions.

Apart from this, professionalization and institutionalization also emerge as critical issues in the study of NGOs. Breaking down of development projects into smaller goals with timelines is a fundamental approach for all NGOs which function in the development space.

Even though the members of Sri Aurobindo Society maintain that their primary identity is that of a spiritual organisation, legal requirements of the country led to the Society being registered as an NGO. NGOs entered the social welfare space in the 1980s and 1990s, during the early phases of liberalisation, privatisation and globalisation. This also led to the state's flight from the social sector and the entry of the market in the social welfare sector. It thus created an enabling environment for NGOs to thrive.

The main critique of NGOs contends that they turn beneficiaries into consumers. Arundhati Roy argues that NGOs diffuse political anger which is the first major step towards change. In fact, Roy describes NGOs as the 'Missionaries of secular missions of the modern world'. Their reliance on funds from donors and corporate organisations has made NGOs more accountable to the funders than to the people.

Further, NGOs implement most social welfare activities as projects. The process of projectization and professionalization dilutes the humaneness of an NGO. Breaking down a social welfare programme in fragments, milestones and timelines, depoliticises activism. Professionalization in social welfare activities works well for the neo-liberal regime as it increases control over the community through NGOs. Project logic also prioritizes the roles of technocrats and administrators over social workers thereby, defeating the whole idea of social welfare for the community.

In the case of Sri Aurobindo Society, its spiritual identity remains central to the functioning of the organisation. As mentioned previously, the staffs on payroll are paid salary with money that the organisation obtains from running the ashram school, guest houses, and from individual donations. Since these are the three main sources of income, there is no institutional obligation to any donor or corporate body. Thus, Sri Aurobindo Society remains faithful to its spiritual objective while focusing on the primary stakeholders. On instances when the Society collaborates with corporate and other international donor organisations, there is no change in the functioning of the Society. Transition from a spiritual organisation to an NGO entails change in discourse and practice. For Sri Aurobindo Society, these have remained constant and unchanged since its inception.

Further, due to the ineffectiveness of NGOs in bringing about total transformation in the lives of the community, there is a vacuum that could be filled up by spiritual organisations. The ineffectiveness of NGOs in the social sector space emanates from the fact that urban, middle class members of the community exercise power and hegemony over grassroots activities. In simple terms, professionalization creates hierarchy which leads to concentration of power in the hands of few. The approach of Sri Aurobindo Society is a critique of this perspective as it aims to convert communities from passive recipients to active partners in the development process.

Thus, we can assert that spiritual organisations function differently even while being part of the non-state segment of the social welfare sector. First, spiritual organisations, as a subcategory of NGOs, in some way retain one of their fundamental characteristics in their spiritual affiliation. This helps in building trust, empathy and a relationship of honesty between the organisation and the beneficiaries. Second, the managerial style of the organisation depends greatly on the funding sources. In this case, the spiritual organisation raised most of its funds from members of the community due to which, the functioning of the organisation steered clear of being absorbed in bureaucracy and professionalization.

c) Ethics of Sadhana

In this study it was observed that the ethic of sadhana motivates members of the organisation to engage in transformation of their own lives and consequently, transform the society around them. Their work is overwhelmingly regarded as offering to the guru (72.47 percent), as participation in a noble mission (9.14 percent), or as giving meaning to life and existence (9.34 percent), and building a sense of communitas (anthropologist Victor Turner's concept which talks of community or the 'we' feeling) with fellow followers and the organisation. In terms of sadhana, majority i.e., 51.62 percent did office work pertaining to social service projects of the organisations, and 23.89 percent undertook field site volunteering.

Conclusion

In a society of organisations, Sri Aurobindo Society can be identified as a spiritual organisation which is engaged in human transformation through social welfare programmes. It is based on the ethics of experience, motivation and faith. It is only after individuals enter into the realm of experience that the world of spirituality opens up before them. While trying to understand the unique value that spiritual organisations add as partners in the development sector, we must also not lose sight of the aspect of the relationships within the organisation and how members work to translate spiritual ideals into practice.

The past two decades have witnessed burgeoning research on the subject of faith-based organisations and the social welfare sector. Such studies mostly take religious organisations as their field of study. There is, however, a lacuna in empirical research investigating the value that spiritual discourses impart to development work. This study represents an attempt to capture the significant role played by spiritual organisations in social welfare programmes. The rise of a charismatic leader, the building, stability and sustenance of a spiritual organisation, and the work ethic derived from the spiritual philosophy, together position the spiritual organisation as an important partner in the development space.

This essay thus, seeks to make a meaningful contribution to the anthropology of organisations in the context of spirituality and social welfare. There are numerous studies of Sri Aurobindo as a spiritual leader, and his charismatic personality no longer comes as a revelation to those who have read, interpreted and analyzed his works from various available sources. This study will hopefully add yet another dimension to the understanding of spiritual philosophy and the way in which it is interpreted and institutionalised.

EXPLORING THE 'OTHER' IN HINDU MYTHO-EPIC IMAGINATION

A Gendered Rereading

Kamalini Mukherjee

Introduction

In *The Womb of Mind: A Sociological Exploration of the Status-experience of Women in Delhi*, Prof. Singh writes, 'It is believed that religion had been instrumental in developing and maintaining morality. It has influenced, since times immemorial, the behaviour, and the majority of life of individuals. By and large, the religious patterns and beliefs may guide the behaviour pattern in the family, community and society.' (1990. pp.128) This correlation of maintenance of morals and religious perpetuity is a core value-system of social regulation in our society. Religion plays a vital role in every individual's life, either directly or indirectly, and much of the perpetuation of religious ethics and morals occurs through the dissemination of mytho-epic storytelling. Religious mythologies depict vivid stories of heroes, warriors, philosophers, and sages alongside those of terrible monsters, abominations and similar shadow[1] manifestations—with the overarching theme of providing the reader with an epic[2] journey culminating at a grand moral gesture. The aim, therefore, of a mytho-epic imagination is to provide the reader with a continuing perception of varied perspectives, to enable conscious self-reflection through structured internalisation. Thus, it is essential here to put forth the two main inspirations for deconstructing the mytho-epic imagination—Levi-Strauss and Jung: the former, a structuralist, for his semiological[3] approach to social reality, and the latter, an analytical psychologist, for his theories of the social psyche[4]. Both provide (although often oppositional) views of the *unconscious* '(...) and agree that only when its function is clearly revealed will modern man acquire the self-understanding so lacking in contemporary existence.' (Gras, 1981. pp. 471) That, there is an *unconscious* disconnect between the 'modern man' and his 'contemporary existence', is seemingly evident. This disconnect also permeates the social psyche of our times; and creates categories of meaning around 'self understanding'—thereby locating both the 'self' and the 'other' in a symbolically meaningful religio-historic context. Society thus imparts meaning to an undefinable category, through the symbolic sense it derives out of the collective mytho-epic imagination. Therefore, this work is an attempt to explore the structure of 'self-understanding' arising out of Hindu mythological storytelling, so as to locate the 'other' within current sociopolitical interpretations of the *epics*.

Romila Thapar defines an 'epic' as 'essentially a literary crystallisation of the heroic ideal. By its nature, therefore, it is not to be taken as factual evidence, but as the representation of an ideal.' (1979. pp. 199) But in the cultural tradition of reproduction of values, norms and ideas, Indian society relies significantly on the imagination derived from great Hindu epics such as the Ramayana and Mahabharata: which '...may not have been, strictly speaking, historically real events, and we are not concerned with whether they really happened or not. This peculiar indifference to assigning chronology to ancient Indian works is (…) symptomatically an Indian attitude.' (Jha, 2016. pp.185) Therefore, the systems of symbols and meanings that have risen from the popular dissemination of mythological epics have reinforced their hold on society, and have subsequently created structures of *othering* built around associations that fall outside the popular imagination. Additionally, the disregard for historical accuracy or authenticity in these imaginations purports them to an arena of divine quality—one that is beyond question and reproach.

The religious character of mytho-epic imagination in the Indian subcontinent provides the basis of a shared *collective unconscious*[5]: for Jung, it is a structural layer of the human psyche containing inherited elements, distinct from the personal unconscious. 'The collective unconscious contains the whole spiritual heritage of mankind's evolution, born anew in the brain structure of every individual.' (Jung, 1959) The large numbers of Hindus living in India, and around the world, associate their spiritual heritage with the interpretations of popular Hindu mytho-epic texts like the Ramayana and Mahabharata. The effective role of religion in social behaviour determines not only how structures are built around ideals interpreted through mytho-epic imagination, but also how the individual 'self' is ordered within society. Both Ramayana and Mahabharata provide ideals of *personhood* through storytelling: in the context of gendered rereading, both texts present masculine and feminine *ideals,* but it also provides the space for the 'neither' and the 'in-between' on the gender spectrum.

In *Gender and Narrative in the Mahabharata,* Brodbeck and Black propose a realistic connection between studying gender in mythological narratives: '(…) due to the complexity of the Mahabharata and the probability that it contains material composed in different historical periods (...) it is very difficult to establish concrete connections between the text and the social worlds from which it might have emerged, particularly since those social worlds are not directly accessible and must be reconstructed in the first place largely on the basis of texts. Thus, while discussing gender as it intersects with social factors such as dharma, varna, marriage practices, family relations, and soteriological paths, it is important to emphasize that the world of the Mahabharata is a literary world, and not a direct reflection or representation of the ever-evasive 'reality' of ancient India. (...) Furthermore, any discussion about gender in a literary product like the Mahabharata must necessarily address much more than the degree to which the text represents real life. Gender roles in narrative literature are not merely reflections of or instructions for the real world; they are always also artistic and metaphorical literary devices, and sometimes, gendered symbolism in the text gives added meaning at a textual level without necessarily referring to a social reality.' (2007. pp. 13-14)

Their view bluntly states three distinct outlooks: first, the mytho-epic imagination is *not* a textual catalogue of history, second, it is *not* a direct reflection of social reality, and third, it *is*—to an extent—an artistic creation or a metaphorical tool of imparting social ideals. However, this view will be vehemently rejected by Indian scholars, as it is broadly argued that the cultural ancestry of the Indian subcontinent is deeply entrenched in its religious mythology (Chakraborty, 2014; Doniger, 1975, 2009; Jha, 2016; Thapar, 1979): and it is more than merely fantastical literature meant for lessons in morality. The Hindu mytho-epic imagination is a vast spectrum of belief-systems, whereby our society draws meaning, logic, and structure. It is the imagination that both creates hierarchy and patriarchy in our society, as well as, provides the very instruments to fracture the order.

The imagination of Shiva (and Kali in some stories) in Hindu myths as both, the embodiment of creation and destruction, is reflective of the balance of oppositions that Hindu mythology often anthropomorphizes as interpretative tools.

One can argue that the interpretation of such texts is, therefore, crucial to the shared imagination. For Jung, the collective unconscious appears to consist of mythological motifs or primordial images, and therefore the mythological traditions of nations, societies and communities are its real exponents. Thus the conceptual analogy in Jung's understanding of mythology could be taken as a sort of literary projection of the collective unconscious of epochs (Jung, 1959). One can hence study the collective unconscious in two ways, either in mythology or in the analysis of the individual.

The Structure of Mytho-Epic Imagination

In the introduction to *Hindu Myths*, Doniger writes, 'Every Hindu myth is different; all Hindu myths are alike (...) each myth celebrates the belief that the universe is boundlessly various, that everything occurs simultaneously, that all possibilities may exist without excluding each other.' (1994, pp.11) This is therefore either an archetypal opportunity for constructing individual interpretations of self-reflection or a tautological fallacy: using universality to momentously placate one's specific view of the ideal as *divine*. One widely observed practice of focusing on certain aspects of mytho-epic imagination to put forth a religious narrative of social order, and the use of the overtly simplified and often myopic interpretations, is to enforce patriarchal views of women's role in society—as purported by the archaic traditionalist revivalism of Indian political movements in recent years (Luthra, 2014). The recurrence of Sita as a *feminine* ideal-type, the *pativrata*[6] (dedicated to the duties of home and husband, Rama the virtuous) entity of the Ramayana—one who never leaves her husband's side, until she is abducted by Ravana. The feminine ideals put forth in the socio-political interpretation of Sita in Ramayana, portrays her as an obedient wife—who leaves behind the grandeur of riches to follow Rama on a path of isolation, insecurity and exile. However, it rejects the premise that by choosing to follow Ram, Sita is self-actualising: in other words, the romance of Sita's sacrifice is relegated to a 'duty' expected of the wife. Even after the great battle between good and evil, as Rama emerges victorious, Sita never really manages to regain her status quite as Rama's wife—as an abductee, her virtue was stained. In the Mahabharata, Draupadi's demure acceptance of literal sharing of conjugality with all five Pandava brothers because of a simple miscarriage of context, is popularly depicted to focus on the virtue of the brothers who are sworn to carry out *any* instruction given by their mother. Kunti's puerile decision to ask the brothers to divide in five ways 'whatever they brought home' at the end of each day, did not deter the brothers from apportioning Draupadi's ownership five ways. She too is seen to comply with a higher patriarchal imagination that befalls women to this day in our society. Apart from the myriad ways, this approach to morality is problematic. The Ramayana and the Mahabharata, as objects of imagination, have become even more relevant today with overt social and religious ideals being directly drawn from them (Kumar, 2016a). Similar tropes exist for men as well: Rama's unrelenting dedication to his parent's wishes; Arjuna's unwavering ambition to reach the pinnacle of achievement; Yudhisthira's resolute pledge of truth; and many more such illustrations of ideal-types paint the mytho-epic imagination of Hindu traditions[7]. Similarly, systems of symbols and meanings that are structured around gender and sexuality are also drawn from the same mytho-epic imagination: the characters of Sita and Draupadi or Rama and Arjuna are evoked as ideals even today in perceptions of loyalty, duty and valour (Kumar, 2016a, 2016b): in other words, systems of social structure in our society are fundamentally enveloped in a series of symbols and meanings derived from mytho-epic imagination. In defining social dynamics, Levi Strauss derived his analysis of social structures from stories and myths, and established how symbols are meaningful to people—this desire to derive meaning from myths is essentially a human quality. For him, the power of mythologies came from its oral trajectory: the generational transmission of mytho-epic storytelling created the shared beliefs that in turn created structures of meanings. For Levi Strauss, 'myth *is* language' (1955. pp. 430): therefore the language of the mythological imagination is fundamental to its location in the social psyche. In other words, the linguistic ability of mythological storytelling to engender value to social experiences validates its existence. However, as Levi-Strauss observed, the linguistic disposition of mythology also allows for diverse interpretations: 'Myths are still widely interpreted in conflicting ways: collective dreams, the outcome of a kind of aesthetic play, the foundation of ritual. (...) Mythological figures are considered as personified abstractions, divinized heroes or decayed gods. Whatever the hypothesis, the choice amounts to reducing mythology either to an idle play or to a coarse kind of speculation.' (Ibid. pp. 428) It is the latter, therefore, which calls for greater introspection, as the interpretation of these mytho-epic texts becomes more relevant in the discussion.

In the introduction to the first volume of *The Valmiki Ramayana,* Bibek Debroy writes: 'The Ramayana and the Mahabharata are known as *itihasas*. The word *itihasa* means 'it was indeed like that'. Therefore, the word is best rendered as legend or history, and not as myth. This does not mean everything occurred exactly as described. In a process of telling and retelling and oral transmission, embellishments are inevitable. However, the use of the word itihasa suggests a core element of truth. There were two great dynasties—Surya Vamsha and Chandra Vamsha (the solar and the lunar dynasty).' (2017) Thus, these two mytho-epic narratives might be considered as textual chronicles of ancient dynasties: the Ramayana tells the story of the Surya (solar) dynasty and the Mahabharata depicts the story of the Chandra (lunar) dynasty. This dynastic understanding of mytho-epic history reinforces the structural politics that Levi-Strauss observed in his study of myths. Let us take, for example, the relationship, an entire generation of Indians built with the television rendering of the epics (Ramanand Sagar's Ramayana and B.R. Chopra's Mahabharata) through the depictions of duty, love, loyalty, bravery, cunning, revenge and retribution, bordered on the edge of obsession (Verma, 2019). The imagination of a great ancestry creates the perception of divinity and meaning in *Hindu* life. In Devdutt Pattanaik's illustrative and stylistic interpretations of the Puranas, Vedas and epics from Hindu mythological literature, he often oversimplifies the contexts, or his stylistic liberties reject the original ambiguities of the texts. Debroy's critique on Pattanaik's publication *Ramayana versus Mahabharata: My playful comparison*, states: 'For both Ramayana and Mahabharata, there are Sanskrit and non-Sanskrit versions. (...) Devdutt's strength is in retelling stories from non-Sanskrit versions of Ramayana and Mahabharata too, as evidenced in his earlier books. In this particular case, since he not only talks about the Sanskrit Valmiki Ramayana and Mahabharata, but about the respective critical editions brought out in Vadodara and Pune, do we take the book's statements to be about these, or about non-Sanskrit versions?' (2019) Debroy's critique of Pattanaik's choice of using specific source materials to inform his work stems from a historical concern: mytho-epic literature often allows the cultural imagination to take over and consequently unravels the prospect for various trajectories of interpretation to take their own course—incidentally, in our case, whatever compliments the politics of the time.

Therefore, the structure of mytho-epic imagination in India is embedded in its historicity: imparting worldly knowledge, morality, conviction of duty, and social order through the generations. In other words, it is a system of disseminating religiocultural propaganda, which has over centuries been relied on to negotiate public opinion and inspire masses against or in favour of specific socio-political objectives. In *The Structural Study of Myth,* Levi-Strauss rejected Jung's interpretation of myths as 'pre-scientific' and argued instead that: 'Social life in effect was a system of messages or codes all of which were homologous because they reflected the human mind which had engendered them (...) whereas Jung's originality lay in psychologizing mythic tales and religious dogma, in making them the externalization of unconscious psychic processes, Levi-Strauss psychologised every aspect of culture. Nothing is exempt from the unconscious structuring of the human mind.' (Gras, 1981. pp. 476) Levi-Strauss' semiological approach to analysing social realities provides the opportunity to interrogate the *collective unconscious* of Jung's imagination—by analysing the gap in interpretation of the mytho-epic imagination in the social psyche. In the gendered context, one may argue: if mytho-epic imagination shapes our social interpretations of gender, gender roles and gendered identities, what limits our perception to only allow any one or few specific ideals while relegating the rest to obscurity? In other words, the question thus arises: what makes *Sita* the favoured feminine ideal but not *Kaikeyi* or *Surpanakha*?

The Archetype of The 'Other'

In manifest form, the influence of mytho-epic imagination on social psyche essentially creates categories of socially accepted identities and patterns of behaviour: apart from creating ideals of 'self' through codes of morality and hierarchy, it also cultivates the antithetical category of the 'other'—which is borne out of negatives[8]. There is a specific *undesirability* to the symbolic meaning attached with the category of the 'other': understood as an archetypical association of *evil* or unwanted. In both the Ramayana and the Mahabharata, the narratives follow archetypical characters on their journeys to predestined ends; however, these primary stories are almost always illustrated with sub-plots of secondary characters who are metaphorically used to elucidate the shadow areas of the imagination. The monsters (rakshasas), the half-humans (borne of union between humans and rakshasas), the demigods (borne of humans and gods) and the animation of inanimate objects (rivers, mountains, forests, etc.), and the socially undesirable (the destitute, the criminal, the pariah, etc.)—all of these provide symbolic meaning to an association of the 'other' in the social psyche. In mythological illustration of these categories, the stories often view them in sympathetic context: the *othering* occurs retroactively, that is, through its internalisation in the social psyche. Although Sita and Draupadi, the two primary female protagonists of the Ramayana and the Mahabharata respectively, are complex characters, their popular perception however, embodies the patriarchal gaze of interpretation: beauty, devotion or piety: making these women seem one-dimensional archetype of the feminine ideal. On the other hand, the eventual plot-resolutions of sub-characters such as Kaikeyi, Manthara or Surpanakha in the Ramayana, and Gandhari, Kunti, Bhanumati or Hidimba in the Mahabharata, are considered as contrasts, and as cautionary tales—as women who represent defiance, disloyalty, deformity or cruelty.

As discussed earlier in this work, Hindu mytho-epic imagination is vast and diverse, and it acknowledges multiplicities of meaning and possibilities, thereby rejecting the phenomena of *othering* that occurs in society based on religio-cultural interpretations. In a gendered context, the attitude towards the queer in our society has an overt religio-cultural overtone, and the laws regulating this approach is deeply embedded in India's colonial past, in the 'sodomy' laws of the British imperial policy (Human Rights Watch, 2020). This signifies that the laws of our society are not entirely based upon the cultural history it represents: the Sanskritic traditions of the Vedas clearly puts forward three distinct categories for gender—*Nar* (man), *Nari* (woman) and *Napunsak* (queer)—and allows for the interpretation of the queer category to be ambiguous and inclusive (Alisha, 2018). This also indicates that the category was not considered as unacceptable in social order or to be undesirable in any sense. In contrast, until very recently, the queer community in India has been largely left out of public policy and economic considerations undertaken by the Central or individual state governments. However, it is important to note here, that the gender *and* sexuality aspects of an individual are considered on a dissimilar plane in the public imagination: the *gender* aspect only considers the *trans*-identities and the *sexuality* aspect relegates all other sexual non-normativity into another dispersed realm (Agoramoorthy, 2018). This attitude was reflected in the archaic law of Section 377 of the Indian Penal Code[9], whereby heteronormativity was set as the ideal, and anything 'other' was considered criminally deviant (Mukherjee, 2017; Saraswat, 2018; Tiwari, 2019). Therefore, disconnect between the Hindu mytho-epic imagination of gender and sexuality, and the manifest reality of queer experience in our society is great, and indeed, fraught. A historically isolated category, the queer have an oppositional mytho-epic imagination internally and externally: in India the current interpretation of the mythological tradition '(...) represents a general consensus of perception. It also provides the backdrop of locating gender-sexuality as categories, first as historical, then social and lastly political—in such as: binary categories of gender incorporates sexuality within the structure based on its functionality, then the category is disrupted by the individual identity that removes itself from the strict structure by defying the binary model and its functions, and finally it seeks to express its desire to exist independently of the structure as well as the functions.' (Mukherjee, 2017. pp. 96) Therefore, borrowing Jungian logic, this desire to exist *outside* structured social forms and create new meaning for symbols and experiences, is the conceptual process of the 'other' archetype. To explore this approach further, it is critical to engage with the Jungian conception of the psyche, and the collective unconscious.

Both Jung and Levi-Strauss argue that the essence of human function is to impart meaning to its experiences, and they both use the tradition of mytho-epic storytelling to illustrate how the collective unconscious within human psyche operates to ascertain meaning to experiences and symbols. 'Both interpreters are motivated by a sense of crisis. If the future is to be liveable, they say, man must stay in touch with the archaic and unconscious psychic levels.' (Gras, 1981. pp. 478) In Jungian understanding, the *psyche* is the totality of all psychic processes, conscious and unconscious: therefore the social categories that arise out of the archaic collective unconscious have entrenched themselves into the very fabric of social reality in our society. For Jung, the collective unconscious is the 'psychic residue' of evolutionary development, a consequence of repeated experience over many generations. This perception illustrates how and why the Hindu mytho-epic imagination is a core element of the social psyche or at least a version of it over generations.

Jung's arguments for the psychic nature of human beings has been used to define and study various facets of social and personal life, but his use of archetypes is perhaps the most widely used to focus on individuals and their psychic location in society (Atre, 2011). Therefore, trying to locate the gendered 'other' in our society brings us to social perceptions of the *deviant* in gender-sexuality paradigms. The queer community in our society is composed of varied identities from across the spectrum, each associating a specific symbolic meaning to their existence, thereby ascribing to specific archetypical conditioning. Let's take for example the *trans* community in India: when I say *transgender*, in the popular Indian imagination, it representatively signifies the *transwomen* of the category, as *transmen* do not possess much visibility in our society, even in modern urban India (Mukherjee, 2016). The Western notions of 'queer' or 'trans' do not fit well with the cultural imagination of its manifest form in Indian society. The social psyche understands established symbols and meanings, so the historic record of 'hijras' (essentially represents—transwomen, cross-dressing men, effeminate men, and as well as inter-gendered persons—in the popular imagination) has created a space within society, albeit marginal, for all the undesirable persons (or the 'other') to be understood as a monolithic category. However, the Hindu mytho-epic imagination is ubiquitously resplendent with queer tropes: to explore this in the simplest form we look at Pattanaik's (2014) cataloguing of the archetypes in *Shikhandi and other Tales.* In his queering of the Hindu mytho-epic textual content '(...) Pattanaik lists the chapters according to the popular tales of queer identities, experiences and folklores' (Mukherjee, 2017). In the mytho-epic imagination of the queer, our society has evolved into categorical chaos of meanings and symbols, creating an overall archetype of an 'other'—where all non-normative aspects are discarded.

Narratives of *Othering*

In this section, I will attempt to bridge the arguments proposed earlier in the paper: especially when it comes to the perception of the 'other' in manifest form compared to its imagined form. To do this, I will be borrowing heavily from my field diary and notes from my doctoral work, parts of which have been published as separate papers and referenced in this work as well. Conducted over four years, my field was vast and difficult to locate spatially; ultimately, I collected personal stories[10] from individuals who self-identified as queer and all resided in the Kolkata area. They came from diverse backgrounds and identified with a varied range on the gender-sexuality spectrum, and their stories[11] elucidate the experience of being *othered* in our society.

> (1) I am a forty two year old man, I have a wife and daughter, and we live with my parents in our ancestral home. I got my degree in Bengali honours with distinction, but could not find a job in academia or a publishing house, like I wanted. So I started to intern for small corporate offices, and eventually landed an office accountant's position, where I have worked for 12 years. But I also have a secret life. I am a transsexual lesbian[12]. I was born with a man's body, but I *am a woman.* My body is a cage, and I feel trapped in it forever. My wife did not understand my condition, until one day she saw me wearing her *sari.* From that day on, she views me as less of a person, or in her eyes as 'less of a man' perhaps. Her

> interactions with me now are different; she looks down at me, and verbally abuses me as *napunsak* and *hijra*. Despite this, I feel immense love for her, I want her to love me too. My daughter is old enough to understand that I'm not like other fathers, and the situation at home does not help either. She has grown distant, and does not share the same sort of closeness we had even a few years back.
>
> My father is a religious man, and would reject the premise completely, calling it unnatural and blasphemous to feel like a woman when one is born as a man. My mother, who loves me a lot in her own way, knows or suspects a little bit of what I feel on a daily basis. But she's always careful not to broach the subject with me, I think she hopes if we all ignore it I will forget about it and move on with my life. She also holds a lot of validity over her bearing a son—me—and she does not take kindly to me trying to unseat her grace of motherhood.
>
> For years, I have struggled with my own self, leading to destructive decisions in my teenage years, abuse from 'friends' as the *effeminate* person in the group, prejudice from the fairer sex for not being 'manly' enough, self-doubt, repressed anger and addiction. But I have also felt love, and passion, and longing. I feel I have seen it all: both the highs and the lows of humanity. And what I have observed is, we humans have very little empathy for others. Especially in our society, we are so involved in controlling others in our lives that we forget that we too live in shackles.
>
> I am a woman. I will always *be* a woman. How society perceives me is not my concern anymore. I have two lives, one that I live for others, and one that is my own. As long as this balance persists, I can survive in this society.

This record of an 'other's' experience of being *othered*, can be analyzed in many ways: first, it provides the view of a gender-sexuality paradigm of non-normative identity located inside a normative structure—which is oppressive in its isolation of the 'other'. The narrator's view of their life as having a 'secret' aspect, that is deeply personal, yet political, speaks of the desire to attain dignity and self-worth external to their source of *othering*. Second, it provides a context for the non-normative located as culturally opposed to the normative—in other words, the dissociation of the non-normative identity from its own Nature (Jung, 1964). The narrator clearly talks about feeling trapped in their physiological 'self'—that of a *man*, a privilege in patriarchal societies, whereas their psychological 'self'—that of a *woman*, a considerably lower socio-cultural caste in our society, is nonetheless assertive and desires to exert its own selfhood outwardly rather than inwardly: therefore creating the 'cage' within their own consciousness. Third, it allows one to delve further into the psyche of the spatial location of the non-normative identity—the family, core value-structure and kinship ties. The narrator's relationship with their family is crucial to understanding their outlook on universal elements of existence, such as love, friendship, loyalty, faith, etc. The mother's lack of empathy for her 'son' is contrasted only with her attachment to the social parlance of her having borne a son (still largely considered the epitome of a woman's existence). And lastly, it provides a commentary on the collective dislocation of meanings attached to the 'other's' existence—vis-à-vis the chaos of survival and lack of self-actualization of the non-normative identity. 'Napunsaka' literally translates to 'not quite a man', but in common usage, it represents a man who has lost his manhood (Gannon, 2011). The 'hijra' as a category, on the other hand, stands for an oversimplified understanding of the gendered 'other', and as a common slur in our society. Both terms are often used as insults to a man: used as a retort for expressions of cowardice or *un*-manly behaviour. Both categories are historically relevant, and deeply embedded in our social psyche through the mytho-epic imagination. Interestingly, both these terms are being used to humiliate the narrator at the level of their physiological 'self', but the psychological 'self' remains unaffected by the derogation—perhaps because the narrator is experiencing life as a woman, and not a man. The consequence of this is a rupture in the narrator's experience of life, living simultaneously together *and* apart.

> (2) I am a 36-year-old architect, successfully running my own design firm for 3 years, with my business associate, who is also my civil partner. We are both gay asexual *cis*-men[13]. And I'm quite at peace with who I am. My partner and I have a wonderful relationship; we are hopelessly in love, but neither of us desires sexual gratification through physical expression. We connect with our minds. Fortunately, it's a mutual feeling.
>
> We have been together 5 years, and in these I have felt loved and respected like I have never before experienced. I was a pariah in my own family and community, being a gay man in a conservative religious community is extremely oppressive. I hid my sexuality for years, not even my closest friends knew what tremendous turmoil I managed to hide internally on a daily basis. I lost my mother when I was young, and my father remarried soon thereafter. My relationship with my father was ruined forever, although my stepmother and I now share a very close bond. She stood by me when I came out to my father. My father is a forceful dominating man, and has always been verbally vicious. Whenever things got heated, I pleaded with my stepmother to leave; but she stood by my father, like she did with me.
>
> Meeting my partner changed my outlook on life, helped me move on from a lot of repressed anger and pent up emotions. I could open up to him about my sexuality and still be accepted, on equal terms. He showed me a level of compassion I did

> not imagine was possible to experience. Even his ex-wife and children have a very positive outlook towards our partnership and lifestyle choice.
>
> The city also presented more problems when it came to us living together, or being open about our relationship. We bought a house together because it was so difficult to find a rented apartment as a gay couple in the city. Even then, we had to find a neighbourhood that would be accepting of a gay couple living amongst them. Very few places like that in the city, to be honest. I consider us *lucky* in that respect as well.
>
> Even so, life is neat and orderly. We have found our *Zen* [sic] moment in life, and I would hold on to that as long as possible.

The purpose of including the above narrative in this work is to elaborate on the diversity of the gender-sexuality spectrum explored in the mytho-epic imagination. The narrator here is a self-identified gay man, a *cis*-man, and asexual by preference. Asexuality is often equated with impotence, which is another element a *napunsaka* embodies. The tale of Samavan, who was a man who pretended to pose as his friend Sumedhas's wife to receive gifts by pretence, but at the end of the story both choose to remain in the marriage, even though they were both men. This can be read as a culturally accepted imagination of homosexuality (Pattanaik, 2014. pp. 71). Or take the story of Alli: the warrior princess, who refused to marry any man, and refused even (the Great) Arjuna's romantic advances (Ibid. pp. 145). Perhaps this is a subliminal suggestion towards asexuality: because, in Hindu mytho-epic imagination, Arjuna has been cast as the epitome of virility any mortal woman would find impossible to resist. However, in stories like these, the society of the mythological space recognizes and accepts the deviations from the norm without hesitation. Whereas in this account, at the manifest level, the narrator's own family and community consider their unorthodox identity unacceptable. The isolation felt by him as a homosexual man in a conservative society is evident in his emotions about home. However, his sexual preference would also further sequester his potential for a fulfilling romantic companionship—as asexuality is still largely misunderstood, even within the queer community (Mukherjee, 2016).

> (3) I am 45, I am a designer and I run my own boutique shop. I have a daughter, and we live with my mother. I am a lesbian, but I've only been aware of it for the past 6 years. I was married off when I was 21. I had my daughter at 23, and lived with my husband and his parents in their apartment. My in-laws were very traditional people, I wasn't allowed to have friends over or go out without my husband. My daughter was also treated similarly. My own parents were not exactly liberal but they allowed me more freedoms. After my father passed away, I wanted to live with my mother for a week or so. There, after many years, I met an old school friend. I had almost forgotten how it felt to have a frank conversation with another woman.
>
> By the end of that week, something had changed in me, and I began to think more independently. The following year I started my own business, it was my only escape from my failing marriage. The same year, I met my partner, and when we met, I felt an instant connection with her. We started talking, and that conversation hasn't finished yet—we tell each other all the time. After a few months of talking, we met at her house. That night I lied to my in-laws and stayed the night with her. I didn't go back after that. I met my daughter and told her the truth. I also decided to tell my husband that our marriage had failed, and I was leaving him because I was in love with a woman. He did not stop me, but my in-laws

> made very clear they wanted nothing to do with a 'mad' woman and wanted both my daughter and I to leave. My daughter supported my decision to leave, and she has been by my side since. My mother has supported my choices as well; in fact, my mother found her own sense of freedom after my father died. Sometimes we call our house 'Brindavan', because we seem to be so free and happy without the men in our lives trampling over us, drawing *lakshmanrekha* around us, and controlling our feelings. I know, not many people understand it, but we live in a small bubble of acceptance, and I wish it wasn't so rare.

Women have been 'othered' historically in our society: never considered as equal with men (Brodbeck, 2007; Chaudhuri, 2012; Luthra, 2014). Therefore, to include this above narrative, the attempt is to locate the queer woman in the mytho-epic representation and to juxtapose the social reality pertaining to the imagination. In this narrative, we are exposed to three generations of women who have felt oppressed by social practice of patriarchy, which disallows them the right to self-actualization or independence.

A 'lakshmanrekha' is an imaginary boundary that Lakshman drew around Sita (to keep her safe) while she was alone, which prevented anybody from stepping inside the line, but it also kept Sita from stepping outside. The comparison to *Vrindavan* is also symbolic, as in some mytho-epic stories it is seen as an open space for feminine expressions, where Radha and her *gopinis* indulged each other in *raas-lila* (love games) even in Krishna's absence (see. GALVA). The imagination of this mysterious place, where only women entered (except Krishna, of course), and practised love, and its forms in all its glory—is subjective of the feminine desire to express passion, often to each other. Hindu mythology is rife with such permissive approaches to gender and sexuality experiences; however, the lived experience is far-removed from those.

In the course of writing my doctoral thesis, I encountered and recorded many such narratives: each resplendent with its particular intrigue of character, plot and events. However, the focus then was on the politics of queer 'experience', and not so much its relevance in epic texts or its imagination in common parlance. Later, on rereading them as stories (similarly like the mytho-epic texts of the Ramayana and the Mahabharata) one begins to observe the patterns that emerge from the repetition of concepts and contexts, drawing out the similarities in the living histories. Thus, the primary aim of including these specific narratives in this study was to draw out the manifest experiences of 'others' in our society: where the imagination of the *queer* already exists in ancient religious texts, but it allows not only ambiguity of its conceptualization but also, its dissemination through generations. Thus, it is imperative to explore 'how, why, and when' the fissure, between the mytho-epic text and its relevance in current social psyche, occurred.

Conclusion

The ideals about love, sexual intimacy, masculinity, femininity, our sense of family, community, faith, as well as our notions of honesty, respect, courage, valour, charisma, and ultimately, the 'self'—referenced, are profoundly structured around our sense of culture and tradition; yet the imagination of the 'other' archetype in our social psyche is referenced from external cultural inputs. Historically, the Indian subcontinent has been absorbing peripheral cultures and their mythologies into its system, therefore, the existing mytho-epic imagination largely reflects all the external influences that have shaped, reshaped and contorted the originality of the textual reference (Janaky, 1992).

Over time, many versions of the Sanskrit texts have emerged, and with them, the imagination evolved into simplistic themes that are easily acceptable to the layperson. The current re-imagination in our society, therefore, is the product of generations of cultural interpretation, fuelled in the last few decades by primarily two sources of misrepresentation: televisation of the epics (the Ramayana and the Mahabharata) in the 80s and 90s, and the subsequent popular dissemination; and secondly, the various literary readings with specific interests of focus. In both, the central interpretative instrument has been the patriarchal gaze: creating the language of *othering* in our society. The use of terms like *napunsak* and *Brihannala* (Agoramoorthy, G. et al., 2015) remains a part of colloquial usage all over India, as do comparisons of Draupadi, Kunti, Radha and Sita, and of Rama, Ravana, Krishna and Arjuna, in most Hindu cultures. Here I agree with Barthes, that the mytho-epic imagination is primarily used to naturalize specific perceptions (1972): thereby imparting a sense of ancestry and tradition within the collective unconscious.

Therefore, the answer to my original question as to why there exists such a gap between the Hindu mytho-epic imagination of society and the current social psyche in our nation—it remains a composite of many factors emanating from various cultural, historical and political conditions. Barthes considers myth as a 'mode of signification': a language that takes over reality'. And I agree that the modern mythmaking process in our social psyche has created differentiations based on the categories rising out of our times. It is, however, a dynamic process and will keep evolving. With newer more nuanced interpretations, these categories will likely evolve further and embody newer symbols and meanings. One can hope, that in this movement of imagination, the 'other' will regain some of its original ambiguity and acceptance in the Hindu mytho-epic continuity.

Authors Note

Writing an essay in honour of Prof. Renuka Singh's academic career is a difficult but, undeniably exciting prospect. Her academic practise ranges from gender, culture, and society, to extended philosophical discussions on life, spiritualism, and the 'self'. Of these, the study of 'self' has greatly affected me as a researcher (and as an academic later on). The recurrence of 'self' as a concept, and the consequent chaos of attempts at defining it, locating it, and thereby regulating its context, has revealed a plethora of possibilities for creating new discourse within the discipline and practice of sociological inquiry. The sociological endeavour to understand the 'self' ultimately brought me to the pursuit of the 'other': as I attempted to locate the 'other' in social perceptions of gender in our society for my doctoral research. Prof. Singh's encouragement and enthusiasm for her students' research, and any curious mind, is a rare gift that I experienced: having had the opportunity to work with her during my university years. She inspired me to continue questioning existing literature and opinion, and to strive to find the fissures in present discourses; this rigour for the discipline, along with subjective curiosities, developed into a detailed narrative-based exploratory thesis on the queer experience in our society. This paper is, therefore, an effort to find, what I would argue, is a gap in the knowledge and interpretation of gender (especially when it comes to the queer) in Hindu mytho-epic imagination.

References

Agoramoorthy, G. and Hsu, M. J. (2015). Living on the Societal Edge: India's Transgender Realities. Journal of Religion and Health. Vol. 54(4). pp. 1451-1459. https://www.jstor.org/stable/24485502

Alisha, O. (2018). Tracing the Elements of Queerness in Indian Mythology with reference to the select short stories of Devdutt

Pattanaik's Shikhandi and Other Tales They Don't Tell You. Journal of Emerging Technologies and Innovative Research. Vol. 5(11). pp. 154-160.

Atre, S. (2011). The Feminine as Archetype. Annals of the Bhandarkar Oriental Research Institute. Vol. 92. pp. 151-193. https://www.jstor.org/stable/43941279

Barthes, R. (1972). Mythologies. Lavers, A. (Trans.). Hill and Wang.

Brodbeck, S. & Black, B. (2007). Gender And Narrative In The Mahabharata. Routledge.

Chakraborti, A. (et. al.). (Eds.). (2014). Mahabharata Now: Narration, Aesthetics, Ethics. Routledge India.

Chaudhuri, M. (2012). Indian 'Modernity' and 'Tradition': A Gender Analysis. Polish Sociological Review. No. 178. pp. 281-293. https://www.jstor.org/stable/41969445

Debroy, B. (2017). The World According to Valmiki Ramayana: Rama and Dharma. The Open Magazine. https://openthemagazine.com/lounge/books/theworld-according-to-valmiki-ramayana/

___(2019). Devdutt should be careful with Indian epics. The Sunday Guardian. https://www.sundayguardianlive.com/news/devdutt-carefulindian-epics

Doniger, W. O. (Ed.). (1994). Hindu Myths. Penguin Books.

___(2009). The Hindus: An Alternative History. Oxford University Press.

GALVA (Gay And Lesbian Vaishnava Association). Same-Sex Love and Affection in the Spiritual World. Tritiya-Prakriti: People of the Third Sex Understanding Homosexuality, Transgender Identity, and Intersex Conditions Through Hinduism. https://www.galva108.org/singlepost/2014/05/02/SameSex-Love-and-Affection-in-the-Spiritual-World Gannon, S. (2011). Exclusion as Language and the Language of Exclusion: Tracing Regimes of Gender through Linguistic Representations of the 'Eunuch'. Journal of the History of Sexuality. Vol. 20(1). pp. 1-27. https://www.jstor.org/stable/40986353

Gras, V. W. (1981). Myth and the reconciliation of opposites: Jung and Levi-Strauss. Journal of the History of Ideas. Vol. 42(3). pp. 471-

488. http://links.jstor.org/sici?sici+0022-5037%28198107%2F19 8109%2942%3A3%3C471% 3AMATROO%3E2.0.CO%3B2-S

Human Rights Watch. (2020). Lennox, C. & Waites, M. (eds.). This alien legacy: The origins of 'sodomy' laws in British colonialism. Human Rights, Sexual Orientation and Gender Identity in The Commonwealth. https://www.jstor.org/stable/j.ctv512st2.7

Janaky. (1992). On the Trail of the Mahabharata: A Response. Economic and Political Weekly. Vol. 27(37). pp. 1997-1999. https://www.jstor.org/stable/4398882

Jha, V. (2016). The Mytho-epic Reimagination. Indian Literature. Vol. 60(6/296). 21st Century Poetry and Other Writings from Gujarat. pp. 183-193. https://www.jstor.org/stable/44754735

Jung, C.G. (1946). Psychological Types. Kegan Paul & Trench Trubner.

___(1947). On the Nature of the Psyche. Ark Paperbacks.

___(1948). The phenomenology of the spirit in fairy tales. The Archetypes and the Collective Unconscious. Vol. 9(1). pp. 207-254.

___(1959). The Archetypes and the Collective Unconscious . Collected Works of C.G.Jung. Vol. 9(I). Gerhard Adler and R. F. C. Hull (Eds.). R.F.C. Hull (Trans.). Princeton University Press.

___(1964). Man and His Symbols. Garden City.

___(1969). Essays on a Science of Mythology. Princeton.

Kumar, P.P. (2016a). Chitra Banerjee Divakaruni's 'The Palace of Illusions': Revisiting the woman through the eyes of an extraordinary woman. Research Journal of English Language and Literature (RJELAL), Vol. 4, No. 1 , 432-435.

___(2016b). The fascinating world of retellings: Retellings of the Indian epics. Research Journal of English Language and Literature (RJELAL), Vol. 4, No. 2 , 793-797.

Levi-Strauss, C. (1955). The Structural Study of Myth. The Journal of American Folklore. Vol. 68(270). pp. 428-444. http://www.jstor.org/stable/536768

___(1963). Structural Anthropology. Jackobson, C. (Trans.). Hachette.

Lodhia, S. (2015). Deconstructing Sita's Blues: Questions of Mis/representation, Cultural Property, and Feminist Critique in Nina Paley's Ramayana. Feminist Studies. Vol. 41(2). pp. 371-408. https://www.jstor.org/stable/10.15767/ feministstudies.41.2.371 ?seq=1&cid=pdf-reference#references_tab_contents

Luthra, R.(2014). Clearing Sacred Ground: Women-Centered Interpretations of the Indian Epics. Feminist Formations. Vol. 26(2). pp. 135-161. https://www.jstor.org/stable/43860745

Meadow, M. J. (1992). Archetypes and Patriarchy: Eliade and Jung. Journal of Religion and Health. (Fall, 1992), Vol. 31(3). pp. 187-195. Springer. https://www.jstor.org/stable/27510694

Mukherjee, K. (2016). The Silent Opposition: Dissent and the sexual subaltern in India. SOAS South Asia Institute Working Papers. Open access: https://www.soas.ac.uk/south-asia-institute/publications/workingpapers/file118427.pdf

___(2017). Exploring the subversive Indian: sexual dissidence and the 'queer' in Indian popular culture. Journal of Gender and Power. Vol. 8(2). Open access: http://gender-power.amu.edu.pl/JGP_Vol_8_No_2.pdf

Pattanaik, D. (2014). Shikhandi: and other tales they don't tell you. Zubaan Books and Penguin Books India.

Rossi, I. (1973). The Unconscious in the Anthropology of Claude Lévi-Strauss. American Anthropologist. Vol. 75(1). pp. 20-48. https://www.jstor.org/stable/672338

Saraswat, S. (2018). Myth & Gender: A Critical Reading of Chitra Banerjee Divakaruni's Before We Visit the Goddess. International Journal of English Language, Literature in Humanities. Vol. 6(2).

Singh, R. (1990). The Womb of Mind. A Sociological Exploration of the Statusexperience of Women in Delhi. Vikas Publishing House.

Thapar, R. (1979). The Historian and the Epic. Annals of the Bhandarkar Oriental Research Institute. Vol. 60, No. 1/4. pp. 199-213. http://www.jstor.com/stable/41692304

___(2019). They Peddle Myths and Call It History. The New York Times. https://www.nytimes.com/2019/05/17/opinion/india-elections-modihistory.html

Tiwari, K. (2019). (Ed.). Queer Voices Deconstructing Gender binaries: Indian Myths and Modern Reality. Gender and Popular Culture: Identity Constructions and Representations. Cambridge Scholars Publishing.

Vanita, R. & Kidwai, S. (2008). Same-Sex Love in India: A Literary History. Penguin Books India.

Verma, R. (2019). The TV show that transformed Hinduism. BBC Culture. https://www.bbc.com/culture/article/20191022-the-tv-show-thattransformed-hinduism

Young-Eisendrath, P. (1995). Struggling with Jung: The value of uncertainty. Psychological Perspectives, 31(1), 46-54.

DEBATING CASTE AND DERA ASSOCIATION IN PUNJAB

Introducing an Alternative Narrative

Geetanjali Atri

Introduction

The sacred geography of Punjab has always been a complex reality. Sikhism is a relatively new religion with its own share of conflicts and contestations. From the period of Sikh gurus itself, there ran multiple discourses of Sikh religious identity. The challengers to the succession of gurus, like the Udasis, Gulabdasis, Nirmalas, Dhirmaliyas, etc., were seen as religious deviants; for not falling in line with the recognition of Khalsa as the ultimate Sikh identity. With them is identified the historicity of the modern-day Guru-led religious organisations in Punjab, known as 'dera' (Singh, 2016; Singh, 2017; Singh, 2009). The first to be identified as a dera, were the Udasis, who are followers of Sri Chand, the eldest son of Guru Nanak, instead of Nanak himself. Gradually, with a shift in the socio-political and economic conditions of Punjab, many more religious organisations emerged in the state. Rapid urbanisation, migration, Green Revolution and the Khalistan movement played crucial roles in this development. The term 'dera', in contemporary context therefore, has been broadened to refer to all these religious organisations which did not fit into the Khalsa framework.

While the generic term remained 'dera', it was classified into different genres to accommodate all such organisations depending upon their core beliefs, values and origins (Jodhka 2008; Singh 2016; Singh 2017; Ram 2004, 2007; Kumar 2012). The organisations which followed Sikh *rahitmaryada* (Sikh code of conduct) became the Sikh deras, and those which adopted any theological innovation became the non-Sikh ones. Prominent Sikh deras include Nirmal Dera, Dal Baba Bidhi Chand, Dera Nanaksar, Dera Baba Rumi Wala, and Gurdwara Rampur Khera, among others. Non-Sikh deras include Dera Bhaniarewala, Dera Baba Jaimal Singh, Nirankari Dera, Dera Sacha Sauda, Dera Sachkhand Ballan, Divya Jyoti Jagrati Sansthan, et al. This classification points towards a significant debate over the appropriateness of absorbing the non-Sikh organisations within the fold of 'deras'; but this essay delves deeper into the problem and examines caste as the perceived foundation on which the edifice of contemporary deras is believed to be standing. Methodologically, in order to examine the significance of caste in the social construction of Punjab, this essay offers an analysis of available secondary literature on the issue. Later, in order to make a case for alternative discourse on the subject, it resorts to primary ethnographic observations at one such religious organisation in the state named, Divya Jyoti Jagrati Sansthan.

Henry Lefebvre, one of the most important theorists on the production of space, believed that the idea of space is not produced in the definite measurements as have been developed for material goods, like one yard of cloth or the way it is for sugar in kilograms. Rather, the phenomenon of space is actually a result as well as a pre-condition of certain social structures (Lefebvre, (1991 [1974], p. 85). This idea of space being both, a result as well as a pre-condition of social structures, is widely adopted by contemporary thinkers to theorise the experience of caste in the case of deras. According to them, deras develop as a social space in response to the practices of caste in the state, but end up reinforcing caste identities (Ram 2004, 2007, 2008; Lal 2009; Jodhka 2009, 2008; Singh 2017; Singh 2009; Kumar 2012; Verma 2014; Juergensmeyer 1979, 1982; Judge 2014). Therefore, caste continues to be the most important conceptual tool to study deras in the contemporary context. Following this idea, they limit the understanding of such spaces as mere socio-religious organisations promising social equality and dignity to backward castes. Viewed from this perspective, fissures in the egalitarian promises made by the Sikh gurus paved way for the rise of deras in the modern-day Punjab.

Caste in Pre-Nanak Punjab: Socio-Political Influences

Caste system in pre-Nanak Punjab was dynamic. While on one hand, evidences from eleventh century suggest that the caste system remained largely ossified, on the other hand, socio-political changes from then onwards speak of the rigidity of caste hierarchies in Punjab. This dynamism has caught the attention of many scholars, commentators and ethnographers alike. There are several socio-political factors that influenced how caste was practiced in the period. For instance: the tribal pockets stayed longer and stronger in Punjab, as compared to the rest of the country, as also observed by famous philosopher Alberuni during his stay in Punjab, within the Ghaznavid empire, in around eleventh century (Habib, 1969, p. 9-10). Even the first census enumeration of Punjab, carried out by Denzil Ibbetson in 1881, points out that religious practices of erstwhile Punjab were more Mohammedan than Hindu and consequently, it were the social and tribal customs that guided the socio-religious life of the people instead of any caste-based norms of purity and pollution, as practiced in rest of the country (Ibbetson, 1987[1916], p. 14-15). Later, the *Glossary of the Tribes and Castes of the Punjab and North-West Frontier Province* (1990) also described Khokhar as a prominent tribe of the thirteenth and fourteenth century Punjab. As Dumont's seminal work *Homo Hierarchicus* (1970) would sum it, the caste system and its accompanying hierarchy based on the principals of purity and pollution would not exist at all, or would lack in rigidity, in the tribal societies. This could be considered as a possible factor leading to ossification and institutionalisation of caste in Punjab.

On the other hand, the most important political factor that affected the caste system from eleventh century onwards was the dislodging of Rajput rulers by the Turks. Before the advent of the Ghaznavid Turks, the Hindu Shahi family (Shahiya) led by King Jayapal was dominant in the Punjab, with the Satlej-Jamuna divide under the Tomar Rajputs (Grewal, 1990. p. 4). The existing Hindu society was already experiencing rigid enforcement of the caste system, large scale perpetuation of untouchability, restrictions of free social intercourse, prevalence of blind faith and superstitions, and the supremacy of Brahminical priesthood. All these were bi-products of the privilege that the Brahmins enjoyed under the patronage of Rajputs. Caste and its resultant incoherence has in fact, been viewed as one of the leading factors in the downfall of the Hindu monarchy (Jackson, 1999. p. 14). Under the reign of the Turks, with the devolution of the Rajputs from the status of power, both Rajputs and Brahmins faced social degeneration, paving way for the other castes to improve their social status. This translated into a sharp break from the traditional duties of Brahmins, who were now forced to look for new professions. The social status of the Brahmins was further affected by the fact that unlike their counterparts in other parts of the country, especially in southern India, they did not enjoy land rights in Punjab.

In late twelfth century, with the systematic invasion of Muhammad of Ghori, the Delhi Sultanate annexed the territories of Peshawar, Multan, Lahore, Uch and Delhi. The initially annexed territories, known as the Ghurid province, started expanding its frontiers into what was later to be known as the Delhi Sultanate (*Ibid.* 24-44). Although the Delhi Sultanate is described, primarily, as being agriculturally dominant, it also involved large-scale domestic, intra-Asian and Asian-European trade. This was handled largely by port-based merchants from the Baniya caste which was divided into a number of sub-castes. According to Habib (1990, p. 371-9), indigenous bankers who specialised in land trade, though belonging to the Baniya caste, were a category separate from the maritime traders. According to Schrader (1997, p.77), the establishment of the Delhi Sultanate had profound effects on sub-categories within the Vaisya castes. One such sub-caste that appears to have prospered the most under the sultanates, both Delhi and Lodhi, is the Khatri sub-caste. The Khatris were artisans, money-lenders, traders, and sometimes land-owners in Punjab, who played a significant role in the subsequent history of the state as all the Sikh gurus came from this caste group, which also provided for a large number of initial converts to Sikhism.

By the beginning of the fourteenth century, the Turks had organized the economy, resulting in expansion of crafts production and commerce. This, according to Habib (1969), led to an expansion of the artisan classes. Increased demand for certain goods by the ruling classes paved way for the adoption of newer professions by the indigenous population. The lower castes readily took to these as it gave them a sense of dignity within the caste hierarchy. Here, Habib makes a case for the liberation of the low-caste craftsmen, under the influence of the Delhi Sultanate. The egalitarian ideology of Islam caught the fancy of the urban low-caste craftsmen who wanted to break free from the shackles of caste. On the flip side, this, according to him, provided the foundation for easy political success of the Muslim invaders. This social milieu, in which the economic prosperity of the lower castes failed to translate in upward social mobility and diminution of discrimination, prepared the bedrock for the monotheistic movement of Guru Nanak.

Caste under Sikhism: A Brief Critical Overview

Emergence of the Sikh movement was the most significant occurrence in medieval Punjab. Understood from the perspective of caste, Sikhism began primarily a reform movement under the call of Guru Nanak. He proclaimed:

> जानहोजोती, जातपूछोना
>
> Know people by the light illuminating in them and do not ask their caste
>
> (Singha, 2000, p. 42)

Such an egalitarian origin of Sikhism not only had a demoralising effect on caste-rigidities and the institution of untouchability, but also helped in improving the social status of the depressed classes. In the existing social milieu of the time, the foundation of Sikhism was thus laid, as a religion opposed to Brahminical orthodoxy and caste system. This tradition was further strengthened by subsequent Sikh Gurus. Second in the line, Guru Angad developed the Gurumukhi language in order to disassociate from the Sanskriti religious tradition dominated by the Brahmins, and make education as well as religious texts accessible to members of the lower castes. At another level, he encouraged people from all sorts of social locations to compete in the wrestling bouts in the *mal akharas*. This was an innovative way of countering the taboo of untouchability. Similarly, in contrast to caste exclusivism, the practice of *langar* (community kitchen) as initiated by Guru Amardas, which involves partaking in communal meals irrespective of caste distinction, was a radical statement against Brahminical domination (Jodhka 2001: 41-6). Guru Amardas spoke boldly against the caste system, 'This body is made of five elements. It is subject to hunger, thirst, joy, sorrow, birth and death. It perishes and no caste goes with the soul to the next world. The Guru recognises no caste' (Macauliffe, 1963, p. 84).

The most significant contribution of Guru Arjan to the Sikh faith is the compilation of the holy book, *Guru Granth*. In it, he not only toiled to preserve the preaching and hymns of the first four masters, but also incorporated the words of Ravidas, Namdev, Sheikh Farid, Kabir, Pipa, Surdas, Ramananda, Beni, Trilochan and Jaidev; all of whom belonged to different castes, including the opressed ones. He proclaimed, 'My faith is for the people of all castes and all creeds; from whichever direction they come and to whichever direction they bow' (Pruthi 2004: 70). Similarly, Guru Gobind Singh tried to establish an egalitarian society with no distinction on caste or class lines, in ways more than one. His ideals of Khalsa, Khande-ki-Pahul, abolition of caste based surnames and promotion of the use of universal suffix 'Singh', 'Kaur,'and 'Panj Piyare', are all based on the principle of a casteless society. He declared in unequivocal terms:

> रंगरेटेगुरुकेबेटे
>
> Rangrete Guru ke Bete
>
> (Judge, 2014, p. 122)

Here, Rangretas or the Mazhabi Sikhs are the ones who occupied the lowest rank in the Sikh caste hierarchy, as low in the social status as Chuhras in the Hindu caste hierarchy. Theoretically, Bhai Gurdas best concludes the position of Sikhism on caste system, where he says that under Sikhism:

> चारवरनइकवरनहोये; गुरिसखवरयम, गुरमुखगोते
>
> All four castes have become one. All disciples of the Guru belong to the Gurmukh caste
>
> (Singha, 2000, p. 42)

In the post-Guru Gobind Singh phase, the Sikh movement was characterised by armed movements under the confederation of Sikh chiefs who were the rulers of twelve demarcated territories or the *misls*. These chiefs belonged to different castes, including the Tarkhans or the Ramgarhias, Kalals or the Ahluwalias, Sansis (a Dalit caste) and Jats, who were in the majority. The conversion of Jats to the Sikh faith is significant as it points to the disconnect that the Jats had started to recognize between their economic position and social status. While Jats belonged to the Shudra caste, they had prospered economically as landowning peasants under the patronage of Muslim rulers. It is interesting to note here, the observation made by Judge (2002, p. 179). He suggests that the relationship between Sikhism and the Jats is dialectical: 'While Sikhism helped the Jats to improve their social status, the Jats in turn contributed to the consolidation and expansion of Sikhism'. According to him, it is this dialectic of social change that significantly contributed to the rigidity of caste institution and subsequently, led to social death of the egalitarian values of Sikh gurus. Apart from the Jats, there were other Shudra castes that emerged to the top of the caste hierarchy under Sikhism, like the Sainis, Mehtons, Ahluwalias and Ramgarhias, along with the Khatris and Aroras who were already dominant castes within the Hindu caste structure. In order to maintain their newly achieved social status, they subjected castes lower on the rung to control from above.

Thus, despite their theological particularity, the Sikh community developed a three-tier caste structure over the course of time. At the top of this distinction were the Jat Sikhs, while Mazabis or Rangretas occupied the lowest rank, mirroring the position of the Chuhras in the Hindu caste hierarchy. On the middle rank were the non-Jat castes like Bhatias, Mahton, Saini, etc. Most recently, it was McLeod (2007, p. 184) who pointed out that there existed almost thirty different castes within the realm of Sikh religion, in which of course, Jats are the absolute majority. The caste composition of the Sikhs is characterised by the subsistence of distinct rigidity. Even though, the caste structure of Punjab lacked the rigidity of caste-based practices like purity and pollution or untouchability, it developed its own unique character of discrimination. For instance: separate Sikh places of worship, i.e. Gurdwaras have been instituted for the Dalit Sikh population in Punjab, along with separate marriage halls, cremation grounds, etc. especially in its rural pockets.

The Colonial Contribution

Following the annexation of Punjab by colonial rulers in 1849, a new social structure and caste relations were shaped in the Sikh community. The British initiated several steps that had lasting impact on the caste system. They diluted Jat dominance in Sikh soldiery, confiscated the estates of the most prominent Sikh chiefs, and crushed the priestly castes of Bedis and Sodhis. Consequently, caste emerged as a dominant trope for the colonial administration. In the aftermath of the mutiny, the British Indian Army was re-organised according to the theory of 'martial races'. Dirks (2002) points out that this was the race of the loyals, faithfuls and the manly independents, in contrast to others who were effeminate, coward and inclined to crime (p. 179). The Sikhs were recognised as one of the most prominent martial races of India. However, it was the Jats who were identified as parallel to the term Sikh. So, the term Sikh was now coterminous with Punjabi Jats. Just as the Mazhabi Sikhs were excluded from the religious shrines, and left to the religious administration of the *granthies* of their own caste, they were excluded from serving in the army as well. While later, in 1857, they were recruited in the army, their recruitment was restricted to the Mazhabi regiment.

According to Fox (1985, p.10; 141), the colonial administration deliberately constructed and nurtured an orthodox, saintly yet martial Singh identity, consisting of only the baptised Sikhs. Thus, the British-Indian forces were categorically organised on the lines of caste, tribe and religion. The British administration once again reinforced caste differentiation in the Punjabi society with their project for the development of canal colonies in 1885-1940, which involved allocation of over 4,000,000 acres of freshly developed virgin lands for ownership and cultivation. The land was allocated to the dominant castes; and outcastes such as Mazhabis, Balmikis and Ramdasias (Chamar Sikh)/ Ravidasias were not allowed to own land. This extraordinary privileging of the Jat agriculturalist contributed further to their caste domination and arrogance of privilege. But the discrimination meted out to the already downtrodden sections of the society pushed their members further in the direction of the Christian missionaries and their proselytising activities. As a result, the number of Christian converts rose rapidly. From 3,912 in 1881 to 19,000 in 1891; it registered an increase of 410 percent in merely a decade (Jones, 1989, p.87). The alarming rise in their numbers sparked a series of reform-revival movements in Punjab (Oberoi, 1994, p. 218-22).

Singh Sabha Movement

In the nineteenth century, Arya Samaj became the foremost Hindu reform movement in north India. Faced with identity crisis following extensive proselytisation, it started preaching the Vedas with a military zeal such that it subsequently led to the invention of the 'Vedic golden age' (Jaffrelot, 1996, p.76). They developed their own ritual of re-conversion, or getting back into the Hindu fold, known as *shuddhi.* It not only targeted those Christians and Muslims who allegedly descended from Hindu lineage, but also sought to 'purify' the untouchable Sikh and Hindu castes. To counter the growing influence of the Arya Samaj, and avert the risk of relapsing into Hinduism, Sikhs too launched a movement aimed at identity reformation, called the Singh Sabha Movement during the 1870s, in what Fazal (2015) refers to as 'boundary maintenance' (p.107).

The Singh Sabha Movement was theoretically aimed at total rejection of caste in Sikh religion. The social universe of the Sikhs came to be defined by, what was described as Sanatan Sikh tradition, which primarily posits a priestly religion. Per this, untouchable castes like Mazhabis, Ramdasias and Rahitas were forbidden from entering the Golden Temple. Their offerings of *karahprasad* were not accepted and the Sikhs denied them access to public wells and other utilities. And, those who were found guilty of violating these caste-rules were, as punishment, shunned by the whole society (Oberoi, 1994, p. 106). Others have commented that although the Singh Sabha movement was aimed at abolition of untouchability, it remained more concerned with opening schools and colleges instead of paying attention to caste-based religious discriminations.

The project initiated by the Singh Sabhas was advanced by the Akali movement. Grewal (1990, p. 162) calls the movement the 'third Sikh war,' in which 4000 died, 2000 were wounded and 30,000 men and women got jailed in a war-like movement against the British administration, aiming to liberate Sikh gurdwaras from the grips of Hindu *mahants* and arbitrarily nominated Sikh appointees. Subsequently, the demands of the movement were accepted with the passing of the Sikh Gurdwara Reform Act (1925). It recognised the democratically elected Shiromani Gurdwara Prabandhak Committee (SGPC) as the legal authority for management and control of certain Sikh gurdwaras. The Akali Dal became the political wing of the SGPC. It were the Jats, along with other higher castes, who composed 70 percent of the Akalis, thus ensuring, that social equality and abolition of untouchability and other discriminatory practices remained antithetical to their dominant position within Punjab's social hierarchy.

With the SGPC's association with the Akali Dal, politics of caste was further entrenched within the former institution. Such a trajectory of successive fissures within the egalitarian foundation of the Sikh religion has compelled Dalits to look elsewhere for social justice, a search in which the contemporary guru organisations have come up prominently.

Non-Sikh Religious Organisations: An Egalitarian Hope

The early twentieth century marked the origin of the Ad-Dharm movement against the backdrop of socio-political turmoil among the marginalised in Punjab. Opportunities of economic and educational mobility created by colonial rulers and reform movements were optimised by Ad-Dharmis (or Chamars). For instance: demand of boots and other leather goods, especially in the British army, led to the economic mobility of the Chamars, drawing upon their traditional occupation. This led to the consolidation of the Ad-Dharm movement, which gave a unified direction to Dalit consciousness in the state.

According to the Ad-Dharmmandal's official report (1931, p. 3; also cited in Juergensmeyer, 1975), the key objective of the movement was to unite untouchables of Punjab (like Chamars, Chuhras, Bhils, Sainis, among others) into a distinct 'quam' or a religious community, much like the Sikhs, Muslims, or upper-caste Hindus. However, after the partition, 'the movement found its reverberation among the vast following of Ravidas Dera epitomised by Dera Sachkhand Ballan,' informs Ram (2009, p. 3-4). He further points out that gradually, the Chamars of Punjab, especially those living abroad, started organising Guru Ravidas Sabhas and also established Ravidas shrines known as Ravidas Deras, in Punjab and abroad.

In deploying caste as a lens for looking at the evolution of deras, contemporary thinkers largely refer to this prominent association between a particular Dalit caste and one of the earliest non-Sikh religious organisations in Punjab. They discern Dalit experiences in the state as fundamental to the expansion of twentieth century deras. Juergensmeyer (1979) draws out commonalities in the cultural experience of deprivation among the Chamar caste members, across three different Punjab villages—Bimla, Nalla and Boota Mandi. Sant Ramji Das and the Gogapir sect are revered and followed in Bimla. Nirankari and Radhasoami organisations rule hearts in Nalla while the Ad-Dharm movement is followed in the prosperous Boota Mandi. Regarding the Radhasoami Satsang Beas, Juergensmeyer (1982, p. 213) points out that members of different untouchable castes like the Mahasha use the weekly *satsang* as a medium of building up their business contacts in other communities, and even seek favours to secure education benefits for their children.

Similarly, Singh (2009) connects the emergence of such organisations to the continued social exclusion and pervading inequality in the social and economic order of Punjab. He regards deras, especially the Dera Sachkhand Ballan, as egalitarian institutions which help in raising identity consciousness among Dalits. Jodhka (2009) too, begins by tracing the practice of caste from colonial Punjab while pausing at important points in history to build his case for socio-economic and political mobility of the untouchables in Punjab. He especially credits the Ad-Dharm movement and the Ravi Das deras with carving out a distinct identity for Dalits. He concludes that association between Dalits and the deras primarily reflect the former's quest for stability (2008). Jodhka's observation follows Ram's summing up of the organisations as 'centres of Dalit mobilisation' in Punjab (2007, p. 4067).

An Alternative Discourse

An Investigation into the historicity of the deras provides an alternative discourse to the one referred thus far, positing a framework in which caste politics of the state gets little role to play. In the history of Sikh religion, deras were basically organisations established by deviants who did not comply with the succession in the Sikh guruship. This led to the creation of religious islands, with their distinct beliefs and practices, vis-a- vis the mainstream religion, that is, Khalsa Sikhism. The first of such groups, termed as deras by the writers of Sikh history, emerged sometime around the sixteenth century. It was established by a group of dissidents called Udasis who were more attached to the teachings of Sri Chand, the eldest son of Guru Nanak, electing him as their guru over Nanak himself. After Udasis, another significant group of dissidents arose during the reign of the fifth Sikh guru, Arjan Dev. These were known as Minas.

Although exact periodic account of the origin of such groups has not been documented by writers of Sikh history, a rough chronology can be drawn between them and the reigns of individual Sikh gurus, corresponding to which, they emerged. Then came the Dhir Maliyas who owed their origin to Dhir Mal, the elder brother of Guru Har Rai, in whom the guruship of the Sikh faith was invested after their sixth guru Hargobind. After Dhirmal, it was Ram Rai, the eldest son of Guru Har Rai (the seventh Sikh guru), who established his own sub-sect, known as the Ram Rajya. There were yet others challenging the idea of a homogeneous Sikh faith, by forwarding claims to the guruship of the community from outside the familial clan of Guru Nanak. These include the Handali faction, Bandai Khalsa or Bandei Khalsa and Nirmalas, which according to Ram, were historical deras (2007, p. 4067). Historically therefore, deras have spoken the language of religious deviance instead of caste-based discrimination.

The contemporary understanding of deras as centres of 'caste-mobilisation' raises a few pertinent questions from sociological perspective: is it only Dalits who attend such religious organisations in the state? Do they have following in other castes? What could explain the absence of this other narrative from the hitherto surveyed literature on these organisations? And of course, if it exists, this alternative narrative of association between caste and such organisations, then what could be the possible factors behind it? This essay tries to address these questions through an ethnographic exploration of one such religious organisation in the state called Divya Jyoti Jagrati Sansthan (henceforth, DJJS), which is recognised by contemporary scholars as a non-Sikh dera (Singh, 2016, p.12; Meeta and Ravilochan, 2007, p.1910; Ram, 2007, p. 4067; Kumar, 2012, p. 343; Singh, 2009).

DJJS is a religious organisation, headquartered in Delhi, but originating in the Nurmahal area of Jalandhar district in Punjab. Led by Ashutosh Maharaj, the organisation claims to have emerged, in the early 1980s, against the backdrop of the separatist movement in the state. In the period that observed a strong reaffirmation of the Sikh religious identity as distinct from all hitherto existing religious identities, DJJS propagated the idea of 'Hindu-Sikh unity,' garnering support across both communities. Although largely inspired by the 'Sanatana Dharma' philosophy of Hinduism, the organisation maintains a syncretic approach to its everyday conduct. All this often raises more contestations than genialities from the organised religion of the state.

According to the 2011 census, Punjab with a scheduled caste population of about 31.9 percent against the national average of 16.6 percent, has the largest number of Dalits in the country. This social character of the state reflects in the management committee at the regional head office of the organisation. In the eight-member committee, there are three Dalits who, together with other members, form the second nucleus of power and authority. Power within the organisation flows hierarchically. At the top is the office of the leader, followed by his close confidantes in the governing body in Delhi and in the regional management committee in Punjab, respectively. Situated in a rural area close to Nakodar, Nurmahal Ashram also has maximum following amongst Dalit Sikhs. However, the composition of the followers differs from branch to branch within Punjab. For instance, the branches situated in the urban areas of Ludhiana, Moga and Chandigarh draw fewer Dalits compared to the Nurmahal and Kartarpur branches.

As part of the larger fieldwork for my doctoral thesis, I conducted twenty-five in-depth interviews with followers of the organisation, at its Nurmahal and Moga branches. These were conducted during the weekly *satsang* sessions of the organization. Respondents were identified using a mix of convenience and maximum-variation sampling techniques. A typically small sample was interviewed in great detail so as to ensure a comprehensive representation of the universe. Respondents included Khatris, Baniyas, Sadhana (Jat), Sihra (Ramgarhia), Mazhabi, Rai (Dalit), Brar (Jat) as well as Brahmins. The identification of such a composite sample, even through a mix of non-probability sampling techniques, indicated towards the changing trends in caste composition of the followers. Upper caste Sikh and Hindu denominations were also found among generational followers of the organization. It is thus apparent, that these organizations have followers of non-Dalit denominations as well. This association is however, yet to garner significant attention. Over-emphasis on studying the correspondence between Dalits and the deras also comes from the fact that Dalits, especially of the Doaba region of Punjab where most of these organisations are located, have achieved a significant difference in their economic status owing to large-scale migration. Based on an extensive field survey, Kaur (2019) points out that 'one member in every second Dalit family in Doaba region has gone abroad' (p.2). Data further indicates that 27.5 percent Dalits in the region have recorded a high socio-economic status while 43.7 percent has achieved middle status. However, this turnaround of economic fortunes has yet to translate into social status. Segregation of individual castes or groups of castes still remains fundamental to social organisation in Doaba villages.

On the other hand, for followers from dominant castes, alike their Dalit counterparts, apart from being an inter-generational phenomenon, such organisations also remain important centres of rehabilitation against drugs and substance abuse. According to the Punjab Opioid Dependence Survey (2015), conducted by the National Drug Dependence Treatment Centre of All Institute of Medical Sciences (NDDTC, AIIMS) and Society for Promotion of Youth and Masses (SPYM), there are 2,30,000 opioid dependents in the state out of total 8,60,000 users. The survey carried out in 10 out of the 22 districts of Punjab further reveals that while 80 percent of the addicts tried to quit at some point, only 35 percent could receive professional help. It is gaps like these that such organisations tend to fill for their followers. The social fallouts of drug abuse are manifold and beyond the purview of this essay, but these fallouts are addressed by these organisations using socio-spiritual methodology which turns the latter into a lucrative catch point.

At a more philosophical level, the upper caste respondents believed that DJJS and other such organisations lacked the ritual rigidity, which according to them was an integral part of the gurdwaras. In the same breath, most of them claimed however, that going to such organisations did not make them any less of a Sikh, as they continued doing '*path*' everyday. In fact, it is their regular attendance at the *satsang* sessions of the organisation, which helped them comprehend the true meaning of the *Guru Granth*, which they believed they were just rote learning earlier. Now they feel that their emphasis has shifted from learning the Granth to understanding it. Furthermore, they argued that this is the reason they do not feel threatened by fundamentalists who insist that following a living Guru is against the dictums of the Sikh faith. Apart from such social and philosophical reasons of associating with DJJS, they also cited 'constructive' peer pressure as a prominent inspiration for their initial association with the organisation.

Conclusion

Caste has always been integral to the social composition of Punjab. However, its nature has changed over time owing to various socio-political factors, be it the invasion of Mughals, genesis of Sikhism, or religious reform movements in the state.

These developments make caste an appropriate lens to look at the various socio-political developments in the state, from the origins of Sikhism, to the trends of migration. It is however, the pioneering association between a particular marginalised caste of Ad-Dharmis with the Ravidas temples or deras, that caste is discerned as a root factor contributing to the rise and expansion of non-Sikh religious organizations in the state. This has resulted in studies on such organizations getting attached to the Dalit factor. This over-emphasis on the association of one particular section of the Punjab society, however numerically dominant, ignores the trends in affiliation of 'other' sections, to such organisations. Filling in these gaps, this essay posits that with their prolonged presence in the state, such organisations have captured the socio-religious imagination of people from all caste groups even though the reasons for their affiliation may vary mutually.

References

Dirks, Nicholas. (2002). *Castes of Mind:Colonialism and the Making of Modern India*. Delhi: Permanent Black

Fazal, Tanweer. (2015). *'Nation-State' and Minority Rights in India: Comparative perspectives on Muslim and Sikh identities*. Oxon: Routledge

Fox, Richard Gabriel. (1985). *Lions of the Punjab: Culture in the Making*. California: University of California Press

Grewal, J.S. (1990). *The Cambridge History of India: The Sikhs of Punjab*. United Kingdom: Cambridge University Press

Habib, Irfan. (1969). The Historical Background of the Popular Monotheistic Movements of the 15th-17th centuries. in Bisheshwar Prasad (ed.). *Ideas in History*. Bombay: Asia Publishing House

___. (1976). Jats of Punjab and Sind. in Harbans Singh and N.G. Barrier (eds.).*Punjab, past and present: Essays in honour of Dr. Ganda Singh. Patiala*: Punjabi University. pp. 92-103

——. (1990). Merchant communities in Pre-colonial India. in James D. Tracy (ed.): *The rise of Merchant empires: Long Distance Trade in the early modern world 1350-1750*. Cambridge: Cambridge University Press

Ibbetson, Denzil. (1987[1916]). *Punjab Castes.* Delhi: Low Price Publications

Jackson, Peter. (1999). *The Delhi Sultanate: A Political and Military History*. United Kingdom: Cambridge University Press

Jaffrelot, Christophe. (1996). *The Hindu Nationalist Movement and Indian Politics, 1925 to the 1990s: Strategic Identity Building, Implantation and Mobilisation (with special reference to Central India)*. London: Hurst

Jodhka, Surinder. (2001). Caste in the Periphery. Seminar. No. 508. *Special Issue on Exclusion*. Symposium on Caste, Race and Dalit question. pp. 41-46.

——. (2008), *Of babas and deras.* Retrieved from http://www.india-seminar.com/2008/581/581_surinder_jodhka.htm

——. (2009), The Ravi Dasis of Punjab: Global contours of Caste and Religious strifes. *Economic and Political Weekly*, 44 (24), pp. 79-85

Jones, Kenneth W. (1985). *Socio-Religious Reform Movements in British India, Volume I.*Trumpington Street: Cambridge University Press

Judge, Paramjit S.(2002). Religion, Caste and Communalism in Punjab. *Sociological Bulletin.* 51 (2), pp. 175-194

——. (2014). *Mapping Social Exclusion in India: Caste, Religion and Borderlands.* Delhi: Cambridge University Press

Juergensmeyer, Mark. (1975). *AdDharm: Religion of the Untouchables.* Retrieved from: https://velivada.com/2019/08/22/ad-dharm-religion-of-the-untouchables-mangoo-ram-punjab/

——. (1979). Cultures of Deprivation: Three Case Studies in Punjab. *Economic and Political Weekly*, 14 (7/8), Annual Number: Class and Caste in India, pp. 255-257, 259, 261-262

——. (1982). *Religion as Social Vision: The Movement Against Untouchability in 20th Century Punjab*. Berkley: University of California Press

___. (1991). *Radhasoami Reality: The Logic of a Modern Faith.* UK: Princeton University Press

Kaur, Amanpreet. (2019). Changing Social Status of Dalits in Doaba Region of Punjab. Current Journal of Applied Science and Technology. 37(5), pp. 1-8

Kumar, Ashutosh (2012). Deras as sites of electoral mobilisation in Indian Punjab: examining the reasons that political parties flock to the dera. *Journal of Asian Ethnicity,* 15(3), pp. 335-50

Lal, Madan (2009). Gurudom: The Political Dimension of Sects in India. *South Asia Research,* 29 (3), pp. 223-234

Lefebvre, Henri (1991 [1974]). *The Production of Space,* Translated by Donald Nicholson- Smith. Massachusetts: Basil Blackwell, Inc.

Macauliffe, Max Arthur. (1963). *The Sikh Religion: Its gurus, sacred writings, and authors.* Delhi: Low Price Publications

McLeod, W. H. (2007). *Essays in Sikh History, Tradition and Society.* New Delhi: Oxford University Press

Meeta and Ravilochan. (2007). Caste and Religion in Punjab: Case of the Bhaniarawala Phenomenon. *Economic and Political Weekly,* 42 (21), pp. 1909-1913

Oberoi, Harjot. (1994). *The construction of Religious Boundaries: Culture, Identity and Diversity in the Sikh Tradition.* Delhi: Oxford University Press

Pruthi, Raj. (2004). *Sikhism and Indian Civilization.* New Delhi: Discovery Publishing House

Ram, Ronki. (2004). Untouchability in India with a difference: Ad Dharm, Dalit Assertion and Caste conflicts in Punjab. *Asian Survey,* 44 (6), pp. 895-912

___. (2007). Social Exclusion, Resistance and Deras: Exploring the Myth of Casteless Sikh Society in Punjab. *Economic and Political Weekly,* 42 (40), pp. 4066-74

___. (2008). Ravidas Deras and Social Protest: Making sense of Dalit Consciousness in Punjab (India). *The Journal of Asian Studies,* 67 (4), pp. 1341-1364

___. (2009). Ravidas, Dera Sachkhand Ballan and the Question of Dalit Identity in Punjab, *JPS,* 16 (1), pp. 1-34

Schrader, Heiko. (1997). *Changing Financial Landscapes in India and Indonesia: Sociological aspects of monetisation and market integration.* Hamburg: Lit Verlag

Singh, Joginder. (2016). *Religious Pluralism in Punjab: A Contemporary Account if Sikh Sants, Babas, Gurus and Satgurus.* New Delhi: Manohar Publishers

Singh, Santosh K. (2017). Deras as 'Little Fiefdoms': Understanding the Dera Sacha Sauda Phenomenon. *Economic and Political Weekly,* LII (37), pp. 20-3

Singh, Surinder. (2009). Deras, Caste conflicts and recent Violence in Punjab. *Mainstream Weekly,* Volume XLVII, No. 26

Singha, H. S. (2000). *The Encyclopedia of Sikhism.* New Delhi: Hemkunt Publishers (P) Ltd.

Verma, Neeru. (2014). Rise of Deras in Punjab: A Serious Challenge to Main Stream Sikhism. *Review of Arts and Humanities,* 3 (4), pp. 83-86

URBAN WOMEN AND MATTERS OF LAND

An Analysis of Land Politics in Urban India through Gendered Lens

Anindita Tagore

Introduction

Land is a key social, economic and political asset for families in general. It is a primary vehicle for creating and transferring wealth within the family, for providing sustenance and generating income, for gaining social status and claiming political voice, and for establishing some economic independence (Hanstad et al, 2009). Families with secure land rights feel more confident in making long term investments and production decisions, are more inclined to protect their natural resource base, may benefit from housing opportunities, and are more likely to avail of government programs and financial resources. It creates a conducive environment for fuller engagement as citizens. Hence, land and property are at the heart of various pressing development challenges in contemporary times. It is imperative that women, and not just their families, have secure rights to land as it can enhance their productive capacities and improve their position within the household and the community. It can empower women with direct access to other resources, significantly reduce their vulnerability, and secure greater scope for them in decision making processes.

Half the world's population now lives in cities. While providing housing for the urban poor has climbed higher on the priority lists of governments and international development agencies, women's issues have attracted minimal attention. In 2005, the Government of India amended inheritance laws to ensure that daughters enjoyed equal inheritance rights to their parent's land and property. While changes in Hindu succession laws are progressive, the society in which they operate is traditional and hence, very little actual impact has followed. Similar condition characterises the fortunes of Muslim women in the matter. Despite existing provisions in the Personal Law, Muslim women have largely been left wanting in terms of direct access to land and property of their families. This essay is an attempt to map, first, the history of land rights within India and how they have addressed the issue of gender. Second, the essay focuses on recording similarities as well as differences in land ownership patterns in both, urban and rural spaces by comparing usual impediments encountered respectively, by urban and rural woman, with regard to land rights. Finally, the essay seeks to draw attention to formal and informal barriers for women on the path to land ownership in urban India. Given the utmost importance of securing women's rights to land in a growing economy, this essay further intends to expand the knowledge base within this area, specific to the context of urban women.

Introduction—Gender, Property Rights, and Economic Development

Most works on gender and property rights highlight the dismal record of developing countries in providing women with equal rights, not only to land, but to basic necessities of life. Women have lesser access to shelter, income, water, food, education, and healthcare as compared to men, leading to what is often termed, the 'feminization of poverty.' While women are increasingly heading households, today, women and girls constitute approximately 70 percent of the estimated 1.2 billion people living in abject poverty across the developing world. They are estimated to be subsisting on less than a dollar a day. An obvious factor contributing to the overrepresentation of women in poverty is their largely inadequate ownership of land and other immovable properties. While such assets are generally considered to represent about 75 percent of a nation's overall wealth, women own only an estimated 1-2 percent of all titled land worldwide. While there is a dearth of reliable and comprehensive data on the extent of inequality between men and women with regard to access and control over land and real property, particularly in urban areas, available surveys and studies indicate that the disparity is substantial.[1] The plight of women in poverty seems destined to continue unless there is significant reform and strengthening of laws, policies, and practices relating to ownership and control of property throughout the developing world.

Promoting women's right to property accrues as a matter of human rights and underlines the principal of universal economic development. There is an abundance of research corroborating the link between rise in women's incomes and overall growth of an economy. It implies that women's income substantially boosts levels of household consumption. Men on the other hand, spend much of their income on personal items.[2] In addition, lack of women's property rights is increasingly recognised as contributing to other development-related problems including low levels of education, hunger, and poor health.[3] For women, there is a link between rural and urban poverty. Rural women's incomes could increase if they own or control land, individually or jointly, and have the benefit of legally recognized use and inheritance rights. Ongoing exclusion of women from rural land rights pushes them toward the cities, where they often add to women-headed or women-only households in slum areas where inadequate housing is the norm and homelessness is all too common. While women make up 66 percent of the labour force in urban areas of developing countries, they account for only 10 percent of the income. With urbanisation as well as feminization of poverty on the rise, it is critical for women living in peri-urban or urban settings to have clear rights and independent access, use, and control of property and housing for their own economic benefit and empowerment. This is also required for optimizing women's contribution to the growth of their national economies.

Why Urban?

Cognizant of growing urbanization and its key role in economic development, as well as the particular problems that beset poor women in urban settings, we consider the urban context instead of access to land in rural, agricultural settings. Nowhere are the inequalities facing urban women clearer than in urban slums and informal settlements. Throughout the world, these are the settings where women experience the highest levels of poverty, reproductive health risks, sexual threat, violence, as well as the worst barriers to education, employment, housing, and basic services like water and sanitation.[4]

For the first time in history, more people inhabit cities than the countryside. Cities are going to be the spaces where much of the global population growth in the next fifty years is going to occur. It is correctly estimated that most of this growth will be absorbed by cities of the developing world. A consequence of urbanization is the increasingly concentrated poverty in urban slums. One billion people now live in slums, most in wretched conditions. UN HABITAT estimates that the urban population in developing countries will increase from 1.9 billion in 2000 to more than 3.9 billion in 2030, equivalent to 70 million people per year. On balance, there is general agreement that urbanization should be viewed positively as it is fundamental to sustained national economic growth. Indeed, no country has achieved higher income status without greater urbanization. Nevertheless, while women have more opportunities for work in urban areas, they still typically earn far less than men, partly because they are concentrated in low-paying jobs, and often because they are paid less for the same work.

Women's Access to Land for Housing and Property for Entrepreneurial Activities

Numerous international legal instruments and declarations such as the UN General Assembly's Universal Declaration of Human Rights (1948), the Platform of Action adopted at the Beijing World Conference on Women (1995), and the Millennium Development Goals (2000), have recognized the importance of equal access to property rights.[5] Nevertheless, women continue to own only about 1-2 percent of land and other real property throughout the world.[6] How has this gross disparity come to be, and what perpetuates it?

Throughout history, numerous cultural, legal, political, and social factors have systematically impeded women's access to property. It is imperative that the problem is contextualised against common methods by which real property rights are acquired in developing countries. As with distribution of all resources, the rules, norms, and customs for land allocation are developed through various institutions in society—families, communities, state and the legal system, and economic markets. Gender inequality in access to property continues largely because of discriminatory inheritance and marital laws, women's unequal access to land markets due to income limitations, an inability to obtain conventional financing, and gender-biased and/or gender-neutral land reform policies.

Following are the common methods of gaining property rights, embedded with impediments to gender equality:

A. Inheritance and Marriage

Inheritance and marital laws vary considerably from place to place, and differ in the extent to which they recognize women's rights to property. In both Africa and Asia, the most widely practiced form of customary inheritance is patrilineal—through the male line only. Such systems often relegate women to unpaid labour on family farms or in family businesses while they are married, and push them to extreme poverty, desertion, singlehood, or divorce. Following widowhood, a lot of women are rendered homeless.

Women's rights may be particularly tenuous in cultures where polygamy is the norm, as in much of Africa and in Muslim cultures in the Middle East-North Africa region, and Asia. In Latin America, by contrast, it is more common to recognise, at least partially, women's contributions to the family's assets, in the event of marital breakup. In polygamous settings where women have property rights, wives often jointly inherit a plot of land that is often too small to grow enough food, let alone garner any other economic dividends.

In many countries, statuary laws or even constitutional provisions have been adopted to improve property rights of women. Unfortunately, records clearly show that legislative change does not necessarily translate into real rights given the resilience of customs and social norms that favour men's rights to land. There is often lax enforcement of new laws because longstanding social, cultural, and religious biases against women remain firmly entrenched.

Moreover, there are many legal exceptions in 'personal laws' that apply to marriage and family matters, making the more general rules on gender equality difficult to enforce or subject to evasion. In Kenya for example, the constitution states that any Kenyan of sound mind over the age of 18 may own property. However, in another section the text reads, '...courts shall be guided by African customary law in civil cases...so far as it is applicable and not repugnant to justice or morality'.[7] Even assuming that a woman is aware of her constitutionally guaranteed property rights, and has the wherewithal to take to the court, the latter provision provides judges with enormous discretion to apply customary rules regarding marriage and patrilineal inheritance instead of the letter of the law when adjudicating conflicts over land rights. Since women rarely occupy top-level judicial or enforcement positions, gender-equality perspectives are unlikely to be considered in policy formulations or while implementing new laws aimed at mitigating gender bias. In countries, or communities within countries where the Hindu or Muslim faith is widely practiced, courts may be inclined to defer to prevailing religious customs and norms of behaviour regarding marital and inheritance rights. In some places, members of religious groups are exempted from legal sanctions against discriminatory practices.

Needless to say, property rights assume critical importance for women when the household breaks down—through male migration, abandonment, divorce, polygamy, death, or natural disaster. Particularly in urban settings, where women are less likely to have access to the support of their natal family, independent, actuated property rights could determine the difference between a life of poverty and the ability to develop a viable, self-reliant women-headed household.

Many development programmes have been successful in mitigating the spread and the effects of HIV/AIDs which kills more men than women, leaving thousands of women in charge of their households. Integrating advancement in tenure rights for women in HIV/AIDs programmes might ensure their overall effectiveness and sustainability of results. Similarly, civil war or other major conflicts usually result in the creation of more women-headed households. Programmes to bolster economic development in post-conflict areas should take into account women's property rights. When men die in natural disasters their families are often left without a roof over their heads. When property rights are unclear, or do not extend protection to the widow, she may be unable to rebuild her family's shelter or engage in any meanigful economic activity on her late husband's property.

B. Communal and Joint Ownership

Communal ownership of land and property exists in some parts of the world, particularly sub-Saharan Africa, where customary land systems coexist with more formal titling systems. Under customary law, communal ownership and usage rights are usually vested in lineages or clans. While rights to use the land may be conferred upon both men and women, customs ensure that actual control of the land rests with senior men of the clan. Subplots are usually allocated to male members of a family or tribe when they marry, and are reabsorbed within the husband's family's stock upon his death.

While most countries have adopted laws prohibiting gender bias in communal land assignment under formal and customary systems, women's rights to communally owned land are often not honoured at the community level or even by way of law.

The exact type of rights that would improve women's access to property and economic productivity has been intensely debated over the past several decades. While individual rights are crucial for elevating women's positions, joint rights or titles are easier to attain in the near-term given the complexity and costs of revising formal tenure systems. This is also likely in light of continuing resistance to female ownership of lands. Given the importance of domestic ties in the lives of poor women, their interests may be better served through mechanisms that secure and extend their rights to the collective resources of the household. In any case, titling reforms are context-specific and so, requires careful examination of local laws and customs before deciding on a tailored approach.[8]

In other contexts, women's interests may be best served if they hold group rights in land, constituting a land trust in which women are designated as co-holders of rights. In a similar vein, women often join cooperative groups to access microfinancing in order to acquire and develop property.

C. Land Reform

Land reform[9] efforts, even when well-intended, have not always succeeded in achieving greater equality. Most early efforts, particularly those in Latin America and South Asia, targeted patriarchs of families. In Africa, land titling policies have largely focused on individualization of rights to former customary or communally held lands. The process most ostensibly favours family patriarchs, sometimes excluding women who formerly held customary rights. More recently, innovative practices have been adopted to ensure gender-sensitive policies and outcomes. In Guatemala for example, the state-sponsored land redistribution program requires that names of both spouses appear on documents establishing property rights.

India: Barriers to Women's Land Ownership

The acknowledgment that women have different needs than men, and that culture-specific constraints limit women's access and control over land and housing, has dawned quite recently in policy circles of developing countries. Consequently, these issues have acquired prominence in research in and on South Asia only in recent years. It has since been documented through multiple sources of evidence, mostly in the rural context in South Asia, that women's ownership of land and housing provides vital security against poverty that other forms of income do not afford (Agarwal,1994a; Carr, Chen, & Jhabvala, 1996; Chen, 1998). Since private ownership of landed property occupies a privileged position in the South Asian context, it has also been suggested by several researchers that property ownership strongly influences gender relations both within and outside the household. Basu (1999) writes that property often emerges as the cornerstone of women's capacity to challenge numerous oppressors: the state, contractors, landlords, husbands and parents. Despite such compelling evidence, governmental responses to women's needs in South Asia have continued to concentrate largely on health, nutrition, and poverty alleviation schemes over gender-focused reform of landed property rights, legal literacy, and political equality. Despite compelling evidence and repeated assertion by scholars, of the fundamental value that property rights holds for women's empowerment, governmental responses are mostly marked by reluctance to engage in an issue that is largely shaped by traditional and customary factors (Agarwal, 1994b, 1997; Chen & Dreze, 1992; Sen, 1999; Sen & Grown, 1988; Nussbaum, 2000). Even feminist organizations with avowed aim

of improving women's economic status, have over-engaged with matters of employment and wages while sidelining property ownership.

Urban research in the developing world is increasingly acknowledging the fact that women's access to house and land is a key determinant of their empowerment in urban areas (Tinker & Summerfield, 1999). Mearns (1999) describes how women are excluded from land rights through either legal or cultural means. They emphasize that this lack of access and control is a key determinant of women's economic status and poverty. In India, although women enjoy equal legal rights to own property, many cultural traditions deny them inheritance or management rights. Since struggle for women's property rights requires legal, institutional, and cultural transformation, tenure reforms without express guarantees for women can disadvantage them even further.

In India, seven factors variously impact women's ability to own land: lack of legal knowledge, gendered norms and attitudes about land ownership, lack of formal recognition of women's right to own land, gender biases in family inheritance, lack of formal documentation, difficulties encountered in interactions with government officials, and vulnerability to changes in the family.

1.1 Legal Knowledge

In India, women's rights to own and inherit land are largely determined by family laws which vary among communities. With that in sight, this section considers domestic awareness of relevant laws: the Hindu Succession Act and the Muslim Personal Law.

1.1.1 Hindu Succession Act (HSA)

The Hindu Succession Act (HSA) (1956) consolidated existing succession laws establishing a uniform and comprehensive system of inheritance for Hindus. The Act particularly aimed at guaranteeing women's inheritance rights. Under the HSA, when a man dies without leaving a will, his personal property devolves first and equally to 'Class I' heirs, a category including widows, sons and daughters. Should no Class I heirs exist, the property passes on to Class II heirs in the order delineated in the HSA. While daughters and widows gained rights to equal inheritance of personal property, one oversight in the HSA was the failure to establish women's equal right to inherit joint family properties. Ownership of joint family property was conferred on the group designated as 'coparcenary'. Membership of the latter is limited to male heirs thereby, excluding daughters from a share of this inheritance. Later, state amendments to the HSA, known as the Hindu Succession Act Amendments (HSAA), addressed this discrepancy, recognizing daughters of coparceners as coparceners themselves.

1.1.2 Muslim Personal Law (MPL)

The Muslim Personal Law Application Act of 1937 represents the formal codification of Sharia in India.

1.2 Norms and Attitudes

In communities that rigidly define economic activities and social responsibilities along gender lines, social norms can influence women's ability to own productive assets such as land. If the prevalent norms around land ownership are gendered and sufficiently strong, they can constrict women's economic choices by making it too onerous to deviate from what her family and community consider socially acceptable conduct.

1.13 Recognition of Women's Land Ownership

Since women's rights to land are legitimate only if they are recognized by relevant public actors, we asked women and their husbands whether women's rights to own and inherit land were recognized by three overlapping authorities: the state and political actors, religious leaders, and village leadership which represent local recognition.

1.1.4 Religious Recognition

About half of the women, Hindus and Muslims, reported that their community leaders do not recognize women's right to inherit land from their parents or in-laws.

Acquisition Methods

Having established that women are much less likely to own land than men, we now explore avenues through which households come to own land, and the extent to which these avenues are gender biased. Review of literature suggests that inheritance is by far, the most frequent mode through which families acquire their homestead plots. Inheritance also varies depending upon religion, caste and class. Families hailing from lower middle class backgrounds invariably depend on ancestral property compared to those who have white collar jobs and are able to maintain financial stability.

2.1 Government Allocation

India has a long and varied history of state-level land allocation programs, many of them targeting women. They have also managed to reach some of the most vulnerable sections of the population as the literature reveals that those receiving government land were mostly from backward castes.

2.2 Documentation

Obtaining a title deed for a property in India can be cumbersome and onerous, often involving circumvention of the formal process, going instead by 'white paper' transactions. Even when formal processes to record land allocations or purchases are initiated, they are seldom followed through. The results vary according to state, religion and mode of acquisition. Another point to note is that joint-titling was virtually non-existent. Formal documents list either the woman's name or her husband's, but not both. It therefore creates yet another imperative to check how often women figure as title holders in such formal documents.

2.3 Interactions with Government Officials

Registering land ownership requires interacting with government officials to record land transfers, or to ensure that paperworks are in order. If women are not deft in navigating these interactions it might significantly affect their ability to gain access to and/or maintain control over land. Literature allows us an estimation of how often women venture to these offices alone or with an accompanying male relative.

Role of Women in Urban Economic Development

Women and girls are migrating to urban areas across the developing world in numbers greater than ever before. As of 2008, women constitute nearly half of the bulk of urban migrants, and those numbers continue to grow. While many accompany their husbands, shifting base to the urban for work purposes, a growing number of women are shifting bases in pursuit of their independent aspirations. Fleeing threats, discrimination, or simply lack of opportunity, women arrive at urban centres with little to no capital, believing that cities hold out opportunities for better life and livelihood. Unfortunately, this is not a truism for poor urban dwellers, especially women, who often lose out to men through a combination of legal, social, and economic factors when competing for similar positions.

In many developing societies women's economic rights are limited and they encounter legal, economic, and social constraints when attempting to find formal employment. Far too often, women are not considered long-term or safe employees in the formal job market. Employers fear that marriage, pregnancy, or husband's demands might compel a female worker to quit. Consequently, apprehensions of potential loss in training time and investment often disincentivize prospects of hiring women employees.[10] To make matters worse, the legal restrictions women face when accessing land and capital make it difficult for them to start a formal businesses themselves.

A recent study by the World Bank found that in a pool of 128 countries, ranging from OECD high-income economies to gradually developing ones, only 20 had legal systems that treated men and women as equals.[11] While legal hurdles vary in degrees, all contribute to a cumulative constriction of scope for women's economic independence. Irrespective of type and level, legal restrictions correlate with decreasing levels of female business ownership and management. It is therefore unsurprising that while women make up more than 50 percent of the global population and shoulder 66 percent of the labour, they garner only 10 percent of world income and own an infinitesimal 1-2 percent of the land.[12] These hurdles figure even while implementing the Millennium Development Goal of promoting gender equality and women's empowerment. While some significant headway has been made, for instance, in arresting gender disparity in primary education, the progression from education to employment, especially in the non-agricultural sector, is still difficult for women. Progress in this respect is also difficult to assess due to the high occurrence of informal employment and the resulting poor wage reporting. Lack of progress can be discerned from the disproportionately high representation of women in poverty, as also the relatively dismal financial profiles of matriarchal households in urban areas. In Nairobi for example, poverty incidence in female-headed households was 48 percent in 2001, compared to 31 percent in male-headed households.[13]

Given the anxieties surrounding employment of women in the formal sector, bulk of the urban women workforce is compelled to stagnate in the informal sector. The latter sector is characterized by small enterprises, generally unregistered, with work conducted by casual or intermittent labourers.[14] Paucity of employment and overcrowding of the sector often result in trivialization of worker's rights and protections while wages remain woefully low. Informal work has no minimum wage requirements, no mandatory break times, and no safety standards. Informal labourers are usually the first to be fired, and are most vulnerable to economic shifts such as the current global economic downturn.[15] In addition, women lacking land and capital ownership are far less likely to pay taxes on income, assets, or capital, while simultaneously facing greater barriers to diversification in terms of employment.[16] This gap in taxation can be significant when a large percentage of a country's population works in the informal sector, and can lead to diminishing public revenue and lower investment in infrastructure, education, transportation and healthcare.

For women, working in the informal sector most frequently means working as a street vendor, or directly out of the home as a vendor or piecemeal worker. In many developing countries, 85 percent or more of home-based workers are women, with a similarly high percentage of women running hawking stands. Both categories of informal work are directly affected by a pervasive lack of tenure rights, especially in urban areas. As noted previously, home investments are more likely to occur if the property is secure from seizure by local authorities or land ownership can be formally transferred. If informal wages and profits account for 45 to 50 percent of non-agricultural GDP, as in some African countries, augmenting productivity by roping in women ought to be an obvious imperative.

Evidence shows that women's economic independence often positively impacts living standards of the family. Several studies by the International Centre for Research on Women indicate that women are far more likely to spend their own money on food and other family necessities than on personal luxury goods and consumables such as cigarettes or alcohol. They found that for better impact on children's nutrition and health, a monthly increment of 10 dollars to women's income would have to be matched by an increase of 110 dollars to men's income. [17] This finding makes it amply clear that greater female employment and improved rights over their own finances have significant effect on improving human capital and family well-being.

Conclusion

Women contribute significantly to the entrepreneurial world. They produce and consume goods, earn salaries, borrow and save, and manage households, businesses and employees. In Africa, Asia, and Latin America, women account for at least half of the informal workforce. But also quite importantly, women-run businesses are perceptibly on the rise across the developing world, and according to USAID, women entrepreneurs are likely to prove fundamental as developing economies transition from primarily agricultural to industrial production and become urbanized.'[18] It is therefore essential that expansion of women's ability to own property and access markets be an important facet of pro-poor economic development plans.

References

Agarwal, B. (2002). Are we not peasants too? Land rights and women's claims in India. SEEDS, 21. Population Council.

Allendorf, K. (2007). Do women's land rights promote empowerment and child health in Nepal? World Development, 35(11), 1975-1988.

Bell, K. C. (2011). Integrating gender issues into bank land projects. Presentation at World Bank Annual Conference on Land and Property.

Chen, M. A. (2001). Women and informality: A global picture, the global movement. SAIS Review, 21(1), Winter-Spring.

Chowdhry, P. (2011). Reduction of violence against women: Property ownership and economic independence in rural Haryana. UN Women.

Deininger, K. W., Ayalew, D., & Yamano, T. (2006). Legal knowledge and economic development: The case of land rights in Uganda. World Bank Policy Research Working Paper, 3868.

Field, E. (2006). Property rights and investment in urban slums. Journal of the European Economic Association Papers and Proceedings.

Field, E., & Terero, M. (2006). Do property titles increase credit access among the urban poor? Evidence from a nationwide titling program. Harvard University.

Field, E. (2003). Fertility responses to land titling: The roles of ownership security and the distribution of household assets. Harvard University.

Field, E. (2002). Entitled to work: Urban property rights and labour supply in Peru. Princeton Law & Public Affairs Working Paper No. 02-1.

Food and Agriculture Organization of the United Nations (FAO). (2002). Women's right to land: A human right.

Giovarelli, R. (2009). Gender and land tenure reform. In R. L. Prosterman, R. Mitchell, & T. Hanstad (Eds.), One Billion Rising: Law, Land and the Alleviation of Global Poverty. Leiden University Press.

Grown, C., et al. (2005). Taking action: Achieving gender equality and empowering women. Earthscan Publications.

Gupta, J. (2006). Property ownership of women as protection for domestic violence: The West Bengal experience. In Property Ownership and Inheritance Rights of Women for Social Protection—The South Asia Experience. International Center for Research on Women.

Haddad, L., Hoddinott, J., & Alderman, H. (1997). Introduction: The scope of intrahousehold resource allocation issues. In L. Hassas, J. Hoddinott, & H. Alderman (Eds.), Intrahousehold Resource Allocation in Developing Countries: Models, Methods, and Policy. The Johns Hopkins University Press.

Hanstad, T., Prosterman, R. L., & Mitchell, R. (2009). Poverty, law, and land tenure reform. In R. L. Prosterman, R. Mitchell, & T. Hanstad (Eds.), One Billion Rising: Law, Land and the Alleviation of Global Poverty. Leiden University Press.

International Center for Research on Women. (2008). One woman = One business: Why business and management education for women is essential to economic development.

Katz, E., & Chamorro, J. S. (2002). Gender, land rights, and the household economy in rural Nicaragua and Honduras. Paper prepared for USAID/BASIS CRSP.

Khan, H. (2011). Sindh land distribution program: Impact and challenges. Paper presented at 'Gender-based Violence and Justice in South Asia.'

Panda, P. (2006). Domestic violence and women's ownership: Delving deeper into the linkages in Kerala. In Property Ownership and Inheritance Rights of Women for Social Protection—The South Asia Experience. International Center for Research on Women.

Panda, P., & Agarwal, B. (2005). Marital violence, human development and women's property status in India. World Development, 33(5).

Saxena, N.C. Women and forests in India. Draft.

Steinzor, N. (2003). Women's property and inheritance rights: Improving lives in a changing time. USAID.

Tertilt, M. (2006). Polygyny, women's rights, and development. Journal of the European Economic Association, 4(2/3), 523-530.

UNICEF. (2004). Gender equality-the big picture. Retrieved from http://www.unicef.org/gender/index_bigpicture.html

USAID. (2005). Enhancing women's access to markets: An overview of donor programs and best practices.

USAID. (2006). Women in the economy: A review of recent literature.

United Nations: Department of Economic and Social Affairs. (2009). 2009 World survey on the role of women in development: Women's control over economic resources and access to financial resources, including microfinance.

Uy, W. J. (2006). Medium rise housing: The Philippines experience.

World Bank Group. (2003). Gender issues and best practices in land administration projects—A synthesis report.

World Bank Group. (2010). Jordan NOW: Building confidence, creating job opportunities, changing lives.

World Bank Group. (2010). Women business and the law 2010—Measuring legal gender parity for entrepreneurs and workers in 128 economies.

World Bank Group. (n.d.). Why is women's economic empowerment important for development. Retrieved from http://siteresources.worldbank.org/INTGENDER/Resources/womens_economic_empowerment.pdf

WOMEN AND VIOLENCE IN THE WORKPLACE IN INDIA

A Socio-legal Perspective

Ellina Samantroy

The Context

The Sixty-fifth Commission on Status of Women (2021) concluded that women's full and effective participation and decision making in public life, as well as elimination of violence, is critical for achieving gender equality and empowerment of women.[1] The Global Sustainable Development Goals (Goal 5) aims to eliminate all forms of discrimination and violence against women in public and private spheres, undertake reforms to actualise women's equal rights to economic resources, and promote gender equality and empowerment of women.[2] Violence and harassment, including sexual harassment, constitute a serious human rights issue that negatively affects individuals, workplaces and society. It also creates hurdles for women and men seeking decent employment. Data from the World Employment and Social Outlook: Trends for Women, 2019, revealed a wide gap between South Asia and rest of the world in terms of percentage of women's representation in the labour market. For the year 2018, women's participation in South Asia charted 27.6 percent, compared to 48.5 percent of the global average, while men's participation stood at 79 percent against the global standard of 75 percent. (ILO, 2019).

In India, female labour force participation has declined, from 44.2 percent in 2004-05 to 24.0 percent in 2018, in the productive age group of 15-59 years, as reported by the National Sample Surveys (NSS) under the Ministry of Statistics and Programme Implementation (MoSPI), Government of India. Though there are several reasons underlying the above trends, there is valid concern that owing to restrictive gender and cultural norms, women in India are more constrained in their options of paid employment. Majorly, high probabilities of harassment and violence at workplace discourage women from joining the workforce. Though official statistics on violence and harassment in the workplace is limited, available data show that women who face discrimination because of their race, ethnicity, national and social origin, religion, health condition, or other grounds such as class, caste or sexual orientation, are also susceptible to violence and harassment.

As signatory to a number of international human rights treaties and declarations including, the Convention on the Elimination of All Forms of Discrimination against Women (CEDAW) 1979, India is committed to elimination of violence against women. Recent decades have witnessed progress in improvement of legal and regulatory environment with adoption of the Sexual Harassment of Women at Workplace (Prevention, Prohibition and Redressal) Act in 2013. Regardless, workplace harassment remains a prominent hurdle in the way of women's empowerment. The Convention on Violence and Harassment, 2019 (C190), pioneered by the International Labour Organization (ILO), revisited the issues of violence and harassment, recognizing them as human rights violation, and as threat to equal opportunities and promotion of gender equality.

From a theoretical perspective, a feminist understanding of violence is critical for uncovering mechanisms of systemic violence perpetuating across generations. This position considers gendered structures and imbalance of power existing in society, as responsible for promoting cultures of violence (Lidman, 2018). It provides a broader understanding of the term 'violence' by focusing on intersectionality. Noted radical feminist Catharine MacKinnon describes women's position as a 'structural problem' and of enforced inferiority, a condition which is substantively produced and sustained through sexual harassment (McKinnon, 1979). Scholarly works on feminist jurisprudence highlights an imperative to constantly review the role of courts, and the need for more pragmatic, broad-based approach to ensure that sexual harassment is adjudicated in a principled manner (Scott, 1999). Other feminist scholars point out that sexual harassment is a phenomenon which closely corresponds to agonistic workplace dynamics and functions as a means of establishing male control and expressing or perpetuating masculine norms in the workplace. Moreover, gendered nature of women's employment, like their concentration in traditionally low paying jobs, has provided men with an economic edge, emboldening them to find it appropriate to monitor and comment on (women's) physical presentation (Abrams,1998). The issue of violence against women acquired prominence only in the late 1970s, during the second wave feminism, popularly dubbed 'radical feminism'. Proponents of the second wave interpreted violence as resulting from the hierarchy of sexes and as a consequence of accepted practices in society. Advent of feminist worldviews also reflected in legislation, and the year 1975 was marked International Women's Year. Shortly after, 1979 witnessed the foundation of the Convention on the Elimination of All Forms of Discrimination Against Women (CEDAW). Later yet, gender-based violence gets recognised as an issue of human rights (Lidman, 2018)

In an attempt to highlight systemic gender discrimination, this essay seeks to locate the workspace at the intersection of violence and opportunity. It seeks to examine the existing legislative framework for addressing workplace violence and harassment, which are committed to aligning with international labour standards. It also aims to understand the challenges in implementation of legislation, and the roles and responsibilities of different stakeholders in terms of preventing, responding and addressing issues of violence and harassment at the workplace. The essay is largely based on intense desk review of literature drawn from secondary sources including review of legislations, international labour standards, and discussions with stakeholders. The essay also includes secondary data drawn from labour force surveys (National Sample Surveys, Periodic Labour Force Surveys), for estimations on labour market.

Evidence from Literature

The issue of harassment and violence against women at workplace has been central to discourses on human rights. Some of the studies within the Asian context have highlighted the importance of legislative reform for protection of women against workplace violence (Malla, 2005). Studies in the Indian context highlight experiences of women as victims of workplace harassment across organizational hierarchy, and the urgent need for protection of women workers in the burgeoning informal sector (Dasgupta 2019 & Sahgal and Dang 2017). The vulnerability of migrant women workers and domestic workers to sexual harassment at workplace has been highlighted in a study conducted by the Participatory Research in Asia (MFI, not dated). Further studies point out gaps in legislation and reveal harassment as borne out of and closely related to the nature of work conditions and power hierarchy in the workplace (John, 2014 and Sarpotdar,

2016). While introduction of the new ILO Convention (C190) on Violence and Harassment augurs hope for women's emancipation, it needs to be compared with existing legislations on workplace harassment.

Conceptualizing Violence and Harassment within the Framework of International Labour Standards: ILO Convention 190

The ILO had already developed a system of labour standards with the express aim of promoting gender equality in employment opportunities.[3] This comprehensive yardstick, developed out of tripartite discussions among governments, employers, and workers representatives from across the world, provides guidelines for policy formulation and legislation on workers' rights and social justice. These standards inspire governments and employers to maintain a minimum degree of labour standard so as to gradually diminish low skill and low wage employment. The ILO standards are periodically ratified by nations. The new Convention (C190) recognises universal right to non-oppressive workspace, free from violence and harassment. However, in context of the reality of systemic gender-discrimination, the Convention recognizes that women and girls are disproportionately affected by gender based violence and harassment. It advocates an inclusive, integrated and gender-responsive approach which may tackle underlying causes and risk factors including gender stereotypes, multiple and intersecting forms of discrimination and unequal gender-based power relations.[4]

The Convention (C190) defines the term 'violence and harassment' in the world of work as 'a range of unacceptable behaviours and practices, or threats thereof, whether a single occurrence or repeated, that aim at, result in, or are likely to result in physical, psychological, sexual or economic harm, and includes gender based violence and harassment'[5]. The scope of the Convention is amply wide and covers employed personnel, irrespective of contractual status, persons in training, interns and apprentices, terminated employees, volunteers, jobseekers and applicants, and individuals with authority, duties and responsibilities of an employer.

The Convention applies to both, public and private, as well as formal and informal sectors, and across the rural-urban divide. It takes into account the involvement of third parties and observes legislation, policy formulation, development of tools for enhancing awareness, education and sensitisation on gender issues, and inspection and investigation of reported cases through labour inspectorates or other competent bodies. It also guides development of remedial and support systems for victims.[6] One of the standout features of the Convention is its recognition of psychosocial risks associated with violence and harassment, and includes the same in management of occupational safety and health. Article 12 of the Convention states that 'The provisions of the Convention shall apply by means of national laws and regulations as well as through collective agreements or other measures consistent with national practice, including by extending or adapting existing occupational safety and health measures to cover violence and harassment and developing specific measures where necessary'.

The Convention is followed by a body of recommendations, Violence and Harassment Recommendation, 2019 (R 206) which makes it imperative for legislations and policies to incorporate non-discrimination instruments like equal remuneration, and checking for discrimination in employment and occupation.[7] It further recommends aligning legislations with international labour standards on occupational safety and health.[8] It draws attention to cultural and social norms as frequent factors producing and sustaining workplace discrimination. It marks night time working hours as meriting special attention to neutralize risks of violence and harassment. With an eye on effective remedial methods, the recommendations include establishment of crisis centres, 24 hour hotlines and psychological counselling along with medical care.

The Convention has currently been ratified by thirty-six countries. Although India is yet to ratify the C190, its comprehensive legislation in the form of The Sexual Harassment of Women at Workplace (Prevention, Prohibition and Redressal) Act, 2013 (POSH) predates the Convention by six years. It bears mention that much of the provisions of the Convention already figures in the Act. The Convention however, is much broader in scope and merits comparison with the POSH Act specifically, of the extent of effective implementation on ground.

The Sexual Harassment of Women at Workplace (Prevention, Prohibition and Redressal) Act, 2013

The genesis of the POSH Act can be traced to the landmark 1997 Supreme Court judgment of *Vishaka vs State of Rajasthan.*[9] Other international conventions/instruments ratified by India include the Universal Declaration of Human Rights (1948), International Covenant on Economic, Cultural and Social Rights (1966), UN Declaration on Elimination of Violence Against Women (1993), and the Beijing Platform for Action (1995). As signatory to these conventions, India is committed to abolishing violence and harassment in all forms.[10] The POSH Act was developed with these commitments in sight. It defines sexual harassment as violative of women's fundamental right to equality guaranteed under Articles 14 and 15 of the Constitution of India, and the right to life, and to live with dignity guaranteed in Article 21 of the Constitution.[11] The legislation contains eight chapters and thirty sections, followed by certain rules.

The concept of sexual harassment, as defined in Chapter I, includes any one or more of the following unwelcome acts or behaviour (whether directly or by implication) namely: (i) physical contact and advances or (ii) a demand or request for sexual favours; or (iii)making sexually coloured remarks; or (iv) showing pornography; or (v) any other unwelcome physical, verbal or non-verbal conduct of sexual nature'.[12]

The definition of 'workplace' included in this section is broad, including any department or organization directly or indirectly under the government, local authority, public company, corporation or a co-operative society. It also includes private sector organisations, hospitals, nursing homes, sports institutes or any place visited or accessed by the employee during the course of her work, including transportation provided by the employer for undertaking the journey. In order to prevent sexual harassment at the workplace, the Act outlines certain circumstances: (i) implied or explicit promise of preferential treatment;(ii) implied or explicit threat of detrimental treatment;(iii)implied or explicit threat about her present or future employment status; (iv)interfere with her work or creating an intimidating or offensive or hostile work environment and; (v) humiliating treatment affecting her health and safety. The legislation includes development of redressal mechanisms through the constitution of Internal Complaints Committee (ICC) and Local Complaints Committee (LLC). ICCs are mandated for establishments with ten or more employees. Each committee is constituted of four members comprising of a Presiding Officer (woman employed at a senior level in the organization), two members from the employees, with experience in social work or legal knowledge, and one member from a non-governmental organization. In case of LCCs, it is the responsibility of the district officer to constitute such committee to receive complaints of sexual harassment from establishments that have fallen outside the ambit of ICCs due to workforces of less than ten employees. An LCC is a five member committee comprising of the Chairperson (nominated from among eminent women in the field of social work), one member nominated from women working in block, taluka, tehsil or municipality in the district, two members from non-governmental organizations (at least one woman and with legal knowledge) and an ex-officio member (dealing with social welfare or women and child development in the district). Both LCC and ICC can initiate inquiry and carry out conciliation and settlement. They have the same powers as a civil court and can summon individuals, requisition documents and submit inquiry reports within a period of ninety days. Apart from this, employers are required to organize workshops and seminars to sensitize employees to issues of workplace harassment, and impart knowledge about related laws.

Irrespective of its apparently comprehensive nature, effective implementation of its provisions has yet to go a long way. As of now, the Act is enforced under the Ministry of Women and Child Development (MWCD) Government of India, and not by the labour departments.

Challenges in Implementation: The Role of Stakeholders

The C190 clearly outlines the role of labour departments in dealing with workplace violence and harassment. It pursues governments to 'ensure that labour inspectorates and other relevant authorities, as appropriate, are empowered to deal with violence and harassment in the world of work, including by issuing orders requiring measures with immediate executory force, and orders to stop work in cases of imminent danger to life, health or safety, subject to any right of appeal to a judicial or administrative authority which may be provided by law'.

These provisions recognize the effective role of the labour inspectorates in implementing the POSH legislation. The Ministry of Women and Child Development maintains an online portal called 'She Box' for registering complaints related to workplace harassment.[13] Any woman, irrespective of status of employment, whether working in organized or unorganized sector, can register online complaints which will then be forwarded to the ICC or LCC. For registering complaints through the portal a valid email id is required. Though the electronic complaint mechanism is faster, its coverage of the unorganized sector is extremely limited. A recent UN report revealed that a large majority of informal women workers (domestic workers, farm workers etc.) are unaware of the legislation, and in many cases, redressal bodies like the ICCs and the LCCs are not fully functional. Moreover, several districts are yet to even have LCCs (UN Women, 2020).

Increasing concentration of women in the informal sector, and resulting surge in vulnerabilities associated with the conditions of employment, makes it extremely challenging to implement the relevant laws in this sector. As per the recent Periodic Labour Force Survey 2018-19, women (91.1 percent) are still overrepresented in the informal sector as compared to men (88.7 percent) (GoI, 2018). These women are mostly self-employed or are engaged as own-account workers. It is also found that there is underreporting of cases of workplace harassment among informal sector workers due to fears of stigma, loss of employment, and absence of any complaint mechanism at the workplace (Samantroy and Sarkar, 2020). Further, access to the online complaint system is limited as many of the women in the informal sectors are illiterate and lack access to digital technology.

It is also evident that the monitoring mechanisms under the

legislation are weak as the Central and State Governments have not developed any effective oversight mechanism for supervising the remit of ICCs and LCCs. On the basis of discussions with some of the stakeholders, certain gaps in implementation of the legislation were highlighted. Officials in the Ministry of Labour and Employment point out that unlike majority of the labour legislations in the country, the POSH does not outline powers and duties of labour inspectors. Rules within the Act provides that appellate authorities (Deputy Chief Labour Commissioner or Joint Labour Commissioners in the State) appointed under the Industrial Employment(Standing Orders) Act, 1946, which is now merged with the new Labour Code on Industrial Relations (2020), can entertain appeals under section 18 of the Act. Though this provision assigns nominal role to the labour department, strict enforcement of laws is still lacking due to absence of dedicated labour inspectors. The officials also pointed out that penalty for non-compliance under the legislation needs to be more stringent as presently, it stipulates only monetary penalty in the form of fine up to fifty thousand rupees for the employer in cases of non-compliance.

The unions have a different perspective altogether on the matter of implementation. One of the prominent trade unions in India highlighted the lack of unionisation among women in the informal sector, and the resulting lack of awareness. The employers' representatives emphasised a need to incentivise good practices through further investments. The civil society representatives focused more on preventive mechanisms which are important in order to avoid cases of workplace harassment and violence. They noted that some of the challenges in implementation emerge out of inadequate training of the members of ICCs and LCCs.

However, the role of ICCs and LCCs in implementing the

Act has been reiterated by the courts. In the Delhi high court ruling on *Dr Punita Sodhi vs Union of India & Ors.* on September 9, 2010, it was established that the role of ICCs is extremely important, and the constitution of the ICC in accordance with the *Vishaka* guidelines is essential[14].

The Provisions on Coverage of Issues of Workplace Harassment in the New Labour Codes

The process of simplifying labour laws following the recommendations of the Second National Commission on Labour, 2002, was initiated in the country through labour reforms. In the process, twenty-nine existing labour laws were amalgamated into four Labour Codes namely, The Code on Wages (2019), The Occupational Safety, Health and Working Conditions (OSH) Code (2020), The Industrial Relations Code (2020), and the Code on Social Security (2020). OSH 2020, which has now permitted night work for women, has clarified in the draft rules (notified by the Central government) that the POSH Act will apply to all establishments covered under the Code.[15] Though the Code is aimed at preventing workplace harassment through inclusion of the above provisions, it remains silent on aligning these to the C190. As mentioned in the section above, the labour inspectorate in the country has not been entrusted with the responsibility of implementing the POSH Act. Further, the Act itself does not include issues of occupational health and safety for ensuring the safety of women workers.

The need for incorporating occupational and health issues in legislative considerations, as highlighted in the R206, expands the coverage of such legislations considerably. It reiterates the need for revisiting the POSH Act and identify any scope for aligning it with international labour standards vis a vis the OSH. However, the OSH code is limited in scope as it applies to establishments covering ten or more workers. Employees figuring in smaller workforces, particularly in the informal sector, fall beyond the ambit of its purview. Though the Act intends to cover women workers in both, formal and informal sectors, the convergence of the Act with the new OSH Code does not pave the way for such universal coverage. With regard to implementation of the C190, the recommendation (R206) clearly highlights the need for gender responsive training of the labour inspectorate or other competent authorities, so that they are able to identify and address violence and harassment at the workplace and discrimination against certain groups of workers. As stated earlier, one of the major limitations of this legislation has been the lack of enforcement. There is however, no denying the fact that the new labour codes open up a plethora of opportunities for ensuring the safety and well-being of workers. But it also merits revision, along with the new codes (OSH), in light of the C190 of the ILO.

Concluding Remarks

On the basis of the above discussion, it can be said that the definition of violence and harassment at the workplace needs to be examined in the context of women's lived experiences. Also, the scope of workplace violence and harassment legislations needs to be broadened in order to include all kinds of behaviour which may be deemed as inappropriate and threatening the dignity of women at the workplace. Further, in many cultures, harassment is normalised through the dynamics of everyday conduct. As a result, disclosures are often dismissed as trivial, and responsibility is shifted from the perpetrator to the victim. Such lopsided responses to disclosures of harassment, particularly sexual harassment, send a clear message to perpetrators that their abuse of power is acceptable (Prakash and George, 2019). This has also been established by scholars of feminist jurisprudence who have clearly highlighted the sway that 'masculine norms' hold over the workplace, normalising violence and harassment in such spaces. Such deeply entrenched social norms emanating from cultural inequalities need to be clearly examined in order to uncover the unequal power relations at workplace for any targeted policy intervention to effectively combat violence and harassment.

In the wake of declining female labour force participation, it is important to address the issues of workplace violence and harassment in order to ensure safe workplaces for women so that they continue to stay employed. An in-depth understanding of the new labour codes, particularly the OSH code, is necessary for exploring the possibilities of aligning it with the POSH Act in an effective manner. The labour inspectorate needs to be empowered with additional responsibility for not only enforcing laws on workplace harassment, but also creating awareness on the matter among the workers. Gender sensitisation training of the labour inspectorate is imperative before entrusting them with the responsibility of implementing any legislation pertaining to workplace harassment.

References

Abrams Kathryn (1998). New Jurisprudence of Sexual Harrasment. *Cornell Law Review,* Vol 83,Issue 5,pp 1169-1230.

Dasgupta, Ananya (2019). Protecting Women's Right to Life and Liberty by Strengthening the Labour Rights of Women Working in the Unorganized (Informal Sector) in India. New Delhi: Multiple Action Research group (MARG).

GoI (2018). Annual Report, Periodic Labour Force Survey 2018-2019, Ministry of Statistics and Programme Implementation. New Delhi: National Statistical Office.

International Labour Organization ILO, (2019). World Employment Social Outlook: Trends for Women. Geneva: International Labour Office.

John Maya (2014).Fears and Furies of Sexual Harassment Time to go Beyond Vishaka. *Economic and Political Weekly,* Vol XLIV, No15. pp 29-32.

Lidman Satu (2018). *Gender, Violence and Attitudes: Lessons from Early Modern Europe.* London and New York: Routledge

Malla, Sapna Pradhan (2005). Sexual Harassment in the Workplace in Asia, Paper prepared for Expert Group Meeting on 'Violence Against Women: Good Practices in Combating and Eliminating Violence Against Women', Austria: UN Division for Advancement of Women.

Mc Kinnon Catherine(1979).*Sexual Harassment of Working Women.* New Haven and London: Yale University Press.

MFF, Martha Farrel Foundation (not dated). *Sexual Harassment of Domestic Workers at their Workplaces* MFF. PRIA :New Delhi.

Prakash Neha and George Sonia (2019). ILO Convention 190, Gender Based Violence and World of Work. *Economic and Political Weekly,* Vol 54,Issue no 51, 28 Dec, pp 13-16.

Sahgal, Punam and Dang Aastha (2017). Sexual Harassment at Workplace: Experiences of Women Managers and Organizations. *Economic and Political Weekly,* Vol LII, No 22,pp 49-57.

Samantroy E and Sarkar K (2020). Violence in Times of Covid 19 Lack of Legal Protection for Women Informal Workers. *Economic and Political Weekly Engage https://www.epw.in/engage/article/violence-times-covid-19-lack-legal-protection*

Sarpotdar, Anagha (2016). Implementing or Ignoring the Law on Sexual Harassment? *Economic and Political Weekly,* Vol L1, Nos 44 and 45, pp 27-29.

Scott, Julianna (1999). Pragmatism, Feminist Theory and the Reconceptualization of Sexual Harassment. *UCLA Women's Law Journal,* Vol (10)1, pp 203-234

UN Women (2020). Sexual Harrasment in the Informal Sector: Farm Workers and Domestic Workers. New York: UNWomen.

MARRYING OUT

Why Khasi Women Marry Non-Khasi Men?

Sarah Jayal Sawkmie

> 'For sale
> our young, nubile girls, beautiful like the land itself:
> we prefer men from the lowlands,
> or even from across the seas,
> with a modicum of integrity
> (marital status, religion or caste no bar)
> only those owning a potbelly now,
> or in the near future, need apply.'
>
> –Paul Lyngdoh[1]

Khasi society is epitomised as a matrilineal society where women reign supreme. Unlike the rest of India and the western world, children bear the surname of their mother and women inherit property. As Khasi society moves ahead with the times, urbanisation, migration, globalisation and illegal influx from across the border are increasingly perceived as threats to the Khasi way of life. This fear manifests particularly in the unanimous disdain towards Khasi women who are 'castigated for their eagerness to embrace the so-called illegal immigrant' (Mukhim, 2013, para. 1). In recent years, there has been a perception developing in Khasi society that more and more Khasi women are marrying

'Dkhars' or outsiders. At stake is the purity of Khasi Pnar blood (Mohrmen, 2013, para. 5) Organisations like the Khasi Students Union (KSU) have accused non-tribals of 'taking away all 'our' jobs, 'our' land and 'our' women' (Mukhim, 2014, para. 7).

The Khasi Hills Autonomous District (Khasi Social Custom of Lineage) Act 1997, which received the Governor's assent on 23 February 2005, defines who is a Khasi. It recognises offsprings of cross-cultural marriages as Khasi, provided they follow the Khasi way of life. More importantly, the marriage must not be a means for the non-Khasi partner to attain the Scheduled Tribe status and accrue benefits with respect to reservation in educational institutions, government jobs, exemption from Income Tax, freedom to conduct business, and purchase of property in the state which is governed by the provisions of the Sixth Schedule of the Constitution.

A stronger legislation, the Khasi Hills Autonomous District (Khasi Social Custom of Lineage) (Second Amendment) Bill, 2018 was notified on 24 July 2018. As per this bill, a Khasi woman marrying a non-Khasi[2] will lose her Khasi status/ privileges, and offsprings borne from such a marriage will be deemed as non-Khasi (KHADC Passes Bill to Prevent Khasi Women From Marrying Non-Khasis, 2018). This bill,[3] which was awaiting the Governor's assent, has been sent back to the government for its comments (Govt Returns Lineage Bills to KHADC, 2018).

The crux of the matter is that cross-cultural marriages between Khasi women and non-Khasi men is a matter of great concern resulting in unprecedented steps being taken to curb such marriages. This essay seeks to explore possible reasons behind the growing number of Khasi women marrying outside the community. The views of the members of the Khasi community, selected through a sample survey covering the six Khasi majority districts, have been included. This has been supplemented by case studies involving Khasi women married to non-Khasi men.

In every society, the choice of spouse is not unlimited but is subject to certain restrictions. This is universally manifested in the incest taboo which refers to the 'rules which prohibit sexual intercourse between certain categories of persons' (Holy, 1996, p. 124). For Lévi-Strauss (1969), the incest taboo differentiates humans from animals and denotes the transition from nature to culture. It is a taboo to marry those persons with whom sexual relations are prohibited.

From the perspective of marriage and group membership, J.F. McLennan uses the terms endogamy and exogamy to refer to the two rules of marriage. The endogamous rule requires one to marry within a defined group except with a certain range of kin. Castes, racial, ethnic and religious groups (e.g., Jews) are instances of endogamous groups (Mair, 1971). Endogamy is embraced by isolated groups to avoid geographical dispersion, maintain their distinct way of life and to reinforce group solidarity and identity (Cerroni-Long, 1985). Exogamy refers to 'the rule that one must find one's marriage partner outside a defined group' (Mair, 1971, p. 23). It 'prohibits marriage within a specific group or category, usually defined in terms of kinship, descent or locality' (Holy, 1996, p. 125) such as a lineage, clan or village. It was practiced by societies which struggled to survive in harsh and hostile conditions. The cooperation of other groups was required to collectively hunt for food and defeat mutual enemies. Marriage was a means to establish alliances. Women from one group were married to men from other groups uniting the groups through ties of affinity (Mair, 1971).

Cross-cultural marriages, inter-marriages, and mixed marriages are terms which refer to exogamous marriages where an individual marries outside her membership group.

Cross-Cultural Marriage

'Cross-cultural' or 'mixed' marriages are 'taken to mean marriages between two people from different linguistic, religious, or ethnic groups or nations' (Breger & Hill, 1998, p. 7). The term intermarriage, 'is generally applied to those married persons whose religious, racial or ethnic background is or was different from each other's, either prior to or after the marriage' (Gordon, 1972, p.6).

The types of intermarriages are further elaborated. 'Interethnic' marriage describes a marriage 'in which each of the parties to the marriage was reared in a cultural and nationality environment which differs from that of the other' (Gordon, 1972, pp. 6-7). 'Interracial marriages are those in which the parties to the marriage belong to different races' (Gordon, 1972, p. 7). The term 'mixed marriage' designates only those unions in which separate religious ideologies are maintained by the parties post-marriage (Gordon, 1972). However, this description is not subscribed to by most sociologists who use the term mixed marriage 'indiscriminately to mean any form of intermarriage: racial, ethnic as well as religious' (Barron, 1972, p. 9).

In this study, the terms cross-cultural marriage, mixed marriage and inter-marriage are used interchangeably to refer to inter-ethnic marriages in which a Khasi man or woman is married to a non-Khasi spouse from a different ethnic community.

Studies on Cross-Cultural Marriages

Cross-cultural marriage, as a field of research became popular in the USA only by the end of the First World War (Barron, 1951). Between 1880 and 1930, America was perceived as the land of opportunities and attracted immigrants from south, central and east Europe. Research on cross-cultural marriage was considered to be important for the insights it gave in studying a multi-group society like the United States. Most research on cross-cultural marriage has examined its causes, patterns and consequences.

A significant amount of research has focussed on the causes or reasons which increase the likelihood of such marriages. Members of groups with a small population and an unbalanced sex ratio are often compelled to marry out due to the paucity of potential marriage partners. Thus, the numerically preponderant gender is pushed to marry outside the group (Barron, 1951; Cerroni-Long, 1985). Among the Chinese immigrants in the USA, the gender imbalance in the sex ratio resulted in women marrying out more than men (Sung, 1990).

In pluralistic societies, certain physical spaces increase the likelihood of frequent contact between individuals from diverse communities (Cerroni-Long, 1985). One such area is the residential space(s) which is inhabited by people of different races and nationalities who have economic and cultural similarities. This residential propinquity facilitates premarital contact between persons of different cultural groups, which leads to cross-cultural marriages (Barron, 1951). Similarly, educational institutions and workplaces facilitate interaction of young people who are of diverse identities but share a common educational and economic status. This creates in-groups with a 'consciousness of kind.' The educational and economic propinquity also increases the likelihood of cross-cultural marriage between them (Barron, 1951). Therefore, among Chinese men and women, those who married out were more educated (Sung, 1990).

Compatibility in value orientation and role expectation, also known as 'psychological availability,' creates similarities between groups. This can result in cross-cultural marriages which are directly proportional to it (Cerroni-Long, 1985). Social processes like egalitarianism, secularism, increasing women's choice, rejection of group norms over personal choice and view of marriage beyond procreation, are conducive for cross-cultural marriages. Where individualism and freedom of choice of marital partner prevails, more cross-cultural marriages take place as marriage fulfils the individual's emotional needs guided by notions of romantic love (Cerroni-Long, 1985).

Immigrants or persons residing abroad can find potential mates only from the out-group, resulting in cross-cultural marriages by members of the diaspora, expatriates, diplomats, and their families etc. Similarly, in the 'war brides' phenomenon, military personnel temporarily stationed in another country in a war zone marry local women, e.g., American troops in Vietnam (Cerroni-Long, 1985).

The attainment of economic rewards is a strong motivation for cross-cultural marriages. Some people marry a person from a higher social status to achieve upward social mobility (Cerroni-Long, 1985). Merton's (1941) social exchange theory shows how cross-cultural marriages usually occur between men of a higher socio-economic status but from a 'lower' racial group status, and women with low socio-economic status but of a 'higher' racial group status. There is an exchange of the black man's high socio-economic status for the white woman's high racial status and vice versa. This alliance is mutually beneficial to both parties (Merton, 1941). In white-black marriages, white women married black men who were more educated than a white man they might have married. Similarly, black men marry white women who are likely to be less educated than a black woman they might have married. Thus, men and women from majority groups marry partners from minority communities for socio-economic status gains (Kalmijn, 1998; Kalmijn & Wooldredge, 1989).

Research on immigrant communities reveals a correlation

between the immigrant's generation, gender, education status, income, and cross-cultural marriages (Sung,1990). The personality traits of people who marry cross-culturally have also been identified (Khatib-Chahidi et al., 1998; Romano, 1988; Sung, 1990). A study of women who met and married their foreign spouses in the host country reveals that they were unconventional, adventurous, uninhibited, liberal, free-thinking and more emotionally stable. They were independent enough to reject their parents' choice of spouse. Some married out to escape the feelings of structural, social or personal marginality. For women from liberal families with a 'jet set' lifestyle, marrying out is a natural extension of their lives involving global travel and new experiences (Khatib-Chahidi et al., 1998). This was corroborated by a study that reveals that Chinese individuals who married cross-culturally are unconventional, rebellious and marry more than once. Their non-Chinese spouses tend to be Sinophiles who patronise Chinese businesses, augmenting the possibility of meeting and befriending Chinese people, culminating in marriage (Sung, 1990).

Some marry to prove their unorthodox or rebellious nature against group norms, parental authority or guilt towards subordinate groups (Cerroni-Long, 1985). Romano has identified seven personality types who tend to marry cross-culturally as outcasts, rebels, mavericks, compensators, adventurers, escapists and unstables. Most people fall into more than one category or see parts of themselves represented in all of them (Romano, 1988).

Some of those who married out had initially wanted to marry within their community but due to circumstances, were unable to find a suitable match. Most met their future spouses in college as equals in a neutral environment (Sung, 1990).

The role of the state in influencing the choice of partners, especially in cross-national marriages, by granting or withholding permission to marry, awarding work permits, controlling job access, rights, and even through revocation of these rights in case of divorce, including access to children, has also been examined (Breger, 1998).

In contemporary times, globalisation is a significant factor contributing to cross-cultural marriages. It has opened job opportunities in other countries, and technology has enabled communication with people in distant places. This has resulted in a generation that chooses to travel the world in pursuit of their dreams, jobs, and personal goals rather than stagnating in a single location. This has changed the notion of romance and marriage, leading to a rise in intercultural or multicultural families (Williams, 2011). Globalisation and modernisation have also resulted in cross-cultural marriages by Indians who travel abroad for study, work and visits. There is a visible pattern in which the educated, professional, and modern marry out and the semi-literate, unskilled and traditional marry in (R. Singh, 2010).

Conventionally, studies on cross-cultural marriages in India have focussed on inter-caste or inter-religious marriages between Hindus and Muslims. In North India, the gender imbalance stemming from male child preference, combined with female foeticide, have compelled men to seek wives from outside the caste and community, usually from poorer states like West Bengal, giving rise to a 'Bengali bridal diaspora' who are colloquially classified as 'marriage migrants.' These women achieve the twin goals of marriage and work where sexual and reproductive labours merge with economic labour (Kaur, 2010).

A popular theme of studies on cross-cultural marriages is the consequences of such marriages. Some studies have explored the family's reactions to those who intend to or have married out, including the society's attitude towards them for breaking the rule of endogamy (Joshi & Krishna, 1998; Sung, 1990). The adjustment problems arising from cultural differences, and efforts made by the partners for the marriage to endure, have also been studied (Romano, 1988; Rosenblatt & Stewart, 2004). Difficulties experienced by foreign brides living in a joint family in India indicate how differences in cultural ideals and expectations make cohabitation difficult (Joshi & Krishna, 1998).

The experience of the offspring is also a popular theme of study (Kich, 1982; Maxwell, 1998; Sung, 1990). The attitude of parents towards their children, the role of culture in child-rearing, and the choices made by the parents for their children, have been researched (Joshi & Krishna, 1998). A later study has investigated the role of parental education while choosing the group affiliation of their offspring (Finnäs & O'Leary, 2003).

At a wider level, the role of cross-cultural marriage in facilitating sociological processes such as assimilation, and in maintaining data on each racial, ethnic, and religious groups and the degree of social distance between them, especially in pluralistic societies like the USA, has been an important research area (Barron, 1951; Barron,1972; Hirshman,1983; Kennedy, 1952).

Background of the Matrilineal System of the Khasis

Before understanding the dynamics of marriage and cross-cultural marriages among the Khasis, a brief background of the Khasi matrilineal system is in order. The ideological basis of the Khasi matrilineal system is rooted in the Khasi view of human reproduction. A mother has rights over her child because she nurtures the unborn child during incubation by contributing flesh and blood (*ka kmie ka ba ai ia ka doh ka snam*) which is the life-giving force. Man contributes to the stature and form (*u kpa u ba ai ia ka rynieng*) of the child through semen which is regarded as pus that can be drained out and is thus, deemed inferior. This blood bond between the mother and the child forms the basis of the matrilineal system which revolves around the woman (Nongbri, 1993).

The Khasi social organization centres on the *'kur'* or clan system of social organization. A Khasi takes her/his mother's clan name and belongs to her clan. Although residing with his wife in his mother-in law's house post-marriage, the Khasi man continues to belong to his mother's clan. Members of the same *kur* accept each other as siblings and therefore, clan exogamy is strictly observed. The *kur* has social, economic, religious and political functions. It comprises smaller units like the *jait* (sub-clan), *kpoh* (lineage) and the *iing* (family unit). The *iing* is the smallest unit of clan segmentation and comprises of a grandmother, her daughters (married or unmarried), and sons (married, unmarried, widowed or divorced). It is the most basic and functional unit. These kinship units regulate the day-to-day life of a Khasi (Giri, 1985; Pakeyntein, 1996).

The rule of succession is strictly matrilineal. While authority passes from the mother's brother to the sister's son, property, particularly ancestral *(ka nongtymmen)*, is handed down from the mother to her youngest daughter *(khadduh)* who is the heiress. Other daughters may inherit jewellery, land or gifts (Gurdon, 1914). Each clan has its own council (*Durbar Kur*) which settles inter-clan and intra-clan disputes and cases like adultery, theft etc., for which it awards punishment. It regulates marriage and social relations between kins (Pakeyntein, 1996).

Marriage Among the Khasis

Khasi marriage is guided by the principle of clan exogamy. Violation of this rule is *'sang'* (taboo) and is regarded as incest. The consequences include ex-communication from the clan, loss of inheritance rights, and refusal to perform funeral rites by the clan upon death (Cantlie,1934; Gurdon, 1914). Some clans are interconnected (*iateh kur*) and marriage is forbidden between members of such clans. A man is also prohibited from marrying his maternal uncle's daughter during his maternal uncle's lifetime. Marriage with his father's sister's daughter, though viewed unfavourably, is nevertheless permissible, but only after the father's death. A man cannot marry his father's brother's daughter (*u para kha*) or the daughter of his father's paternal uncle. A man who is divorced cannot marry his divorced wife's sister during his divorced wife's lifetime (Cantlie, 1934).

According to Nakane (1967), spouse selection is primarily based on personal choice. Thus, 'The network of marriage relations among the Khasi seems in no way to follow any set principle' (Nakane, 1967, p. 119). Except for the strict rule of exogamy, every marriage 'is ruled simply by temporary personal liking' (Nakane, 1967, p. 119).

However, for Nongbri (2013), Khasi marriage is not a chance encounter but is guided by certain norms and principles. As the youngest daughter is the heiress and caretaker of her parents in their old age, it is in their interest that she marries a responsible man who will elevate the family's status. Although the mother's brother (*kni*) is the formal head of the family, 'the ideology of the providing husband and institution of resident son-in-law prevailing in the society not only makes the husband a member of the wife's household, uxorilocality could also, over time, provide the son-in-law access to its property' (Nongbri, 2013, p. 415).

In the absence of an arranged marriage system, the role of courtship is integral in uniting a couple. It takes place under controlled conditions where parents can subtly encourage or discourage a potential union and ensure that the marriage is outside the prohibited limit. A group of eligible young men visit the houses of marriageable girls to get acquainted with them and their families. If a girl is interested in a boy, they try to meet separately during the day after which the family elders arrange for formal negotiations. If everything goes well, a date is fixed for the union. Although Khasi girls are free to choose marital partners outside the prohibited degree of kin, the gender ideology and the family's protectiveness result in them conforming to parental choices (Nongbri, 2013).

Today, the traditional courtship system is on the wane. Youngsters are preoccupied with their studies. They also prefer to meet outside their homes, away from prying family members. A girl invites her suitor home only when they are sure about their feelings. This has reduced parental control in mate selection. However, the core ethos remains unchanged (Nongbri, 2013).

After marriage, the form of residence is uxorilocal, where the husband lives with his wife in his mother-in-law's house. If the wife is not a *khadduh* (heiress), they can move to their own house (neolocal residence) after the birth of one or two children (Gurdon, 1914).

There also exists 'a system of concubinage in which the couple seek to settle down without a formal marriage' (Bareh, 1974, p. 75). This occurs when a couple inform their parents that they want to marry but both sets of parents withhold consent (Bareh, 1974). The terms *hap, ia hapmon* or *sushong* describes a form of union wherein a man and a woman cohabit without their parents' awareness and without conducting any ceremony (Das Gupta, 1984). In *ia loi hi*, on a pre-decided date, the man, along with his friends and relatives, go to the woman's home where they are welcomed with food and liquor. After the friends and relatives leave, the man and the woman start living as a couple.

Here as well, no rituals are performed. However, friends and relatives are involved. This usually occurs between widows and widowers or between divorcees (Das Gupta, 1984). Therefore, among Khasis, 'A public living together of a man and woman without any ceremony constitutes a valid marriage' (Cantlie, 1934, p. 75).

Khasi women practise monogamy or at the most, serial monogamy. For men, the rule of monogamy is not as strict. A man can only marry once through a formal ceremony. However, he can have an informal alliance with another woman. The only condition is that she should not belong to the village of the original wife. The legally married wife is called *ka tynga trai*. The other wife is called *ka tynga tuh* or 'stolen wife' and her children are referred to as *ki khun kliar* (children from the top) as they are from the branches and not from the root (*trai*) of the tree (Cantlie, 1934; Gurdon, 1914). There is no serious social disadvantage of being a secondary wife because wives, irrespective of their position, continue to enjoy socio-economic independence as opposed to the condition in patrilineal systems (Nakane, 1967).

Due to the matrilineal principle of reckoning descent, a Khasi child cannot be deemed illegitimate whether borne out of a formal marriage or otherwise (Cantlie, 1934). Therefore, among the Khasis, 'The child is the heir of its mother whoever may be the father' (Cantlie, 1934, p. 75).

For Khasis, the main purpose of marriage is to beget children. Therefore, barrenness is a ground for divorce apart from adultery, incompatibility, lunacy, leprosy etc. A woman cannot be divorced during pregnancy. In a divorce, the custody of the children is always given to the mother. Usually, both parties must agree to a divorce. However, if one divorces the other without his/her consent, the other party must be paid compensation or *ka mynrain* or *ka thnem*. Once divorced, the parties may marry into other families (Gurdon, 1914). Therefore, among the Khasis, the position of the father in conferring legitimacy to the children has never had the same importance as in a patrilineal society.

Studies on Cross-Cultural Marriage Among the Khasis

Cross-cultural marriages have been taking place among the Khasis since time immemorial. However, there is no comprehensive account except for a chapter or a few paragraphs here and there, usually in the context of the Khasi matrilineal system and its accommodative nature in incorporating the offspring of such marriages.

Internationally, studies on cross-cultural marriages have relied on secondary data such as census reports or information derived from marriage licenses or public records to study the trends and patterns of cross-cultural marriages. In Meghalaya, such information is limited. Mathur (1979), in his study on Khasi tribalism and religion, surveyed a hundred Khasi families in the Umsohsun locality of Shillong. Twenty of these families reported instances of cross-cultural marriages where a non-Khasi Hindu man had married a Khasi woman of the family and settled down in Shillong. Since his work focussed on religion, he devoted one chapter to the Khasi Muslims who trace their ancestry to the non-tribal Muslims who would intermittently visit the Khasi Hills from seventeenth century onwards. The progeny of marriages between Khasi women and non-tribal Muslim men are considered to be Muslims only in terms of religion. For all other purposes, they regard themselves as Khasi (Mathur, 1979). Khasi Muslims have also been studied from a demographic perspective (Langstieh, 2001).

Nakane (1967), in her comparative study of matriliny

between the Khasi and Garo tribes, briefly describes cross-cultural marriages in two generations of Khasi women of a border village.

Lobo (2018), in her article on Anglo-Indians, describes how unlike most Anglo-Indians, the Scheduled Tribe/Khasi/Anglo-Indians of Shillong, and the Other Backward Class/Nair/Anglo-Indians of Cochin, continued to stay on in India after the British left. As members of matrilineal communities, they derived their main identity from their Indian mother, and did not suffer from bias towards those of mixed races in India.

Legislative methods of excluding out-marrying Khasi women, and their progenies from tribe membership have been widely documented. Some scholars have tried to uncover the male bias where the bill is seen as an attempt by men to control women, their sexuality and their children (Nongbri, 2003). The legislation is also seen as a means to ensure that land does not fall into the hands of outsiders through women who marry out of the community. Ethnic control over land is thus achieved through control over women's bodies and sexuality (Wahlang & Karlsson, 2022). For some, the bill is a mechanism through which political and economic elites seek to diminish women's ownership of land as women have been instrumental in blocking mining ventures and consequent degradation of land (Wahlang & Karlsson, 2022). For Nag, the bills represent an orchestrated strategy led by male Khasi ethnic tribal elites to neutralize two proven threats to Khasi local sovereignty namely, the ethnic outsider and the insider women (Nag, 2022). These are attempts aimed at excluding women from decision-making processes and hindering their participation in durbars, from which they have been traditionally excluded (Nag, 2022; Nongbri, 1993; R. Syiemlieh, 2018).

Since cross-cultural marriages have been the focus of

the entire community, what could be the reasons for such marriages among the Khasis? Nongbri (2003) points out that the perpetuation of the clan is an important duty for Khasi women and if a suitable Khasi match is unavailable, Khasis have been known to encourage their daughters and sisters to marry an eligible non-tribal man. She also highlights the plight of educated Khasi girls who resort to marrying out due to the absence of an arranged marriage system, and the preference among Khasi boys for younger and less qualified girls.

Interviews with local Khasis have revealed that Khasi women marry non-Khasis because 'Khasi men have failed them' (Chhakchhuak, 2018, para. 14). Khasi men often indulge in 'unofficial polygamy,' (Chhakchhuak, 2018, para. 15). They neglect their responsibilities towards their existing families which leaves their wives and children high and dry. Since marriages are unregistered and not legally binding, they are prone to break up easily. Under such circumstances, women have no choice but to marry other men who will provide for them and their children (Chhakchhuak, 2018).

The Syngkhong Rympei Thymmai (SRT) has been advocating a shift to patriliny and regularization of equitable distribution of ancestral property among sons and daughters. The SRT claims that many Khasi women marry non-Khasi men because they are economically better off in the patrilineal system. Khasi men do not own property and hardly get loans since they do not have property as collateral. Their frustration often fosters alcoholism and substance abuse. This further diminishes their appeal to Khasi women (Bhutia, 2013). Non-Khasi men are often blamed for exploiting their Khasi wives for the latter's property rights, and use their name to carry out business and benami (anonymous) transactions. In Meghalaya, while strict laws control transfers of land, it is alleged that non-tribal men are increasingly assuming de facto control of land by marrying tribal women (Saikia, 2018).

Reasons for Exogamy: Primary Sources

In order to gain an insight into the factors that lead to such marriages, one of the objectives of my Ph.D research in 2014 was to seek the views of the respondents on this matter. The research comprises a survey of 290 Khasi households, selected through a multi-stage random sampling design involving simple and systematic random sampling of households, covering the six Khasi majority districts of the state namely, East Khasi Hills, West Khasi Hills, South West Khasi Hills, Ri Bhoi, East Jaintia Hills and West Jaintia Hills districts (total number of districts being eleven). The electoral rolls were used as the sampling frame for selecting the households as they are updated more regularly than census documents. The assembly constituencies, polling stations and households from each district were selected through the method of simple and systematic random sampling in a proportion that was representative of the universe of study. The interview schedule was used as the method of data collection, making use of a combination of open-ended and closed-ended questions that were put to this sample. Although the households were selected randomly as detailed above, the respondent could be any available member of the household.

Out of the sample of 290 respondents, 178 respondents (61.38 per cent) were female and the remaining 112 (38.62 per cent) were male. A reason for this could be that the fieldwork was carried out during the day when majority of the men were away at work or in the fields, so only the female members of the household were available.

The following Table 1 depicts the district wise distribution of respondents.

Table 1: District wise Distribution of Respondents

District	No. of Households/ Respondents	Percentage of Households/ Respondents
East Khasi Hills	159	54.83
RiBhoi	38	13.11
West Khasi Hills	36	12.41
West Jaintia Hills	35	12.07
East Jaintia Hills	15	5.17
South West Khasi Hills	7	2.41
Total	**290**	**100**

Source: Field Survey

The age profile of the respondents is tabulated in Table 2 below. The age distribution of the respondents ranges from the 16-20 years age group (which comprises of 5.52 per cent of the respondents), to the 81 and above age group (which comprises of only 0.69 per cent or, in other words, two respondents).

Table 2: Age Distribution of the Respondents

Age (in Years)	No. of Respondents	Percentage of Respondents
16-20	16	5.52
21-30	74	25.52
31-40	60	20.69
41-50	68	23.45
51-60	29	10.00
61-70	30	10.34
71-80	11	3.79
81 & above	2	0.69
TOTAL	**290**	**100**

Source: Field Survey

The majority of 25.52 per cent of the respondents fall in the 21-30 age bracket closely followed by 23.45 per cent in the 41-50 age group and 20.69 per cent in the 31-40 age group. Thus, we can say that 69.66 per cent of the respondents in the survey belong to the 21-50 years age group. 24.82 per cent of the respondents are more than 50 years of age. 4.48 per cent of the respondents are above the age of 70 years.

In the survey, 82.76 per cent of the sample or 240 respondents are married. As far as religious identity is concerned, 83.10 per cent of the sample or 241 respondents are Christians out of which the majority (149 respondents) are Presbyterians, followed by Catholics (65) and other denominations (27 respondents) namely Church of God (11), Church of Christ (6), Full Gospel Fellowship (6), Seventh Day Adventist (3) and Unitarian (1).

The indigenous Khasi religion, (*Niam Khasi* or *Niamtre*) is professed by only 15.86 per cent of the sample or 46 respondents. Following the arrival of British missionaries, and subsequent British conquest of this region, bulk of the Khasis converted to Christianity. 1 per cent of the sample or 3 respondents described themselves as Hindu. These were respondents who followed the religion of their non-Khasi parents although they officially defined themselves as Khasi.

Table 3: Educational Qualification of the Respondents

Educational Qualification	Number of Respondents	Percentage of Respondents
Non-Literate	49	16.90
Class 5 and under	57	19.66
Class 6 to Class 9	64	22.07
Class Ten	32	11.03
Senior Secondary School (11,12)	26	8.97
Graduate	46	15.86
Post Graduate	5	1.72
Professional Degree	5	1.72
Diploma	3	1.03
M.Phil./Ph.D.	3	1.03
TOTAL	**290**	**100**

Source: Field Survey

As per Table No. 3 above, 16.90 per cent of the respondents (49) had had no education at all. The majority of 22.07 per cent have studied between classes 6-9. This is closely followed by 19.66 per cent who have not studied beyond class 5. Thus, 40.70 per cent of the sample (this excludes 1.03 per cent or 3 respondents who are still students and yet to complete class 9) who have entered the schooling process but have dropped out before reaching class 10.

15.86 per cent of the respondents are graduates and only 1.72 per cent i.e., 5 respondents have a professional degree (B.Tech.-1, Nursing-1, Agriculture-1, MBA-1, Theology-1) while

3 have a Diploma. 2 respondents have a Ph.D. and 1 respondent has M. Phil. degree. Interestingly, 17 respondents are still pursuing their education.

Table 4: Occupational Profile of the Respondents

Occupation	Number of Respondents	Percentage of Respondents
Homemaker	64	22.07
Farming	50	17.24
Self Employed	41	14.14
Government Servant	34	11.72
Wage Labour	31	10.70
School Teacher	19	6.55
Student	17	5.86
Private Employment	9	3.10
Unemployed	9	3.10
Carpenter	6	2.07
Driver	5	1.72
Lecturer	3	1.03
Tailor	2	0.70
Total	**290**	**100**

Source: Field Survey

A perusal of the occupational profile of the respondents in Table 4 above, indicates that a majority of 22.07 per cent of the respondents are homemakers of which 3 respondents are unmarried and are caring for their old parents or younger siblings at home. 3.10 per cent of the sample comprises of those who are unemployed. 5.86 per cent are students who are still pursuing their education. 17.24 per cent of the respondents are involved in farming. As the fieldwork progressed, the farming season commenced and most of the family members were busy in the fields. Those who remained at home were not involved in farming. 11.72 per cent are government servants, mostly at the lower levels. 14.14 per cent are self-employed. 6.55 per cent or 19 respondents are school teachers.

Reasons Why Khasi Women Marry Out

In the survey, respondents were asked for their opinion on what could be the reason for the increasing number of Khasi girls marrying outside the community. Their responses have been tabulated in Table No. 5.

Table 5: Potential Reasons for Khasis Marrying Outside the Community?

Nature of Responses*	No. of Responses
Fall in love with a non-Khasi, friendship, mutual understanding, personal choice	126
Exposure to non-Khasis, specifically when studying or working outside Meghalaya	76
The cosmopolitan environment in Meghalaya such as in the neighbourhoods, educational institutions, border areas, workplaces-coal mining areas, tea stalls, markets etc. fosters cross-cultural interactions which may result in marriage	69

Such Marriages are ordained by God and it is a product of destiny	51
Khasi men marry non-Khasi women to perpetuate the family name in the absence of sisters	24
Marry out for better economic opportunities or to escape poverty	16
The inability of Khasi women to find a suitable match within the community (especially for highly educated women)	16
Khasi men are irresponsible, laidback or alcoholics who ill-treat their wives. Non-Khasi men are responsible and take good care of their wives and children	15
Broad-mindedness, relaxed social norms and changed outlook toward marriage	10
Khasi women are fooled by non-Khasi men into marriage	8
Friendships facilitated by social media platforms like Facebook	7
Other	12
Not aware/ Have not encountered	20

*Source: Field Survey *Multiple responses*

Since respondents have given multiple reasons for such marriages, it will not be possible to present the data in percentage form. From the table above, it can be observed that a majority of 126 respondents believed that such marriages are guided by love, friendship, mutual understanding and personal choice. 76 respondents are of the opinion that many Khasis meet their

non-Khasi spouses while away from the state for educational or work purposes. Pockets of cosmopolitan spaces within the state were cited by 69 respondents as factors facilitating cross-community interaction between Khasis and non-Khasis. These include cosmopolitan neighbourhoods, educational institutions, border regions, and markets or workplaces. There is greater cross-cultural contact with non-Khasis in these places which increases the likelihood of such marriages. The respondents informed that the roadside tea stalls along the National Highway in Mawryngkneng and Ri Bhoi areas are frequented by non-Khasi truck drivers who befriend Khasi girls working in these stalls. Tea stalls are also present in the coal mining regions of Jaintia Hills where workforce mostly comprises of migrant labourers. These friendships frequently culminate in marital alliances.

Thus, residing outside the state, or being in a cosmopolitan environment facilitates interaction and friendship with non-Khasis. Such residential and occupational propinquity have been cited by academicians as factors behind intermarriage (Barron, 1951).

While 51 respondents opined that cross-cultural marriages are divinely ordained and products of destiny, 24 were of the opinion that the absence of sisters or daughters in some families lead Khasi men to marry non-Khasi women. This ensures that the family name is carried forward, family wealth preserved, and elders cared for. This is a regular practice among the Khasis who inhabit the Ri-Bhoi region where a Khasi man marries a woman from the Assamese tribes like the Tiwa tribe (a tribe from Assam which is very similar to the Khasis) after paying a bride price. After marriage, the Tiwa woman moves into her Khasi husband's maternal home, looks after his family and helps perpetuate the Khasi clan name. The Khasi man does not have to leave his mother's home after marriage.

A total of 16 respondents were of the view that Khasi women marry out because they cannot find a suitable match within the community. This is especially true in the case of highly educated women as education not only qualifies them for better jobs but also changes their outlook.

Alcoholism, domestic abuse, and laid-back attitude among Khasi men were identified as deterrent factors by 15 respondents. Pursuit of better economic opportunities or escape from poverty was cited by 16 respondents as reason for marrying non-Khasi men. The respondents said that this was because non-Khasis have stable jobs, earn well and are better providers. However, 8 respondents mentioned that Khasi women are sometimes duped into marriage by non-Khasi men who want to access their wealth and run business in a scheduled area.

While 10 respondents attributed the trend of cross-cultural marriages to broad-mindedness, relaxed social norms and a changed outlook toward such marriages, 7 respondents believed that social media platforms like Facebook facilitate friendships with non-Khasis which culminate in such marriages.

Another 12 respondents cited assorted reasons which have been classified as 'other'. Out of these, 3 respondents believed that Khasi men married non-Khasi women who would obey and submit to their authority. Two respondents believed that those who married out, looked down upon Khasi people and culture. There was one response each, attributing marrying out to a desire for a white spouse, lack of suitable Khasi boys, *benami* (anonymous) purposes, the globalised world, demise of first (Khasi) husband, tendency of children of mixed marriages to marry out, and desire for intelligent offspring.

Insights from the Case Studies

In order to provide an insight into the more nuanced aspects of cross-cultural marriages, a qualitative method, in the form of case study method, was adopted to supplement the survey. The study includes 10 cases of Khasis married to non-Khasis, of which 8 were of Khasi women marrying non-Khasi men. The non-Khasi spouses are from different communities (including nationalities), generations, economic backgrounds and educational levels. While 6 of the 8 Khasi women met their non-Khasi husbands in Shillong, 2 met their husbands outside the state.

The participants were asked about reasons why Khasi women married non-Khasi men. Most of the Khasi women said that they married out of the community as they did not find a suitable Khasi spouse. They claimed that Khasi men are irresponsible, not well-qualified, and that it is rare to find a good Khasi man. This finding is consistent with the literature on the subject where the same is claimed, especially by organisations like the *Syngkhong Rympei Thymmai* which have attributed this trend to the perils of matriliny where the men suffer from low self-esteem and alcoholism because they are denied good education and inheritance rights thereby, driving Khasi girls to marry outsiders.

During one's youth, one does not consider if a male or female friend or colleague is from a socially acceptable religion or community, before interacting with them. A simple friendship may evolve into a serious relationship leading to marriage. This was observed in all the cases except that of Kong Marina, which was an arranged marriage.

Educational institutions or places of work have provided the backdrops in which Khasi women meet and interact with fellow young people who come from diverse backgrounds. The concept of economic propinquity, which has been mentioned in the literature review, refers to educational institutions/ job settings which provide opportunities for interaction with like-minded students/colleagues from other groups, which culminates in marital ties facilitated by economic propinquity (Barron, 1951).

It was observed that 4 out of the 10 participants met their spouse at their place of study or work.

As in the case of Kong Meena and her sister, many Khasi women who reside in the areas adjoining the Border Security Force (BSF) Camp in Umpling, have married BSF personnel who come from different communities from all over the country. Many of these young men are single or stationed without their families. Often, they get into relationships with local Khasi girls, which at times, culminates in marriage. Thus, specific physical locations (localities or geographical clusters) exhibit high incidences of cross-cultural marriages because they provide a contact point between members of different communities. This has been termed as 'residential propinquity' (Barron, 1951).

Increasing trend of studying or working outside the state means that younger members of the Khasi community are progressively gaining exposure to multi-cultural milieus. Multi-cultural encounters also occur during travels: 5 of the participants met their spouses outside the state. While 3 were studying/working outside the state, 2 were on a visit. Also, as in the case of Kong Bahun, it is difficult to find a like-minded Khasi spouse outside the state. It is anyway, a fairly difficult task to find someone from outside the state who would be willing to change their domicile post-marriage. Due to the lack of job opportunities in Meghalaya, well-qualified Khasis do not usually want to compromise on their careers by going back to the state, just to find a Khasi match. Therefore, when they meet a compatible non-Khasi, they readily prepare for a serious relationship.

As mentioned in the review of literature, the inability to conform to societal norms is one of the reasons for cross-cultural marriages (Cerroni-Long, 1985; Sung, 1990). In the case of Kong Carol, from a tender age, she realised that she did not fit into the society in which she was born. The societal norms did not make sense and she struggled to conform. She knew that she would marry a foreigner one day, and yearned to live abroad. It was her life's mission which she ultimately achieved. Since her parents empathised with her struggles, they were happy for her when she married Jakob, a European. Although she was the youngest daughter, they permitted her to follow her dreams.

Disappointment with the society into which one is born in, is also seen in the case of Kong Bahun. As a *khadduh* (youngest daughter), she was instilled with a strong sense of responsibility. It was only when she was pursuing her medical education in Gujarat that she realised that she had been living in a high-pressure environment with a lot of social constraints in Shillong. In Gujarat, she experienced freedom for the first time. She was disappointed when her mother was rude towards Jasjit (her Punjabi beau) and his parents, when they had come to Shillong to ask for her hand in marriage, especially since her brothers had also married non-Khasis. She said that this incident affected her to such an extent that she became a rebel. She went ahead and got married to Jasjit without her parents' permission. She is bringing up her children as Punjabis and has not given them her Khasi surname. She finds the patrilineal system to be a better system as it makes men more responsible. She is happy to be living away from Meghalaya as she finds the Khasi society to be very oppressive and judgemental.

Interestingly, the Khasi women who were above seventy years of age informed that during their youth, Khasi society was accommodative of cross-cultural marriages as long as the children belonged to their mother's Khasi clan, were brought up as Khasis, and lived on in Meghalaya. Kong Marina, an elderly Khasi lady reminisced how she met her husband. She happened to be vacationing at a family friend's home in Arunachal Pradesh with her parents. A young Bengali man visiting the family saw her and asked her parents for her hand. Since he was a man of good character with a stable government job, her parents gave their consent with the condition that the future offspring would be raised as Khasis. He agreed and they got married immediately. This memory was corroborated by two other elderly Khasi ladies married to a British tea gardener and a Nepali merchant, respectively.

This study has attempted to provide an insight into the possible factors that lead Khasi women to marry outside the community. Cross-cultural marriages are not new in the Khasi society and were never a problem in the past. However, burgeoning numbers of migrant labourers in the coal mines, and the phenomenon of young Khasis studying and working outside the state in pursuit of better opportunities, are believed to have increased the scope of cultural contact between different communities, ultimately culminating in such marriages. This study has presented the views of Khasis selected through a representative sample survey, and includes the insights of Khasi women married to non-Khasi men (case studies), thereby incorporating both, quantitative and qualitative elements. It is hoped that this study would contribute to further understanding of cross-cultural marriages in Khasi society.

Authors Note

Renuka Ma'am supervised my M.Phil. and Ph.D. research till her superannuation. She is a warm, caring and calming presence in my life. She is generous with her time and has always given me valuable feedback on any issue ranging from my research work to any topic under the sun. At the same time, she has never imposed her opinions upon me. She is a friend, philosopher and guide in personal and professional matters, and has always been there for me.

References

Bareh, H. (1974). *Meghalaya.* North-Eastern India News & Features Service.

Barron, M. L. (1951, November). Research on Intermarriage: A Survey of Accomplishments and Prospects. *American Journal of Sociology, Vol.* 57(No. 3), 249-255.

Barron, M. L. (1972). Introduction to Intermarriage. In M. L. Barron (Ed.), *The Blending American: Patterns of Intermarriage* (pp. 3-5). Chicago: Quadrangle Books.

Bhutia, L. G. (2013, January 21). *Men's Rights in Meghalaya: The Story of a Men's Liberation Movement.* Retrieved from Open: https://openthemagazine.com/art-culture/mens-rights-in-meghalaya/

Breger, R., & Hill, R. (1998). Introducing Mixed Marriages. In R. Breger, & R. Hill (Eds.), *Cross-Cultural Marriage: Identity and Choice* (pp. 1-32). New York: Berg.

Cantlie, K. (1934). *Notes on Khasi Law.* Aberdeen: Henry Munro Ltd.

Cerroni-Long, E. L. (1985, Spring). Marrying Out: Socio-Cultural and Psychological Implications of Intermarriage. *Journal of Comparative Family Studies, Volume 16*(1), 25-46.

Chhakchhuak, L. (2018, August 2). *Why are Khasi Women Being Held Responsible for the 'Dilution' of the Tribe?* Retrieved from The Wire: https://thewire.in/women/why-are-khasi-women-being-held-responsible-for-the-dilution-of-the-tribe

Das Gupta, P. K. (1984). *Life and Culture of Matrilineal Tribe of Meghalaya.* New Delhi: Inter-India Publications.

Feng, Zhiqiang, Boyle, Paul, Maarten van Ham , & Raab, G. M. (2012, May). Are Mixed-Ethnic Unions More Likely to Dissolve Than Co-Ethnic Unions? New Evidence from Britain. *European Journal of Population, 28*(No. 2), 159-176.

Finnäs, F., & O'Leary. (2003, December). Choosing for the Children: The Affiliation of the Children of Minority-Majority Group Intermarriages. *European Sociological Review, 19*(5), 483-499.

Gordon, A. I. (1972). Intermarriage: What It Is. In M. L. Barron (Ed.), *The Blending American- Patterns of Intermarriage* (pp. 6-10). Chicago: Quadrangle Books.

Govt Returns Lineage Bills to KHADC. (2018, August 25). *The Shillong Times*. Retrieved from https://theshillongtimes.com/2018/08/25/govt-returns-lineage-bills-to-khadc/

Gurdon, P. R. (1914). *The Khasis*. London: Macmillan and Co. Limited.

Hirschman, C. (1983). America's Melting Pot Reconsidered. *Annual Review of Sociology, 9*, 397-423. Retrieved from http://www.jstor.org/stable/2946072

Holy, L. (1996). *Anthropological Perspectives on Kinship*. London: Pluto Press.

Joshi, M. S., & Krishna, M. (1998). English and North American Daughters-in -Law in the Hindu Joint Family. In R. Breger, & R. Hill , *Cross-Cultural Marriage: Identity and Choice.* and Krishna, Meena. (1998). English and North American Daughters-in -Law in the Hindu Joint Family. In R. Breger & New York: Berg.

Kaur, R. (2010 , January 30-February 5). 14. Kaur, R. (201 Bengali Bridal Diaspora: Marriage as a Livelihood Strategy. Economic and Political Weekly, 45(5), 16-18. *Economic and Political Weekly, 45(5), 16-18*, 45(5), 16-18.

Kennedy, R. J. (1952, July). Single or Triple Melting-Pot? Intermarriage in New Haven, 1870-1950. *American Journal of Sociology,, 58*(1), 56-59.

KHADC Passes Bill to Prevent Khasi Women From Marrying Non-Khasis. (2018, July 25). *Shillong Times*. Shillong. Retrieved from https://theshillongtimes.com/2018/07/25/khadc-passes-bill-to-prevent-khasi-women-from-marrying-non-khasis/

Langstieh, B. T. (2001). Demographic Structure of the Khasi-Muslims of Shillong, Meghalaya. *Journal of Human Ecology, 12:2*, 121-125.

Leach, E. R. (1955, December). Polyandry, Inheritance and the Definition of Marriage. *Man, 55*, 182-186. Retrieved from https://www.jstor.org/stable/2795331

Lobo, A. (2018). Anglo-Indian Women: A Narrative of Matriarchy in a Global Diaspora. In A. Pande (Ed.), *Women in the Indian Diaspora Historical Narratives and Contemporary Challenges* (pp. 177-180). Singapore: Springer.

Lobo, A. S. (2012). Matrilineal Anglo-Indians. In L. Lumb, *More Voices on the Veranda:An anglo-Indian Anthology* (pp. 203-204). New Jersey: CTR Books.

Lyngdoh, P. (2009). 'For Sale. In R. S. Ngangom, & K. S. Nongkynrih (Eds.), *Dancing Earth: An Anthology of Poetry from North-East India* (p. 171). New Delhi: Penguin Books.

Mair, L. (1971). *Marriage.* Harmondsworth: Penguin Books.

Marshall, G. (1998). *A Dictionary of Sociology.* Oxford: Oxford University Press.

Mathur, P. R. (1979). *The Khasi Of Meghalaya (Study In Tribalism and Religion).* New Delhi, India: Cosmo Publications.

Maxwell, A. (1998). Cross-Cultural Marriage: Identity and Choice. In R. Breger, & R. Hill , *Not all Issues are Black or White: Some Voices from the Offspring of Cross-Cultural Marriages* (pp. 209-228). New York: Oxford.

Merton, R. K. (1941, August). Intermarriage and the Social Structure: Fact and Theory. *Psychiatry, 4*(No. 3), 361-374.

Mohrmen, H. R. (2013, October 28). Taking Influx Issue to the Next Level. *The Shillong Times.*

Mukhim, P. (1994, March 3). Khasi Society in the Emerging Scenario. *The Shillong Times.*

Mukhim, P. (2013, October 4). Jaitbynriew as the Idiom of Deception. *The Shillong Times.* Retrieved from https://theshillongtimes.com/2013/10/04/jaitbynriew-as-the-idiom-of-deception/#

Mukhim, P. (2014, April 26). The Politics of Identity and Location. *The Hindu.* Retrieved from https://www.thehindu.com/opinion/lead/politics-of-identity-and-location/article5948473.ece

Nag, S. (2022). In Search of the 'Enemy': Outsiders, Women, and Political Exclusion in Northeast India. In *Vernacular Politics in Northeast India: Democracy, Ethnicity & Indigeneity* (pp. 311-328). Oxford University Press.

Nagel, J. (2000). Ethnicity and Sexuality. *Annual Review of Sociology,* 26, 107-133.

Nakane, C. (1967). *Garo and Khasi- A Comparative Study in Matrilineal Systems.* Paris: Mounton and Co.

Nongbri, T. (1993). Gender and the Khasi Family Structure. In P. Uberoi, *Family, Kinship and Marriage in India* (pp. 176-186). New Delhi: Oxford University Press.

Nongbri, T. (2003). *Development, Ethnicity and Gender: Select Essays on Tribes in India.* Jaipur and New Delhi: Rawat Publications.

Nongbri, T. (2013). Kinship Terminology and Marriage Rules: The Khasi of North-East India. *Sociological Bulletin*, 413-430.

Pakeyntein, V. (1996). The Khasi Clan: Changing Religion and Its Effect. In J. S. Bhandari, *Kinship and Family in North-East India Vol. II* (pp. 349-372). New Delhi: Cosmo Publications.

Pohshna, W. (2018, July 28). Before I Have a Last Laugh on the KHADC Amendment of Lineage Act. *Raiot.* Retrieved from https://raiot.in/before-i-have-a-last-laugh-on-the-khadc-amendment-of-lineage-act/

Romano, D. (1988). *Inter-Cultural Marriage: Promises and Pitfalls.* Yarmouth, ME: Intercultural Press, Inc.

Saikia, A. (2018, July 27). *In Meghalaya, Khasi Women Who Marry Non-Khasis May Lose Scheduled Tribe Status and Benefits.* Retrieved from Scroll.

Sawkmie,S. J. (2022). *Marrying Out: Cross-Cultural Marriages and the Politics of Identity among the Khasis.* Unpublished Doctoral thesis. Jawaharlal Nehru University.

Singh, K. (1979). Khasi and Jaintia Religion. In H. Roy (Ed.), *Khasi Heritage.* Shillong: Seng Khasi.

Strauss, A. L. (1972). Strain and Harmony in American-Japanese War-Bride Marriages. In M. L. Barron, *The Blending American: Patterns of Intermarriage* (pp. 268-281). Chicago: Quadrangle Books.

Sung, B. L. (1990, Autumn). Chinese American Intermarriage. *Journal of Comparative Family Studies, 21*(3), 337-352.

Wahlang, M. G., & Karlsson, B. G. (2022). The Body of the Land: Women, Ethnicity, and Alter-Politics. In J. J. Wouters (Ed.), *Vernacular Politics in Northeast India: Democracy, Ethnicity & Indigeneity* (pp. 289-310). Oxford University Press.

Williams, W. (2011). *The Globalisation of Love.* London: Summertime Publishing.

AFRICAN DIASPORA IN INDIA

Cultural Hybridity, Memory and Human Ecology

Koyal Verma

Introduction

Eurocentric and Western approaches have dominated the debates on early century African migrations, or transatlantic migrations, and even studies on exchanges within the Indian Ocean. This essay traces the diffusion of people of African origin from the Swahili coast and horn of Africa, to the Malabar Coast in India. It led to permanent settlements of the African diaspora in the states of Gujarat, Hyderabad, Karnataka, Andhra Pradesh and Kerala. Maritime voyages across the Indian Ocean resulted in settlements of African sailors, traders, merchants, artists, slaves, Sufis, saints and missionaries emerging along the coastal regions of India. While human settlements were established on both, ports of East Africa and India, this essay focuses on the latter region. Regrettably, this subject has hitherto, received very little attention in mainstream academic circles due to the prevailing Eurocentric approaches. Hence, studies compiled have been myopic, especially with regard to migrations between India and Africa via the Indian Ocean. These studies have received limited attention within the larger scope of migrations, exchanges and human ecology. Mainstream scholarship has mostly highlighted aspects of trade exchanges and impacts of colonization. However, focus on specific areas concerning the cultural dimensions, specifically of early century migrations, has been scant if not completely missing from mainstream scholarship.

This essay focuses on migration from Africa to India, and particularly, on the cultural aspects of migration. Migration of African peoples entailed import of images, objects, ideas, traditions, and cultural practices from diverse parts of Africa to India. Hence, art history and human ecology perspectives have been employed to understand the impact of early exchanges, social interactions, and socio-cultural assimilation and integration with regard to African migrants. In sum, the essay analyses the cultural migration patterns of the African diaspora.

The African Identity in Retrospect: The Socio-historical Accounts

There is currently, a dearth of dedicated studies on African-Indian identity formation and their subsequent religious, cultural contributions to the Indian subcontinent, from the ancient through the medieval period. This calls for wider and more extensive academic research in the context of African-Indian cultural formations and heritage.

Visual Representation of the African People

This section seeks to re-discover lesser known, diverse forms of African culture, identity and community in India. It describes the African diaspora in India as a unique community with a history and diverse forms of culture, traditions and practices. There is presently a lack of ample understanding and representation of the historical identity of the African peoples in the Indian context.

For instance, in visual culture, the historical representation of African identity portrays the people of African descent as royal slaves. The Siddis no doubt played an important role in the expansion of kingdoms, serving the royalty as administrators, regents, military leaders and foot soldiers, from the thirteenth and fourteenth centuries, right up to India's independence (Khaidi 1989, Harris 1971, Ali 1996). But the representation of the diaspora in mainstream discourse has been limited. Both, present day Siddis and their forebearers adapted, functioned, and assimilated in India. Though they belong to the Indian linguistic and cultural clusters of Gujarat, Hyderabad, Karnataka and Andhra Pradesh, the African diaspora articulates 'subcultures' or 'alternative' cultures through symbolic activities. Academic literature has documented the slave trade, but very limited academic scholarship has focused on the aspects of cultural interaction along these historical migrations.

Cultural Hybridity

This essay posits that cultural intermixing and exchanges have produced hybrid cultural identities. It argues that the African diaspora is not only influenced by the culture of the host society that gives rise to unique cultural identities in the adopted homelands, but also produces forms of cultural hybridization. The ancient historical migrations provide an analytical framework to study African-Indian cultures which may be regarded as hybrid cultures. Trade exchanges and migrations between ports of Africa and India i.e., between Mozambique, Zanzibar and Gujarat, Karnataka, Bombay, have led to cultural diffusion and dispersion, resulting in the emergence of complex forms of hybridity on both sides. Exchanges and migration also imply exchange of religious- cultural art forms, music, dance, customs, practices etc. The early century (ancient, medieval) migrations of African traders, artists, slaves, sailors etc. led to settlements of *Siddi, Chaush* and *Hadhrami* in India (Verma 2023). Interestingly, cultural hybridity has emerged from myriad discourses on globalization (Kraidy 2005, Pieterse 2004). This term has also been widely used to describe multi-layered identities as 'creole', 'syncretic' and 'diasporic'. The term 'cultural hybridity' encompasses ideas such as contact and fusion, conflict and difference, compatibility and rupture, territorialisation and deterritorialization, and dislocation and location across geographical and linguistic boundaries (Cancilini 1995). Theories on cultural hybridity have also been discussed in the context of cultural boundaries which demarcate 'sites' for negotiations, struggles and clashes. Khan (2007) opines that many theories on hybridity also refer to ideas of optimism and emancipation. Acculturation similarly reflects the degree to which immigrants retain their ethnic culture, and the degree to which they are invested in seeking contact and absorption in their host cultures (Bhatia 2011). Notions of acculturation are analysed through the cultural translation model, and are shaped by intersectionality of race, class, gender, religious identities, and forces such as xenophobia and colonization. To understand cultural hybridity in the particular context of the African diaspora, it is important to expand on the analyses of migrations during early centuries through the Indian Ocean, between East Africa and India. These migrations led to permanent human settlements and subsequent emergence of Africanism in the Indian society, giving rise to cultural hybridity in the social, cultural and human spheres. In short, forms of cultural hybridity imply complex patterns of cultural-social practices, behaviour, rituals, dance forms, music and art. Using this multi-dimensional approach, this essay posits that migrations from East Africa to India led to the emergence of complex forms of human settlements and demography. Most importantly, they produced an 'African Indian identity'. It has led to the emergence of hybrid cultures, practices, customs, art, music, dance forms. Further, it gave rise to 'hybridity' in context of community and the production of complex identities of 'African-Indian origin.' These developments were not limited to the territorial or geographical dimensions, but extended to a wider sense of dispersed boundaries, expanding as far as the Indian Ocean. It is important that the significance and contribution of the African diaspora, particularly the *Siddi, Chaush* and *Hadhrami* communities, to the adopted homelands, i.e., the local cultural environment, from the early centuries, be appraised in light of construction and production of hybrid identities (Verma 2023). Significant questions like what constitutes hybridity, specifically with regard to the African-Indian identity, need added scholarly focus. For instance, the musical performances of the diaspora are linked to the religion and culture such as of the cults of Sufi saints, particularly of the black Sufi saint famously known as Gori Pir (Kessel 2008). According to the local folklore, Gori Pir migrated to Gujarat as an African merchant along with his brothers and sister. Gori Pir's shrine is in Gujarat, and one in Bombay. The Pir's shrine is visited by not only the Siddis but also Indians of both, Muslim and Hindu communities. This shows that African cultures have made significant contributions to the host culture. Some members from the Sufi cult have formed a contemporary Siddi Goma group which recite mystical Sufi chants and perform African dances. They perform locally as well as internationally. Frequently, this African diasporic community is referred to as Siddi, deriving from a 'Northern African term signifying respect, particularly an honorific term coined to designate benevolence for descendants of loyal defenders of Muslim rulers in India or an association with black sainthood'

(Basu 2005:5). These traditional practices made the African diaspora unique and outstanding among the local population practicing Islam. Thus, the religious and cultural practices of these ancient communities are important factors to consider while researching processes of identity formations, especially those identities that are hybrid.

Contemporary Representations of the African Identity and Its Historical Link

It has become an established fact, that with the migration of people, culture also migrates. Basu (1998) points out that people of African descent and cultures who migrated to India, were popularly known as Siddi. Siddis were known to be descendants of the Bantu people of East Africa. They were also popularly identified as *Habhsi*, a term belonging to the Arabic-Persian lexicon, literally meaning people belonging to Abyssinia or Ethiopia. However, in the contemporary context, *Habshi* represents a set of stereotypes designating the African community (Verma 2023).This may be linked with how Hawley (2008) traces the arrival of Siddis in India and South Asia, as slaves, brought first by the Arabs as early as seventh century, followed by the Portuguese and the British. Later, during the thirteenth and fourteenth centuries, they were brought in from Ethiopia, Egypt, Sudan and Somalia. They served as soldiers in the armies of sultans. During the sixteenth century, they were plied from even deeper south of the East coast of Africa. They were drawn from Mozambique and the hinterlands of inland Tanzania, Malawi and Congo. Basu (1998) further shows that even after the abolition of slave trade, a small number of slaves continued to be shipped to India, especially to the western coast of Gujarat, where they permanently settled as the Siddi community. They were employed as servants and bodyguards of local rulers. The women were employed as domestic servants for queens and aristocratic women. They were 'given away' as dowries of Rajput brides, and thereafter, moved with their new employers to the new kingdom (Verma 2023). Further, Alpers (2004) shows that the English, the Portuguese, and the French employed African slaves as soldiers and servants in India. Contemporary representations of the African identity resonate with historical representations. The idea is to focus on African identity, and not upon the historiography, but rather, on the construction of the African identity in the Indian historical context.

Migration and Memory: Locating Art History for Cultural Analysis

This section focuses on historical African voyages, in order to understand present African settlements in India and subsequent processes of identity formations. It has been argued that the memory can reflect important dimensions of social, political and cultural identity. It can be identified as one of the most important aspects of identity. Warburg (1905), a historian, for instance, has inspired many anthropologists and sociologists to adopt this methodological tool. Halbwachs (1992) adopts Warburg's approach (1905) to study memory in order to analyse identity and community. He discerns memory as a social event. He interprets collective memory as that which is generated through close interaction of subjects in a social context involving a continuous return to common images, rituals and myths. These help members in reaffirming their in-group identity and status. Further, he analyses the quality of 'dreamlike' production of memory in the same way as Warburg (1905).

Assmann (2006) also talks about a theory of 'communicative memory'. He refers to it as everyday interaction between members or subjects of a group and their contexts. He posits that communicative memory refers to living memories which enable the members of a community to share and produce common ideas in a spontaneous manner. He describes cultural memory in a similar manner and shows how it is more organized than communicative memory, and is a part of long-term memory. He shows that unlike communicative memory, which only extends up to three or four generations, cultural memory provides the members with a sense of unity and identity in a more permanent manner. Assmanns (2006) uncovers the parallels between Warburg's approach and that of Halbwachs (1992). Halbwachs (1992), Assmans (2006), and Warburg (1905) are frequently cited by art historians and cultural historians attempting to understand the significance of memory in history.

Collective Memory and Social Construction of Migration Patterns

With regard to cultural memory, rituals and symbols are seen as critical to analyses of identity. For instance, according to Warburg (1905), cultural forms that are commonly held as symbols, facilitate recollection of aspects of reality and identity. Historians, anthropologists and sociologists such as Halbwachs (1992) and Assmans (2006) demonstrate the significance of symbols and motifs in retracing images and ideas. They demonstrate that the motifs and their emotive impulses have the capacity to communicate the psychology of the era in which they are produced (Verma 2023). Art historians such as Warburg are attracted to classical arts and mythical figures for this reason. Interest in images, and their interpretation outside the canon of fine arts, has received wide academic attention giving rise to transdisciplinary approaches. Recent scholars interpret metaphors and motifs in terms of how they travel across time and space. Hence, this methodology interests scholars across disciplines. The intriguing way of blending art with culture has become a popular model among academic scholars, for interpreting images and objects to understand the identity of a community. The Siddis recollect objects and elements of African heritage and culture such as, musical instruments exhibiting resemblance to African forms, as well as songs, music, traditions, folklores. Interestingly, the dhow culture owes its origins to these early century trade migrations between Africa and India (Verma 2023). The wooden 'dhow' has been studied in various disciplines such as history, anthropology and cultural studies. Its importance as a means of transportation has been recognised, but more importantly, it signifies the value of a cultural object (Sherrif 2010, Basu 2008 et all). Hence, it is argued that the 'dhow' can be studied (Assmann, 2006) (Halbwachs, 1992) as an important object related to the culture and identity of a community. Thus, the significance of the 'wooden dhow' is not only being studied as a historical means of trade and transportation, but also as a means of social interaction and communication (Verma 2023). The dhow was fundamental to trade linkages between East Africa and India. This chapter posits the idea that the wooden 'dhow' was an 'animate' object that marked relations and social interactions between sailors and traders, especially at the ports of Western India and East Africa. More significant to this study is the emergence of the 'dhow culture' among migrants who disembarked and settled at the ports of Africa and India.

This section highlights the aspect of memory in order to understand art forms, objects, cultural practices and traditions that African migrants recollected in India, which helped them significantly in the construction of their cultural identity. Warburg (1905) uses motifs, art, ideas and metaphors as primary subjects to analyse the aspect of recollection of images, practices and religious concepts. His approach signifies a constant self-reinvention of metaphors. His work gave rise to stylistic analysis which is critical of traditional approaches. Warburg's approach demonstrates how the method of art history can be effectively utilised.

Religion, Migration and Cultural Adaptation: The Human Ecological Approach

Historical patterns of migration are important factors in understanding the role of religion in construction of identities and communities. Religion, especially Islam, played an important role in the process of migration and adaptation, for the African diaspora in India. There is a significant presence of African diaspora in the city of Hyderabad. Here, they are known as *Chaush*. They are followers of Islam claiming *Hadhrami* Arab descent. In early centuries, they voyaged through the Indian Ocean, from the Swahili coast and the Horn of Africa, to the Malabar Coast in India, and settled in Hyderabad. They are also settled in other parts of the subcontinent, Pakistan and Sri Lanka. They came to India and integrated with the military forces, especially of the Nizams[1] of Hyderabad. The *Chaush* are known for their rich cultural traditions of music and dance forms called Marfa (Verma 2023). These traditions come to life during festivals and weddings. A sizeable community of African diaspora has called Hyderabad their home since the seventeenth century. The settlements of the African diaspora enabled and ensured continuation of their religious practices, observances, rituals, traditions and customs. Thus, an interrelation can be discerned between religion and the migration of African peoples to India. It can be asserted that religion facilitated a certain pattern of historical migration from Africa to India. Further, it can also be said that it facilitated adaptation and integration of the diaspora (Verma 2023).

Particular to this study, it is important to consider how Islam emerged as a driving force for migration and innovation across the Indian Ocean region since antiquity. Thus, the lens of Islamic traditions, beliefs, ideas, customs, and practices is appropriate for analysing how these communities came together and transformed certain cultural traditions while adapting to new environments. Studies show that irrespective of generational changes and innovations due to cultural adaptation in the host society, there remains continuity of certain customs and traditions since the early centuries. Basu (1998) explains that practices of religious-cultural traditions, rituals, customs, sacred ideas, concepts of devotion and ideas of mysticism have a common descent. Religion is recognised as playing an important role in the everyday lives of the African diaspora even while translating it into different cultural forms and expressions. It is argued that forms of religion and cultural practices undergo change in the host society, and are subsequently subjected to transformation and even innovation. Thus, religion renews itself in the act of drawing from its own tradition in this sense. Park (1915) and Wirth (1945) highlight the significance of studying community as a physical fact. They argue that adaptation to different environments occurs as consequences of demographic shifts and human settlements occurring through displacement, slave-trade, migration and more recently, war.

In this sense, the human ecology perspective highlights the interconnection between the natural, human, social, cultural and the environmental, in studying social life. It derives from the conceptual framework of organising plant and animal ecology in relation to humans, drawing from biological sciences to study individuals and their habitats. In many ways, it facilitates an understanding of social and psychic life. This approach highlights the link between sociology and biology, which is highlighted in order to secure wider scope for analysis of social life and cultural life. Thus, human ecologists have evolved theories for the exploration of human concentrations and the dispersion of people, cultures and identity.

Conclusion

This essay maps the continuities in African traditions that oscillated between the home country and the host country during migration. It analyses the transformations that occurred while the African diaspora adapted to unfamiliar cultural environments of the host society. It focuses on the diversity of religious practices and traditions wherein the rituals and art forms of African origin came into contact with the traditions and systems of the host society. The essay posits that religion played an important role in the cultural adaptation, mediation, mobilization, and rehabilitation, constituting a dynamic force for the migrants in the larger process of integration and resettlement. A historico-cultural analysis of Islamic traditions is undertaken to trace how traditions renew themselves within changed social and political environments, creating indeed, sets of new patterns and cultural innovations. In this context, it also talks about hybridisation. An attempt has been made to outline cultural diffusion and dispersion of African culture in India. A socio-cultural and historical framework is employed to analyse the complex religious engagements across the Indian Ocean. The changing contexts, negotiations and adaptation processes are analysed to study the power of tradition and innovation. To analyse African-Indian identity, it has engaged in a historical, visual and cultural analysis of the symbolism of the *Habshi* through Warburg's approach.

References

Alpers, E.A. (1997). The African Diaspora in the Northwestern Indian Ocean: Reconsideration of an Old Problem, New Directions for Research. *Comparative Studies of South Asia, Africa and the Middle East.*, 62-81.

Basu, H. (2002). Indian Siddi- African Diaspora: A Query. *Cultural Exchange and Transformation in the Indian Ocean World.* University of California.

Basu, H. (2000). Theatre of Memory: Performance of Ritual Kinship of the African Diaspora in Sind/Pakistan . In A.R. Boeck, *Culture, Creation and Procreation in South Asia* (pp. 243-270). Berghahn: Oxford.

Hawley, J.C. (2008). *India in Africa Africa in India: Indian Ocean Cosmopolitanisms.* Bloomington: Indiana University Press.

Wirth, L. (1945). Human Ecology. *American Journal of Sociology*, 483-488.

Park, R.E. (1936). Human Ecology. *American Journal of Sociology*, 1-15.

Cancilini, N. (1995). *Hybrid Cultures: Strategies for entering and leaving modernity.* Minneapolis : University of Minnesota Press.

Khan, A. (2007). Good to think? Creolization, optimism and agency. *Current Anthropology*, 653-673.

Bhatia, S. (2011). Lost in Translation: Cultural Hybridity, Acculturation and Human Development. *Human Development*, 400-407.

Johnson, C.D. (2012). *Memory, Metaphor and Aby Warburg's Atlas of Images.* Ithaca: Cornell University Press.

Warburg, A. (1905). *Artistic Exchanges between North and South in the Fifteenth Century.*

Kessel, W.V. (2008). Retrieved from www.theeastafrican.co.ke: https://www.theeastafrican.co.ke/magazine/434746-470390-dasc6r/index.html Basu, H. (1998). Hierarchy and Emotion: Love, joy and sorrow in a cult of black saints in Gujarat, India. In *Embodying Modernity, Locality and the Performance of Emotion in Sufu cults charism.* Routledge.

Kraidy, M. (2005). *Hybridity or the cultural logic of globalization.* Philadelphia: Temple University Press.

Pieterse, J. (2004). *Globalization and culture: global melange.* Lanham: Rowman and Littlefield.

Assmann, J. (2006). *Religion and Cultural Memory.* Stanford: Stanford University Press.

Halbwachs, M. (1992). *On Collective Memory.* Chicago: The University of Chicago Press.

Verma, K. (2023). *African Clusters in India.* London: Routledge.

COVID-19 AND ITS IMPACT ON WOMEN

Elizabeth Imti

Introduction

The COVID-19 pandemic, which started as a health crisis, rapidly devolved into a human crisis (United Nations Economic and Social Commission for Asia and the Pacific, 2020). It forced governments across the globe to close international borders and suspend international trade. Global transport and communication systems have broken down thus, affecting both international and domestic politics significantly. It has rendered millions unemployed, and many more to the cusp of extreme poverty. Women, especially from the low and emerging economies, experienced the worst of this catastrophe. In the Indian context, the pandemic has led to exponential rise in domestic violence, and has marginalized women further in their homes and communities.

In our society, women are usually assigned tasks of maintaining households and looking after the domestic needs of the family. Their active engagement in community healthcare and nursing services during the pandemic have put them at higher risk of contracting COVID-19, as compared to men. According to a study conducted by the International Growth

Centre, London, it has been observed that in 104 countries, women occupied 70% of the health and social sectors, and 50% of the unpaid sectors (Sili, 2020). But in terms of policies and actions, women mostly remained neglected and deprived, especially during the pandemic. Inadequate health services, weak government programs, along with gender related violence have stood women in utmost precarious position. According to the United Nations, in low and emerging economies, more than 50 %of all maternal deaths occur from complications in pregnancy and childbirth (United Nations, 2020). As essential health services are affected heavily during the pandemic, these numbers are expected to rise thereby, affecting sex ratio within the country.

The pandemic and subsequent lockdowns have led to sharp spike in psychological distress among men due to the loss of employment and limited opportunities. In too many instances, this has led to violent behaviour, often resulting in domestic violence. Apart from further decline in and loss of already marginal economic agency, women have been positioned at the receiving end of physical violence in a yet unfamiliar context.

COVID-19 has an uneven impact on people, especially due to their gender difference, disabilities, ethnicities, socio-economic status, race and age group (Nanthini & Nair, 2020). Cooper and Mosseri (2020) are of the opinion that during the pandemic, women are facing a 'triple whammy': (a) as frontline workers at risk for contracting COVID-19, (b) as workers in industries experiencing greater economic distress, and (c) as caregivers shouldering increased domestic responsibilities due to school and day-care closures.

Moser (1993), with her gender-based approach, attempts to understand the factors responsible for gender inequalities in developing countries. She identifies three main sectors namely, productive and reproductive work, and community activities, in which women are engaged. She also highlights the fact that compared to men, women take on higher responsibilities during global catastrophes like the pandemic.

Similarly, in light of the present pandemic, Fisher & Ryan (2021) are of the opinion that the condition has exacerbated gender inequalities across various domains such as health and well-being, labour, economic stability, relational violence, work and poverty etc.

Violence against Women

Renzetti & Bergen (2005) observed that in the Western world, systematic efforts were underway from 1970 onwards, to understand the factors that are responsible for violence against women. These studies have attempted to understand gender-based violence over the past three decades, introspecting at the local, state, and federal levels.

The phenomena of lockdown has led to higher rates of intimate partner violence, mental illness, and reduced healthcare access, all predominantly impacting women (Bambra, Albani, & Franklin, 2021). Increase in numbers of domestic violence cases is an indirect result of COVID-19. Festering tension, stress, and lack of activities in confined conditions have resulted in a global rise in domestic violence (Nanthini & Nair, 2020).

Women As Frontline Workers and Their Economic Instability in the Pandemic

It was found that among women, the severity and mortality rate from COVID-19 infection is twice as high as men (Jin et al., 2020). According to the World Health Organisation (2019), women comprise 70% of the global healthcare workforce and yet, occupy only 25% of the senior positions in any profession. It was also reported that women professional health workers accrue comparatively lower status and in most cases, are underpaid or unpaid.

During the pandemic, higher percentage of healthcare workers diagnosed with COVID-19 have been women. In Spain, 75.5% (21,392)of infected healthcare workers were women and in Italy, they were 69% (14,350) (UN Women, 2020). Similarly, the Centers for Disease Control and Prevention found that in the United States, 73%(6,603) of infected healthcare workers were women (US Department of Health and Human Services, 2020). Thus, the virus has taken a disproportionate toll on the psychological and physical health of women (Ausin et al., 2020; Szabo et al., 2020). When developing countries like India, Brazil, and Nepal were compelled to reallocate their resources to upgrade health infrastructures on the go, it actually put women's health in further jeopardy (United Nation, 2020).

According to Moreira da Silva (2019), globally, women and girls account for 75% of unpaid care and domestic work in homes and communities every day. But unfortunately, through increase of unpaid work, the pandemic has affected women in different ways than men. In Indian society, domestic and care work in a household are considered exclusive responsibilities of women. As a result, the burden of unpaid works fall disproportionately on women (Chauhan, 2020). Thus, the lockdown has directly contributed to heightened unpaid workload and accountability for women (ibid).

The outbreak of COVID-19 had serious impact on the economic status and security of women. Women are widely employed in industries like travel, healthcare, textiles, retail etc., and during the pandemic these industries were severely affected. Thousands of women are engaged in the informal sector, employed in domestic work and as seasonal agricultural labour. In addition to wage gap and very limited progression opportunities, over-representation of women in the informal sector increases their vulnerability to poverty (Nanthini & Nair, 2020). The situation is hardly different in developing countries. For instance, in the United States, the initial unemployment data revealed that more women than men are losing job in the healthcare sector (Miyamoto, 2020).

Objectives of the Study

Although domestic violence following the lockdown has been globally on the rise, the situation is extraordinarily dire in emerging economies like India. Findings of the National Commission for Women attest to this. Additionally, sexual exploitation, along with lack of proper health care services and education, have ensured that women remain as the most neglected and deprived group in the society. In context of these realities, this study seeks to understand how the pandemic has impacted women to further expand their misery and vulnerability.

COVID-19 and Its Impact on Gender Related Violence

The lockdown ensured that as victims of abuse, women are compelled to stay confined in a shared space with her abuser/s. Domestic violence and physical abuse are universal phenomena but have more currency in developing countries due to low literacy rates along with other myriad socio-cultural factors. Very importantly, the lockdown brought India's law enforcement and judicial operations to a grinding halt. As a consequence, victims were left without timely security and legal recourse, following instances of abuse. Rural areas were observed as being affected more direly than urban areas, in this regard. Largely, India's rural women are not educated enough to use digital platforms such as internet and social media to address their grievances or to seek help through these platforms. Due to this, as well as other socio-cultural factors, domestic abuse mostly escaped unreported during the height of the pandemic.

Numbers published in the reports of the National Commission for Women (NCW) reveal the staggering figures of physical violence on women during the lockdown phase. The Commission received more than 587 complaints of violence between 23 March and 16 April 2023. Out of these, 239 related to domestic violence. Chairperson Rekha Sharma points out that the lockdown has compelled the abused and the abuser to cohabit a space. According to a petition filed in the Delhi high court, it was been observed that within the first eleven days of lockdown, an astonishing 92000 calls were made to report domestic violence (OMMCOM News, 2020). Following the lockdown, there has been a sudden and sharp rise in distress calls related to child abuse and domestic violence. The national lockdown had forced millions of Indians, including migrant laborers and daily wage earners, to return home to their families after a prolonged gap. During this prolonged gap, they developed psychological as well physical apathy towards their families, including women, resulting in physical as well as mental oppression. One of the chief contributing factors to domestic abuse is economic hardship that male family members are experiencing, which in turn, is leading to increased stress levels. Under the circumstances, women appear to be the most readily accessible site of relieving that stress, through violence. Increased alcohol consumption during the lockdown has also contributed to increase in domestic violence. In order to combat domestic violence, the NCW had launched a dedicated WhatsApp number for reporting and registering cases of domestic violence on urgent basis. The Ministry of Women and Child Development and the NCW collaborated to raise awareness on the issue of domestic abuse, particularly during the lockdown. Social media platform Twitter launched a handle #ThereIsHelp, in order to develop widespread consensus against domestic violence among Indian citizens (The Indian Express, 2020). It bears note that the Protection of Women from Domestic Violence Act (Domestic Violence Act) (2005) has largely proven ineffective in dealing with the problem of domestic abuses in India (EPW ENGAGE, 2020). Under this Act, the definition and scope of interpreting domestic violence is limited. The Act principally refers to physical violence, with minimum attention to the psychological, emotional and sexual dimensions whereas the pandemic has entailed a general rise in domestic abuse across the board.

Major facilities for Women Established by the Central Government in India during the COVID-19 Pandemic

Services offered	Aim
One Stop Centres	For redressing domestic violence related cases
Nation Wide toll free no. 181	For quick response to domestic violence cases
Emergency Response Support System	Emergency response to domestic violence related cases
NCW initiated WhatsApp alert	Domestic violence victims can lodge their grievances via WhatsApp no 91 7217735372.
National Legal Service Authority (NALSA) started national helpline no. 15100	NALSA offered legal aid and counselling for women

Source: Ministry of Women and Child Development, Government of India. Data retrieved from *https://wcd.nic.in/acts/facilities-women-during-COVID-19-pandemic*

The Economic Consequences of COVID-19 for Women

There is no denying the fact that the economic fallout of the pandemic has transformed and challenged the global economy post-COVID. Its impact has surely affected women way more adversely than it has affected men. Unlike previous economic crises, the impact of the pandemic was felt much much higher in informal sectors which are predominately occupied by women. Further, the consequences are expected to be even dire for women working in such sectors in the developing countries. Past instances of economic recessions have greatly affected manufacturing, construction and business sectors, but the pandemic has as well affected sectors such as education and healthcare, these being preferable employment destinations for majority of women (World Trade Organization, 2020). At the same time, women working in retail were also severely affected as the pandemic had drastically decreased global purchase capacity and consumption levels.

The economic impact of COVID-19 is much more visible in low and middle income working families, and more disproportionately on working mothers (World Trade Organization, 2020). Circumstances following the pandemic has effected substantive changes in the working hours of women who were also compelled to take unpaid leaves to manage their households. Likewise, employees in many small and medium private companies have been cut loose in order to tide over financial loses. Large number of women lost their jobs or were compelled work sans pay. Compared to men, women who lost jobs experienced greater difficulty in finding alternate avenues of income. Women, who anyway earn less than men for equal responsibilities, had also exhausted their savings in sustaining their families through the crisis. During the pandemic, women had mostly been reduced to contractual or part time jobs owing to severe slump in the job market.

The lockdown has brought global production activities to a grinding halt owing to a combination of unavailability of essential raw materials, shortages of workforce, and declining demands. Sectors such as textiles, clothing, and food production, which employ vast women work forces, have been affected severely due to travel and trade restrictions. According to various sources, manufacturing industries, which are the key areas of global supply chains, such as textiles, leather, retails, heavy machineries etc. are heavily affected following the pandemic (World Trade Organization, 2020). Apart from manufacturing, tourism and travel sectors have also been affected. Across the world, women choose to work in tourism and travel sectors due to high wages and relatively better job security. Similarly, women working in informal sectors within the tourism industry were affected significantly. Besides the current slump, prospects of subsequent employment in these sectors has also been jeopardized due to a largely uncertain outlook of global purchase capacities.

COVID-19 and Its Economic Impact on Women in India

In developing countries, the severe effect of such economic meltdown on women is bound to affect their overall quality of life. There are several important factors which have significant impact on the overall economic position of women in developing countries like in India. These factors are discussed below.

- In countries like India, a substantive women population is dependent upon and working in the service sector which remains highly vulnerable to economic disruptions. Due to severe disruption of export services, sectors such as tourism, health etc., were unable to generate expected revenues, and had to let go of numerous employees in order to balance out the losses.

- The lockdown, and the urgency to get back on track, has persuaded several businesses to shift their operations to the digital medium in order to minimize human involvement and abate risks of further contraction. However, due to inadequate or non-existent digital literacy among large sections of the population, very few have been able to get onboard this novel platform of business and employment. In the north-eastern part of India, which already suffers from technological and infrastructural deficiencies, shifting jobs to digital platforms have significantly affected the population. But the situation for women is more miserable than men. Barring some major cities, for women everywhere, there exists significant inequality in access to digital literacy, and they aren't equipped with the IT and telecommunication skills that are required for venturing into the digital job markets.
- As already discussed above, large numbers of women, especially from the rural areas, are employed in the informal sectors. Even in metro cities like Mumbai, Delhi and Kolkata, women mostly work in informal sectors to support their families. Already sans any protective blanket like pension schemes and such, the pandemic had pushed such families to the brink of financial disaster.
- The ongoing global expansion of the digital platform has persuaded several women entrepreneurs to shift to the digital medium. But here too, especially in developing economies, women are affected by systemic discrimination and biased attitudes which makes the transition more difficult for them compared to their male counterparts.

Quarterly GDP Growth Rate of Three Important Sectors of India

Sector	Q1	Q2	Q3	Q4
Agriculture	3	3.5	3.6	5.9
Manufacturing	3	-0.6	-0.8	-1.4
Production	5.2	2.6	-0.04	-2.2

Source: The Ministry of Statistics and Programme Implementation. Data Retrieved from *https://indianexpress.com/article/explained/gdp-growth-rate-deceleration-tells-us-about-state-of-the-indian-economy-6433491/*
(All Figures are in Percentage)

The above figures show clearly that performance of manufacturing and production sectors are greatly affected. While vast numbers of Indian women are employed in these sectors, a dire projection for upcoming years, as the graph is expected to decline further, have significantly limited the prospects of employment in these sectors in the near future.

COVID-19 and Gender Inequality in India

The pandemic has doubtless exacerbated the existing gender inequalities in India. Unlike majority of men, women working in informal sectors have failed to retain their livelihood during the lockdown. Loss of employment has put their survival at stake. Shift to online education compelled numerous families with utterly limited means, to scourge their resources and if need be, borrow and purchase smartphones just so their children's education do not come to a standstill. Under such circumstances, despite presence of this gadget within the family, women have largely been unable to use them for eking out an income for the family through digital connectivity.

While the household is constructed as the primary site of a woman's remit, the pandemic has definitely turned this space into a sort of workhouse for a vast number of women across the country. Extra responsibilities pertaining to sequestering and caring of patients, along with severely depleted resources, and a pressing need for sanitization and cleaning, increased the domestic workload for a woman by manifolds.

It is duly expected that the coming years are going to chart negative growth in global trade which is going to affect both, the formal and the informal sectors. Given their capacity to access regular resources like infrastructure and capital, however limited for the time, certain industries in the formal sectors are expected to limp back on track, as is evident by the slow consolidation on the digital platform. While efforts are underway to drastically cut down human involvement, it is the human-heavy informal sectors that are going to suffer disproportionately. In the Indian scenario, majority of women are employed in these sectors. While it is going to affect both men and women in their current situation, and in terms of future prospects, given the reality of women's marginalized position, they are going to be hit by this downsizing worse than men. Fundamental gender biases dictate that more women are going to be laid off than men, as a rule. In the unregulated labour market, women would inevitably be compelled to accept assignments on far lower wages than what were existing rates just before the pandemic. Another important development is the emergence of the work-from-home trend. While such an arrangement may work fine for men, for women it is likely to be extremely cumbersome given their traditional responsibilities of home management.

Women generally, and especially in traditional setups, are identified with the quality of 'sacrifice' which builds into the complex of motherhood and homemaking. Under the circumstances, this would often translate into rerouting resources (food and such) meant for own consumption, to fulfilling the needs of the male members and children of the family. For these women therefore, the pandemic is also to be remembered in hunger and steadily declining health.

COVID-19 and Women's Health in India: Current Trajectory and Future Considerations

The pandemic has negatively affected women's healthcare services, including reproductive and family planning services in India. Amidst nationwide lockdown and movement restrictions, essential medical facilities have often been inaccessible despite these services receiving exemption on certain restrictions. In spite of the government's commitment towards uninterrupted reproductive and essential health services, the ground reality has been largely dismal.

There are important factors that greatly contribute to India's declining public healthcare facilities. These are, high chances of infections, inadequate PPE kits in public hospitals, understaffing, shortage of trained staff and nurses, and inadequate health infrastructure including severe shortage of beds (Motihar, 2020). As public hospitals were getting inundated with steadily rising inflow of patients, providing essential health services for women became increasingly daunting. Consequently, the pandemic was expected to witness higher cases of unintended pregnancies, child births, and maternal deaths (Motihar, 2020).

Report from the Global Financing Facility highlighted that due to lockdown and heath service disruptions in India, four million Indian women were without proper medical care required during pregnancy. At the same time, child mortality and maternal mortality rates were expected to rise by 40% and 52%, respectively over the next year (Global Financing Facility, 2020). Marie Stopes International found that more than one million Indian women have missed out their essential health services during this pandemic (Marie Stopes International, 2020).

An all-out health crisis as such, brought out traditional biases, and social preferences and priorities in sharp relief. Lower income populations were far more wanting in terms of essential medical facilities as they were unable to access, and even denied, these services during the crisis period. True to a pattern, rural areas, already largely lacking in basic infrastructure and health facilities, were far worse affected than urban areas. With rising cost of healthcare amidst steadily depleting resources and inundated facilities, women from lower income and rural backgrounds were much worse off.

The situation was much more critical in states such as Uttar Pradesh, Bihar, West Bengal, Jharkhand, Odisha, and Chhattisgarh, which have weak health care facilities compared to other states (Motihar, 2020). It was expected that child mortality and pregnancy related complications were going to increase in these states in the near future, following the pandemic.

Due to limited access to contraception and other preventive measures, family planning took a significant hit during the pandemic. Sterilisation and IUCD services were suspended in public facilities during the lockdown, on orders from the Ministry of Health and Family Welfare, thus affecting the family planning scene in India (Sharma, 2020). At the same time, due to shortage of ASHA and Anganwadi workers in rural areas, availing contraceptives and other measures had become difficult for Women. The Foundation for Reproductive Health Services (FRHS)tried to assess the impact of the pandemic on India's current and future family planning services. FRHS observed that over twenty-four million couples were unable able to access contraceptives in 2020. At the same time, they predicted that lack of uninterrupted services and shortage of contraceptives is likely to result in more than thirty-eight million unintended pregnancies, more than a million abortions, and thousands of maternal deaths (Foundation for Reproductive Health Services India, 2020).

COVID-19 and Its Impact On Reproductive Services in India

Health Issues	Best Case	Likely Case	Worst Case
No. of couples unable to access contraception	24.55 million	25.63 million	27.18 million
No. of Unintended Pregnancies	1.94 million	2.37 million	2.95 million
No. of Live Births	555,833	679,864	844,483
No. of Abortions	1.18 million	1.44 million	1.79 million
No. of Unsafe abortions	681,883	834,042	1.03 million
No. of Maternal Deaths	1,425	1,743	2,165

Source: Foundation for Reproductive Health Services India. Data retrieved from http://www.frhsi.org.in/images/impact-of-COVID-19-on-indias-family-planning-program-policy-brief.pdf

Further, according to sources, within these three months, while nearly four million abortions have been carried out, nearly two million cases were compromised as a direct effect of the lockdown.

Shortage of drugs, essential medicines, and understaffing of nurse and other medical personnel contributed significantly to this aspect. Suspension of services meant that many women were forced to opt for unsafe abortions which may lead to development of serious health complications in the near future.

The Effects of Educational Institution's Closures on Girls' Education

Schools were suspended all over the world, primarily to safeguard the young. Schooling activities were hence, shifted to online classrooms. This abrupt shift to deal with the situation has had unforeseen consequences, particularly across the developing world. Not only did various such economies lack the requisite infrastructure to facilitate a large scale transition to the digital platform, vast sections of populations in these economies lacked requisite funds to purchase communication technologies such as laptops and smartphones. Much more fundamentally, these are spaces marked by sharp gender inequalities where the girl student is often at disadvantage compared to her male counterparts. While the digital platform appeared as a solution on the horizon of so many societies, for people in such developing spaces, it added yet another dimension to their deprivation.

The agonizing prospect of an incomplete education caused young girls to fall prey to depression and in some cases, even take their own lives. In June 2020, a girl in Kerala committed suicide as her family failed to provide her a smartphone necessary for online classroom.This is just one of the many similar incidents playing out in India post-COVID. Incidents as such are stark reminders of the fact that in India, as in so many other parts of the world, access to technology follows a gendered path.

Where girls have accessed the online platform for educational purposes, their attendance and study time had to compete with their traditional remit.Generally, girls are expected to wake up early to do all their domestic chores before attending online classes. Females, as a group and across ages, were at the forefront of reviving normalcy within the household by carrying on their daily chores despite all the unforeseen changes that have beset the society. Quite often, even the intelligentsia of the society, school teachers and professors, are not exempt from such duties. In many instances, teachers were observed as simultaneously delivering lectures and tending to their babies.The enormity of impact on future generations can be gauged from a Global Citizen Organisation report which remarked that the pandemic is causing seven decades of educational growth in India to come undone (Rodriguez, 2020). They identified four important factors compounding the crisis for girls (Rodriguez, 2020).

These are:

- Funding interruptions—especially in rural spaces, families largely depend on government schools for providing education to their children. These educational institutions in turn, are wholly dependent on government funding for operation. Central and state governments in India promote and incentivize education in the villages through periodic grants and funding. These funding and other educational schemes steadily narrowing down, following a general slump in the economy, has sharply increased dropout rates among girl students in these areas. According to the report, nearly ten million secondary school girl students run the risk of dropout due to the pandemic.
- School nutrition—with the Sarva Siksha Mission, the government emphasized the need for universal primary education. In order to increase gross enrolment ratio in primary education, the programme provides free midday meals to primary school students. With this scheme practically suspended and no midday meals enroute, several families have decided to discontinue their girl child's school education.
- It is no secret that in India, families traditionally prioritize boy's education over girl's. In families that can afford digital communication technologies, and have both boy(s) and girl(s) in the household, ostensibly both children are able to access the digital platform to continue their education. But in households with limited resources as well as only girl child, the choice of making such investment to sustain the child's (girl) education might be 'set aside.'

Par for the course, it is likely that in many cases where education has come to an abrupt halt for the girl, and may never pick up again, she will be married off early. This will most likely result in early pregnancy as well as early subjection to domestic abuse and physical violence.

Policy Recommendations and Strategies to Reduce Gender Based Violence

The government would do well to formulate pandemic policies while being cognisant of the immense gender gap across the board, in all matters, that are most likely to disrupt effective implementation of such policies. There is no reason why policies addressing this global catastrophe should not be formulated to simultaneously bridge gender gap while tending to a national population. Careful contemplation is required to understand how men and women are differently affected by the contagion, as well as by the regimes of rules and restriction that have come in its wake. Implementation of policies would require constant monitoring to check any adverse effect and possibilities of deprivation of women from such benefits which they are equally entitled to.

Governments of the world are offering stimulus and relief packages, along with myriad relaxation of financial requirements, in efforts to pull their respective economies back on the feet as also, to get the global supply chain running again. In India, the government has specifically targeted poorer sections of the society such as farmers and blue collar workers. Pradhan Mantri Jan Dhan Yojana, Pradhan Mantri Kisan Samman Nidhi, and Pradhan Mantri Garib Kalyan Yojana are some of the prominent schemes.

Similarly, in order to improve financial condition of women, the government has undertaken cash transfer to women's bank accounts. This is intended to stabilize their finances as well as give them a modicum of economic independence, and increase their contribution to family finances. However, given the vulnerability of women in so many households, this small financial support provided by the government might actually put women in harm's way, from her husband or in-laws. Further, this small, almost token amount of money is not going to go a long way in stabilizing their finances. What is needed is much more fundamental to a social existence. It is therefore, of utmost importance that such financial grants are followed by government assisted restoration of the job market, and special care taken to ensure that more number of women are able to join the workforces.

In light of the pandemic, the United Nations has advised governments around the world to prioritise three important factors which may have substantive positive impact on women's and girl's rights. These three policy measures are (United Nations, 2020).

- Equal & Adequate Representation of women in COVID-19 response Planning and Decision-Making.
- Serious addressal of care economy.
- Targeting greater number of women and girls in all efforts to address the socio-economic impact of COVID-19.

The UNDP and the WHO also propose gender-specific measures to tackle gender-based violence as well as address health related issues of women (UNDP, 2020). These are:

- Ensure availability of sex disaggregated data along with gender analysis of infection rates among male and female.

- Ensure the safety of women working in health services along with providing them necessary medical kits.
- Proper care support for children, elderly women and other dependents of women working in the healthcare sector.
- Rapid skilling programmes to formalize women in the health and social care sectors.
- Special attention to primary healthcare infrastructure, ensuring that access to sexual and reproductive health services is available.
- Adopt strict measures to prevent sexual and gender-based violence associated with quarantine and social distancing.

Concluding Observations

In addressing the impact of the COVID-19 pandemic on women in India, it is crucial that both, governments and citizens recognize the disproportionate and distinct challenges faced by women during crises. Policymakers must acknowledge the multifaceted nature of the difficulties women encounter, spanning from gender-based violence and inadequate healthcare to marginalization in the job market. Governmental intervention is essential for meaningful change, especially considering the exacerbated vulnerabilities of women from low-income backgrounds, those working in informal sectors, and those residing in rural areas.

The pandemic has underscored and magnified existing gender divides, necessitating a comprehensive response that goes beyond immediate health concerns. Women's limited access to public spaces, a challenge even under normal circumstances, requires expanded support mechanisms, such as emergency helplines for reporting health emergencies and domestic abuse.

Financial assistance from the government must be coupled with a commitment to ensure the security and well-being of women recipients.

The pandemic serves as a stark reminder to governments worldwide to recognize how gender inequality can lead to the disenfranchisement of large segments of the population, particularly women. If unaddressed, it can have profound and lasting effects on national prospects and future generations. The lessons learnt during this crisis should guide policymakers to implement more inclusive and gender-sensitive measures, fostering a society where women are empowered, protected, and able to contribute meaningfully to the nation's progress. It is imperative that policies reflect gender awareness, ensuring that the unique challenges faced by women are not only acknowledged but effectively addressed in the aftermath of the pandemic.

References

Ausin, B., González-Sanguino, C., Castellanos, M.A., & Muñoz, M. (2020). Gender-related differences in the psychological impact of confinement as a consequence of COVID-19 in Spain. *Journal of Gender Studies*. Advance online publication. https://doi. org/10.1080/09589236.2020.1799768

Bambra, C., Albani, V., & Franklin, P. (2021). COVID-19 and the gender health paradox. *Scandinavian Journal of Public Health, 49*, 17–26. doi:10.1177/1403494820975604

Bansal, M., & Shukla, S. (2020, August 3). *Understanding How The COVID-19 Crisis Impacted Girls' Education In India*. Retrieved from Feminism In India: https://feminisminindia.com/2020/08/03/girls-education-india-covid-19-early-marriage-crisis/

Chauhan, P. (2020). Gendering COVID19: Impact of the Pandemic on Women's Burden of Unpaid Work in India. *Gender Issues*. doi:https://doi.org/10.1007/s12147-020-09269-w

Cooper, Rae, and Sarah Mosseri. (2020). 'Pandemic Has Impacted Upon Women Most Significantly.' *The Sydney MorningHerald*, June 5. Retrieved April 12, 2021. From https://www.smh.com.au/business/workplace/pandemic-has-impacted-women-most-significantly-20200604-p54ziu.html

EPW ENGAGE. (2020, April 17). *COVID-19, Domestic Abuse and Violence: Where Do Indian Women Stand?* Retrieved from Economic & Political Weekly: https://www.epw.in/node/156784/pdf

Fisher, A. N., & Ryan, K. M. (2021). Gender inequalities during COVID-19. *Group Processes & Intergroup Relations, 24*(2), 237–245.

Fisher, J. (2012). *Envisioning Disease, Gender, and War: Women's Narratives of the 1918 Influenza Pandemic.* New York: Palgrave Macmillan.

Foundation for Reproductive Health Services India. (2020). *Impact of COVID 19 on India's Family Planning Program.* New Delhi: Foundation for Reproductive Health Services India. Retrieved from http://www.frhsi.org.in/images/impact-of-covid-19-on-indias-family-planning-program-policy-brief.pdf

Global Financing Facility . (2020). *Country Brief India: Preserve Essential Health Services during the COVID-19 Pandemic.* Retrieved from Global Financing Facility (GFF): https://www.globalfinancingfacility.org/sites/gff_new/files/documents/India-Covid-Brief_GFF.pdf

Jin, J.-M., Bai, P., He, W., Wu, F., Liu, X.-F., Han, D.- M., Liu, S., & Yang, J.-K. (2020). Gender differences in patients with COVID-19: A focus on severity and mortality. Frontiers in Public Health, 8, 152. https://doi.org/10.3389/fpubh.2020.00152

Manlowe, J. L., & Goldstein, N. (Eds.). (1997). *The Gender Politics of HIV/AIDS in Women: Perspectives on the Pandemic in the United States.* New York: New York University Press.

Marie Stopes International. (2020). *Resilience, adaptation and action:.* London: Marie Stopes International.

Mishra, A. (2020, May 16). *India's Proactive Foreign Policy During COVID-19 Has Given It A Stronger International Position.* Retrieved from Youth Ki Awaaz: https://www.youthkiawaaz.com/2020/05/indias-proactive-foreign-policy-response-during-ncovid-19-pandemic/

Miyamoto, I. (2020). (Rep.). Daniel K. Inouye Asia-Pacific Center for Security Studies. Retrieved April 14, 2021, from http://www.jstor.org/stable/resrep24863

Moreira da Silva, J. (2019). 'Why You Should Care About Unpaid Care Work.' OECD Development Matters, March 18. Retrieved April 14, 2021 from https://oecd-development-matters.org/2019/03/18/why-you-should-care-about-unpaid-care-work

Moser, C. (1993). *Gender Planning and Development: Theory Practice and Training.* London: Routledge.

Motihar, R. (2020, June 25). *The impact of COVID-19 on reproductive health services.* Retrieved from India Development Review : https://idronline.org/the-impact-of-covid-19-on-reproductive-health-services/

Nanthini, S., & Nair, T. (2020). (Rep.). S. Rajaratnam School of International Studies. Retrieved April 14, 2021, from http://www.jstor.org/stable/resrep26875

OMMCOM News. (2020, April 24). *COVID-19 Lockdown: Rise In Domestic Violence & Child Abuse Cases, Petition Filed In Delhi HC.* Retrieved from OMMCOM News: https://ommcomnews.com/india-news/covid-19-lockdown-rise-in-domestic-violence-child-abuse-cases-petition-filed-in-delhi-hc

Renzetti, C. M., & Bergen, R. K. (Eds.). (2005). *Violence Against Women.* Maryland: Rowman & Littlefield.

Rodriguez, L. (2020, July 14). *COVID-19 Is Undoing 70 Years of Girls' Education Progress in India.* Retrieved from Global Citizen: https://www.globalcitizen.org/en/content/covid-19-impact-india-girls-education/

Rossler, A. R., & Moreno, C. G. (Eds.). (2013). *Violence Against Women and Mental Health.* Basel: Karger.

Sharma, E. (2020, May 21). *COVID-19, Sterilisation, and Family Planning: Where Did India Go Wrong?* Retrieved from STATECRAFT:

https://www.statecraft.co.in/article/covid-19-sterilisation-and-family-planning-where-did-india-go-wrong

Sili, L. (2020, April 28). *COVID-19 and the impact on women.* Retrieved from International Growth Centre: https://www.theigc.org/blog/covid-19-and-the-impact-on-women/

Szabo, A., Ábel, K., & Boros, S. (2020). Attitudes toward COVID-19 and stress levels in Hungary: Effects of age, perceived health status, and gender. Psychological Trauma: Theory, Research, Practice, and Policy, 12, 572–575. https://doi.org/10.1037/ tra0000665

The Indian Express. (2020, June 17). *Rising domestic violence in India: National bodies and Twitter launch search prompt for help.* Retrieved from The Indian Express: https://indianexpress.com/article/lifestyle/life-style/domestic-violence-india-national-commission-for-women-twitter-search-prompt-6463505/

UNDP. (2020). *THE ECONOMIC IMPACTS OF COVID-19 AND GENDER INEQUALITY: RECOMMENDATIONS FOR POLICYMAKING.* Panama: United Nations Development Programme. Retrieved from https://www.undp.org/content/dam/undp/library/km-qap/undp-gpn-bpps-gender-Economic_Impacts_of_COVID-19_and_Gender_Inequality.pdf

United Nations. (2020). *The Impact of COVID-19 on Women.* New York: United Nations. Retrieved from https://reliefweb.int/sites/reliefweb.int/files/resources/policy-brief-the-impact-of-covid-19-on-women-en.pdf

United Nations, (2020). Policy brief: The impact of COVID-19 on women. Retrieved April 10, 2021 from https://www.unwomen.org/-/media/headquarters/attachments/sections/library/publications/2020/policy-brief-the-impact-of-covid-19-on-women-en.pdf?la=en&vs=1406

United Nations Economic and Social Commission for Asia and the Pacific. (2020). *COVID-19 and South Asia:National Strategies and Subregional Cooperation for Accelerating Inclusive, Sustainable and Resilient Recovery.* United Nations ESCAP. Retrieved from https://www.unescap.org/sites/default/files/South%20Asia%20Covid-19%20Paper_5.pdf

UN Women. (2020, June 26). 'COVID-19: Emerging gender data and why it matters,' Retrieved April 15, 2021, from umwomen.org: https://data.unwomen.org/resources/covid-19-emerging-gender-data-and-why-it-matters

US Department of Health and Human Services, (2020), Centers for Disease Control and Prevention, *Characteristics of Health Care Personnel with COVID-19—United States, February 12—April 9, 2020 MMWR Morb Mortal Weekly Report 2020* (Atlanta, GA: CDC, 2020), 477-481, accessed April 10, 2021, http://dx.doi.org/10.15585/mmwr.mm6915e6.

World Health Organization. (2019). *Delivered by women, led by men: A gender and equity analysis of the global health and social workforce. (Human Resources for Health Observer Series No. 24).* Switzerland. Retrieved March 31, 2021, from https://apps.who.int/iris/bitstream/handle/10665/311322/9789241515467-eng.pdf?ua=1

World Trade Organization. (2020, August 03). *THE ECONOMIC IMPACT OF COVID-19 ON WOMEN IN VULNERABLE SECTORS AND ECONOMIES.* Retrieved from World Trade Organization: https://www.wto.org/english/news_e/news20_e/info_note_covid_05aug20_e.pdf

NEGOTIATING MASCULINITIES
A Case of Male Sex Workers in Mumbai

Reenu Ram

Introduction

The concept of hegemonic masculinity was coined by Connell and is defined as 'the configuration of gender practices which embodies the currently accepted answers to the problem of legitimacy of patriarchy' (Connell, 1995, p. 77). These practices confirm the domination of women by men as well as domination of some men by men who hold the power. Subordination and marginalisation of certain masculinities is also part of this. In this context, gay masculinities have been marginalised and subordinated historically to ensure the hegemony of compulsory heterosexuality. Many view homosexuality as negation of masculinity and all homosexual men as effeminate. Given this assumption, antagonism toward homosexual men may be used as a parameter to define masculinity. This has been captured by Herek (1986) in the proposition that 'to be 'a man' in contemporary American society is to be homophobic—that is, to be hostile toward homosexual persons in general and gay men in particular' (Herek, 1986, p. 563). The resulting oppression of gay men, as Pleck (1981) observes, provides a symbol for all cases of hierarchy among men. Herek's formulation captures the significance of heterosexual-versus-homosexual relations for heterosexuality. In the same historical process, same-sex sexual contact between men was termed illegitimate by dominant groups of men, and hegemonic masculinity was thus redefined as explicitly and exclusively heterosexual. Closeted gay men enjoy the general advantages of masculine gender. In the Indian scenario, men who have sex with men are generally oppressed, but they are not definitively excluded from masculinity. Rather, they face structurally-induced conflicts about masculinity—conflicts between their sexuality and their social presence as men, about the meaning of their choice of sexual partners, and in their construction of relationships with women and with heterosexual men. These dilemmas of male sex workers constantly disturb them and feelings of inadequacy, low self esteem, guilt, injustice always mire their everyday life.

The concept of hegemonic masculinity has influenced gender studies across many academic fields but has also attracted serious criticism. Evaluating the principal criticisms, the authors defend the underlying concept of masculinity, which in most research application, is neither reified nor essentialist. However, the criticism of trait models of gender and rigid typologies is sound. Treatment of the subject in research on hegemonic masculinity can be improved with the aid of recent psychological models, although limits to discursive flexibility must be recognised. The concept of hegemonic masculinity does not equate to a model of social reproduction; we need to recognise social struggles in which subordinated masculinities influence dominant forms.

Peter Nardi, in *Gay Masculinities* (1999), argues that contemporary research on men and masculinity treats masculinity not as a normative referent, but as a problematic gender construct. Nardi attempts to understand men and masculinity through this lens, providing a comprehensive understanding of gender and gender relationships in the contemporary world. Nardi observes that gay men exhibit a multiplicity of ways of 'doing' masculinity that can best be described by the plural form 'masculinities.' There are range of masculinity stereotypes which varies from the virile and masculine representation through body building and overemphasis of sexual prowess, to a milder or less dominant representation through spirituality or through imitation of other gender. Many simply blend the 'traditional' instrumental masculinity with the more 'emotional' masculinity in their everyday interaction with others. Thus, when they are with partners or friends, there is different interplay of masculinity than when they are in the gym working out. There is no monolithic concept of masculinity but rather, there are 'masculinities' defining men and their diverse interaction in different points in time. Due to postmodern ideas, diversity and difference are acknowledged and privileged over a unifying, shared, homogeneous concept. Gender identities cannot be described in terms of just 'masculinity' and 'femininity'. There may be multiple ways in which we enact our gender roles, and it may take various forms. The very fact that gay men may enact and carry out a different kind of masculinity from their heterosexual counterparts, suggests that there is a plurality of masculinities. There is diversity in the way even gay men display and enact masculinities and therefore, to assume that all of them challenge or contest masculinity in its hegemonic form, would be erroneous. We have to remember that gay men are as diverse as heterosexual men and all of them do not think or act in the same manner.

Male sex workers in India predominantly provide sexual services to male clients, so they have same-sex sexual relations with clients. At the same time, some are married, have children and lead a family-life. Sameer, a kothi identified male sex worker, when asked about his sexual identity, replied:

'Mai waisa hi roop le leta hu jaisa samne wala chahata hai.'[1]

So how do male sex workers present themselves to others? Which aspects of their identities are actually projected to significant others? Erving Goffman notes that in our everyday lives, social actors present themselves to others keeping in mind their knowledge and understanding of their culture and social expectations. This helps to win approval and acceptance from others and deal with the impressions of ourselves that we present to others, and act as artist of a role (Goffman, 1959). The interactional strategies that male sex workers in India engage in with their families, peer, neighbours, clients and larger society demonstrate this process in action. The fluidity of sexual identities that male sex workers articulate, and the extent to which they go in order to present themselves as either sexually conforming or as asexual in the front stage is worth exploring.

Foucault emphasised the role of discourses or networks of ideas in producing and regulating human sexuality. Judith Butler draws on Foucault's work to offer a new perspective on gender and sexuality. Butler thinks that societies that believe in a natural gender order are also organised around the norms of heterosexuality. Heterosexuality is the source of our culture of romance, marriage, and family, and is enforced by our social agencies like family, laws, state, religious bodies, schools etc. Observing men and women as naturally harmonising and complementary makes heterosexuality appear as the natural, normal, and right way of doing things. The system of compulsory heterosexuality can help to understand why societies are divided into two gender types, but it fails to explain how gender and sexual identities are maintained daily. Butler's ideas about gender identity have been very dominant in the sociology of sexual identity. Growing up in a society that classifies feelings, actions, and social roles as either appropriate or inappropriate for men and women, social actors learn how to behave in a gender-correct way.

Butler maintains, as an individual goes by the gender norms, others are likely to read his/her behaviour as manifestation of a core gender identity. For example, most social actors would probably think that an individual who looks and acts like a man (aggressive, competitive or determined) is a man, and that these behavioural tendencies are at the core of his identity. Nevertheless, Butler posits that there is no core gender identity that guides their behaviour. Instead of observing gender performance as an expression of an inner gender identity, Butler suggests that these behaviours are enacted taking into consideration the images of woman or man that one takes over from his/her family and culture. The deception of core feminine and masculine gender identities obscures the social and political forces that mould humans into gendered selves; similarly, the doctrine of a natural gender order camouflages the role of gender in the maintenance of heterosexual dominance (Butler, 1988).

Butler's argument about the 'performativity' of gender is her best contribution to gender theory. Thus, sexualities do not represent any innate behaviour or stable social categories; rather sexualities are outcomes of performance. Butler (1990) demonstrates this with reference to a drag queen who is considered by the audience as having a 'true' gender and sexual identity underneath his 'act'. But she argues that his 'true' identity is another kind of performance like the one represented in drag. Hence, drawing on Goffman's studies, Butler argues that we are all 'on stage' performing, and there is no true self underneath various roles that one performs in various contexts.

Methods

The research is based on 34 in-depth interviews with male sex workers who sell sex to men in Mumbai, and some time, to customers nearby cities. For fieldwork, I approached GAURAV, a community-based organisation of MSM (men who have sex with men) and MSW (male sex worker) working in Mumbai, in the Juhu Koliwada area. GAURAV is run by a dedicated committee of members from the MSM community. Several among its 2200 registered MSMs identify as MSWs. The fieldwork commenced in the monsoon of 2016 and the last four interviews were completed in 2019. Thus, from 2016 to 2019, I spent around 18 months in the field. Since my interviews were sensitive, they were all carried out in GAURAV's office in Juhu Koliwada. Out of the thirty-four male sex workers, thirty were registered with GAURAV and were availing services provided by it. Remaining four male sex workers were not associated with any NGO and were referred to me by interviewees. Of the thirty-four male sex workers, seventeen identified as bisexual, nine as gay, five as *Kothi* and three as versatile. The youngest informant was nineteen years old and the oldest was forty-two years old. The median age of the sample was twenty-six years. All of them were educated: eighteen 12th pass, three graduates, one PhD, and the remaining twelve were 10th pass.

How Male Sex Workers 'Do' Masculinity

Masculinity tension is a common theme in all narratives of male sex workers. Male sex workers constantly experience contradictions, ambiguities, and frustration between sexual scripts and experiences. For instance, Rishi was in a romantic relationship with a boy who was the most important person in his life. When Rishi came to know that his partner was cheating on him, he was shattered:

> For the first time I felt the pain of a wife cheated by her husband. Men are always cheating and I am waiting for a day when women will cheat their men. But I did not lock myself in the house, I wanted to tell my partner that it did not bother me and I entered into sex work. Now, every day I have a new partner.

Entry into sex work was his way of doing away with romantic love and relationship. Instead, he took to an adventure-erotic lifestyle. So the following question asks how male sex workers perceive and enact masculinity. Male sex workers exhibit multiplicity of ways of 'doing-' masculinity that can best be described by the plural form 'masculinities'. In fact, what they do (having sex for pleasure or love) is very close to the masculinity script but the problem is who they do it with (a man) and how they do it (anal sex). Connell (1992) argues that gay men frequently look out for men who personify masculinity. The clients of male sex workers mostly prefer masculine, good looking male body. The materiality of maleness is the most sought after trait. This holds true for male sex workers also who always talk about the strength and good-looks of their clients. The client is always seen as masculine and virile. His sexual prowess is something which male sex workers always talks about. Donaldson (1993) made this observation in following lines: 'It is not 'gayness' that is attractive to homosexual men, but 'maleness'. A man is lusted after not because he is homosexual but because he's a man (Donaldson, 1993, p. 649).

In 'Understanding Masculinity' Chopra et.al (2000) argues that most men make a distinction between sexual pleasures on the one hand and masculinity as a role, on the other. Men talk about *'masti'*, loosely decoded as sexual play or playfulness, and this has no serious consequences in their lives. *Masti* is basically structured as recreational, not 'real' sex. Nevertheless, as soon as sex enters the sphere of procreation, it gets associated with one's positions in sexual act, that is, of penetration (man) and being penetrated (woman), bringing in the whole issue of masculinity. This is noteworthy within MSM relations, where the dichotomy of active and passive are recreated within the same-sex sexual encounters. Within the politics of penetration, the 'panthis' or the active, penetrative partner of the gay dyad is considered more masculine than the 'kothi' who is feminised and is penetrated. However, the transgendered kothi is bisexual so in the gay dyad he is penetrated, but in sexual relation with their wives they are masculine and it is their sexual relations that reopen the question of fluid sexualities.

After closely studying the rate cards of all thirty-four respondents who were part of this research, I found a wide diversity. Rishik, Noor, Daniel, Dev, Satyam, Dhanush, who are good looking tall men with good build and a sense of fashion, dressing up in latest style; they are constantly working on their bodies and looks. According to Rishi, one can only last in sex work until one has good looks and chiseled bodies. Those who are either too fat or too thin are not in demand. Rishi charges rupees 5000 for two hours and rupees 2000 for just going out (escorting), and these rates are non-negotiable. This rate is in contrast to the rates of Aiba, Aapaa, Kumar, Ishq and Samay who identify themselves as kothi. They are effeminate in their behaviour, want to dress up like women, are ready to negotiate their rates, and often do not charge if they like their client. By and large male sex workers play a passive role in their sexual encounters with clients, hence, a kothi identified male sex worker ideally should be more in demand as they like to play passive roles. Narratives of male sex workers illustrate different states of affair. Masculine bodies are more in demand than effeminate ones. Why do clients prefer straight looking guys? Dhanush explained:

> Client wants manly body that can play both top and bottom roles. Clients feel that if they really want feminine sex then there are female sex workers (FSWs) and if a feminine boy is playing top role then it will look quite strange that as a feminine looking man, he has taken an active position. Client's sense of masculinity will suffer a blow. Similarly if client is playing a top role with a feminine MSW then the client will feel that this person is so feminine and it would be better if he does this with a woman. What is wrong with me! So preference is for straight looking man. Client is satisfied when he gets a feeling that he is doing it with a real man.

From the above discussion, one wants to put forward an argument that cultural scripts seem to play a crucial role in the lives of male sex workers. Though there is no desire or attraction for sex with women, pressure from family and fear of being tagged as 'emasculated' pushes them into heterosexual relations. Male sex workers solicit and enjoy sexual encounters with their male clients. Thus, sex work for them serves two purpose: as a means of livelihood, and as articulation of their same-sex sexual desires forbidden by society. This may be responsible for a loose economic exchange between a male sex worker and his client. Thus, we have witnessed this cultural uncertainty surrounding same-sex relationships. But we have also witnessed differential attitude towards same-sex sexual relations by male sex workers and their clients. While clients are not so concerned about their sexual encounters with other men, male sex workers reported constant dilemma and mental stress. The transgenderal role played by male sex workers creates dilemma about their real identity. This also results in increased probability of being discovered by the family and society. Another reason for this tension is their work status that is, sex work. For the good proportion of male sex workers, sex work is a survival strategy.

For most, it is a practice enforced by poverty and deprivation. These existing boundaries are based on social class, education, economic power and gendered behaviour. Clients do not socialise with male sex workers except in sexual environments. Male sex workers do not share their sexual identity or work identity with family members. Therefore, they have compartmentalised their lives. These identities are clearly separated by time and location as well. It is not impossible, therefore, for a man to have several identities: a park identity, a street identity, a home identity, a family identity, and of course a marriage identity. Classifying men who have sex with men as gay men or homosexuals, or even as male sex workers, can be problematic. While there are clear identities such as *kothis, panthis,* and even *do-parathas* or *double-deckers,* these identities are spatially as well as behaviourally constructed. They are not clearly delineated. What do male sex workers think about masculinity or the lack of it? A kothi identified male sex worker, Aapaa, became unusually agitated when discussion about masculinity came up. In my interaction with him for an hour and a half, this was the first instance when he had lost his placid demeanour.

> I lack masculinity? We go to gym so that we look good and we get more clients not to show our masculinity. People (body builder kinds) who think that we (gay) are not masculine...

Then he became agitated and started abusing 'masculine men' taunting them about their size and stamina. He regained his composure after sometimes and stated:

> God has not made anyone perfect. Everyone has some flaws or shortcomings. But everyone can see our flaws because we move around like this (their attire and manifestation) express ourselves and remain who we are. What is going on behind closed doors no one knows. But because of our jokes and

> bantering people locate and identify us and call us name like 'gud' and 'mamu' (popular slang for gay). We disclose our identity a little and therefore people identify us and abuse us.

Samuel, a 19 year old gay identified male sex worker, felt that playing double life was difficult, and there was constant tension that someone will disclose his identity to family and others.

> I do not think that I am perfect. Living two lives is not easy. Playing straight at home with family and a gay here at workplace. I am always afraid, someone will see me. We kill our soul and try to be a man. Guilt, shame, honour—these are the words which haunt us.

Nikunj, a 28 years old gay identified male sex worker, described his fear and tension:

> I am always afraid that I may end up doing something which will create doubt in their minds. It is always there in my mind. Therefore, I always speak in a strong masculine voice. They should never doubt me. I, therefore, control my body and hand movements. These are the ways to protect my identity. As place changes I change my role too.

From the above narratives, it is quite apparent that for a man to enjoy the privileges of his membership to the dominant gender, he will have to present himself in a particular manner to friends, family and significant others. This dramaturgical task guides the members of this 'man' group to do certain things to put up a convincing manhood act (Schwalbe, 2005). To put up a convincing show, they need to master certain acts and practices through which their identity as 'man' is established. Schrock and Schwalbe (2009) argue that the dramaturgical task of establishing creditability as a man and as a member of the dominant gender group is aided by having a male body.

Conventional association between maleness and manhood reproduces the male body as a symbolic asset. It is normally taken as a sign of qualification for membership in the category 'men.' However, it is neither necessary nor sufficient. Therefore, if one wishes to enjoy the privileges of membership to the group 'men,' then he must signify possession of a masculine self. This self is, however, only a virtual reality, a dramatic effect, or a consequence of how an actor's appearance and behaviour are interpreted by others (Goffman, 1959)

Homosexual desires are kept under wraps so that the privileges enjoyed by being men in the family and community remain intact. But several instances were recounted by male sex workers where the mask slipped and role play was aborted. Dhruv, a nineteen years old male sex worker recalled one such incident where he was caught cross-dressing at home. One day, when everyone was out for work and Dhruv was alone at home, he found a saree of his mother along with a few pieces of jewelleries. He closed the windows and the door, wrapped the saree around, and put on the jewelleries and makeup. He clicked few pictures and then, there was a knock at the door. Dhruv froze:

> 'Bhai open the door!' My sister called. I spoke in a strong manly voice—'ok! Wait! I am changing. I am in Bathroom.' 'Bhai I can hear you near the door please! Open the door!' I was so afraid that afternoon. I quickly changed and took off the jewelleries, but the makeup was still on and one earring was still dangling from my ear. She saw me and said, 'What is this nonsense? What are you up to brother?' I said that it was nothing.

Dhruv is pursuing a bachelors degree in banking and wants to have a career in that field. He is the first in his family to pass class twelfth exam. His parents have lots of hopes for Dhruv. But

Dhruv has a constant fear of slipping up, of his manly-masculine mask sliding off while at college. He worries about his final placement in college. He said:

> I know I look like a girl and even the way I talk, it is somewhat girlish. I need to work on my body and the way I speak. I need to look like a man because I do not want to fail in my interview. Everyone is very hopeful and also wants this job desperately. I know many people who get irritated with people like us (homosexual). They hate us and if I encounter someone like this in the interview board then I do not know what will happen.

When similar enquiry was put to Satyam, a versatile (bisexual) male sex worker he replied:

> No, it never occurred to me that I lack masculinity. I have mostly stayed with straight boys and no one is pure straight. There is no boy who has not had sex with boys. I can say this with full confidence. You check Facebook, there is no boy who I cannot woo and have sex with. Being straight is a gimmick and facade. I am a gay but only those who are acquainted with me know this. It is a world of performance. When I will present and showcase myself then only someone will know who I am.

He added further:

> I go to the gym because I am fond of good body and because I want to look good. It is good for my work also. Later I want to work in TV serials on DD1 channel. I know people there and that is why I am interested in body building.

According to Rishi, a versatile male sex worker, masculinity tension is not so important. There are other more important issues like survival:

> It's not like this. Mumbai is one city where you cannot survive without money so we don't think too much when we are doing it. But later on we feel guilty but then we compromise with the situation.

Noor, another versatile male sex worker deconstructed the notion of masculinity and power, and according to him:

> Nowadays one who earns has all the power in the house, everyone listens to him. Even a father loses his power and control if a son earns 25000 rupees a month, then he is the most powerful at home. No matter father is elder but it is son who is earning and therefore power is in his hand.

I have dealt with masculinity tensions of male sex workers and I can clearly delineate three responses to this tension. Kothi identified male sex workers who are effeminate and play transgenderal role with clients, experienced dilemmas, contradictions, ambiguities, and frustration. Aapaa's reaction was manifestation of his frustration. Gay identified male sex workers were constantly trying to mask and camouflage their homosexual desire so that their masculine self is unharmed. Bisexual male sex workers did not show the masculinity tension like kothi and gay male sex workers. They remained concerned with survival and equated masculinity with financial security emphasising their breadwinning role. At this juncture, one can clearly see the performative aspect of sexuality among male sex workers.

Their performance as MSW with clients at the cruising spot, and as a heterosexual man at home, are quite real as they experience them in terms of their personal and social consequences. Though these are performances, there is hardly any choice in the matter as is evident from their interaction. A system of compulsory heterosexuality exerts enormous social pressure on male sex workers to 'perform' the appropriate gender, as a *kothi* in the park and as a 'man' at home, with two distinct sexual identities. *Kothi,* playing the role of enchantress to attract male clients, is nothing but social pressure where their 'man' clients want to have sex with another man but do not want to jeopardise their masculinity, and further, want to maintain their hegemonic masculinity.

Male sex workers are practical in their approach. They know that they have two distinct identities and they live each identity in a distinct style. Though these two lives create conflict in them, they know that nothing much can be done to overcome it. As they experience this conflict, they know that there are no ways to override societal pressure and conception of masculinity. For a male sex worker, to enjoy the benefits that emanate from membership in the dominant gender group, he must present himself to others as a particular kind of social being: a man. 'I believe that there is more to sexual identity of male sex workers. The process of dividing life into many compartments is a good attempt by MSWs to survive. When I am with my wife I never, not even accidentally, refer to myself in the feminine person and when I am with customer I never refer to myself in the masculine person.'

Conclusion

The question of gender and sexual identity transcends the division based on anatomical and physical differences. Mere two categories, that is, male and female do not adequately describe a vast area of overlap. It is in this overlap that categories like effeminate male and masculine female can be understood. It is here where male sex workers can also be located and understood. The 'dramaturgical' term of Ervin Goffman is useful to understand further complexities which result from the compulsion to conceal effeminate male identity and masculine female identity by means of performativity. Recourse to dramaturgical approach for subversion is a pragmatic response from male sex workers who would otherwise face more discrimination, harassment, victimisation, stigmatisation and criminalisation. Such performance becomes part of everyday life to such an extent that male sex workers internalise the multiplicity of identities. Moreover, they also routinise transition from one role to others depending upon the social milieu. Such complexities cannot be explained by erroneous binary division of male and female. Heteronormative division also fails to recognise the underlying tension and different subjective erotic cum sexual desire and behaviour. The fluidity framework offers broader and wider base to understand homosexuality in general, and male sex workers in particular, not only from anatomical plus psycho-physical angles, but also from various other theoretical standpoints. Carl Jung's analytical viewpoint lays strong emphasis on this particular idea of dynamism which cannot be frozen into fixed and static identity especially when it comes to the domain of gender and sexuality. He, through the idea of 'anima' and 'animus' breaks the polarity and underscores the overlap by insightful reference to the interplay of embedded feminine into male and masculinity into female. Jung's answer to the vexing question of identity trouble, which results from conscious or unconscious manifestation of feminine behaviour in male or masculine behaviour in female, lays the foundation for resolution.

References

Butler, J. (1988). Performative Acts and Gender Constitution: An Essay in Phenomenology and Feminist Theory. *Theatre Journal* 519-531.

—. (1990). *Gender Trouble: Feminism and the Subversion of identity.* London: Routledge.

___. (1991). Imitation and Gender Insubordination. In Diana Fuss (Ed.), *Inside/Out: Lesbian Theories, Gay Theories,* (pp 13-31). Routledge.

___. (1993). Bodies That Matter: On the Discursive Limits of 'Sex'. Routledge

Chopra, R., Dasgupta, C., & Janeja, M. K. (2000). Understanding masculinity. *Economic and Political Weekly,* 1607-1609.

Connell, R.W. (1995). Masculinities. Cambridge: Polity.

Connell, R. W., & Messerschmidt, J. W. (2005). Hegemonic masculinity: Rethinking the concept. *Gender & society, 19*(6), 829-859.

Donaldson, M. (1993). What is hegemonic masculinity?. *Theory and society,* 22(5), 643-657

Foucault, M. (1979). The History of Sexuality Volume One: An Introduction. Harmondsworth. Penguin.

Goffman, E. (1959). The Presentation of Self in Everyday Life. Penguin Books.

Herek, G.M. (1986). On heterosexual masculinity: Some psychical consequences of the social construction of gender and sexuality. *American behavioral scientist,* 29(5), 563-577

Jung, C.G. (1989). The Principal Archetypes.'. The Critical Tradition: Classic Texts and Contemporary Trends, 666-676

Nardi, P.M. (1999). Gay men's friendships: Invincible communities. University of Chicago Press.

Nardi, P. M. (1992). Sex, friendship, and gender roles among gay men. *Men's friendships,* 173-185.

Pleck, J.H. (1981). The Myth of Masculinity. Cambridge. MA: MIT Press.

Schwalbe, M.L. (1993). Goffman against postmodernism: Emotion and the reality of the self. *Symbolic interaction, 16*(4), 333-350.

Schrock, D., & Schwalbe, M. (2009). Men, masculinity, and manhood acts. *Annual review of sociology,* 35, 277-295.

JUXTAPOSING THE STATUS AND EXPERIENCE OF INDIAN WOMEN IN COLONIAL AND POST-COLONIAL MALAYSIA

Mahalingam M.

Introduction

Malaysian tourism promotes Malaysia as 'Truly Asia' given its multi-ethnic, multiracial, and multicultural populations. The native Malays and the immigrants, namely Chinese and Indians, are the significant ethnic groups that are numerically higher and omnipresent. The Malaysian Indians are the third-largest ethnic group, constituting 2.4 million or about 8 percent of the total multi-ethnic population of around 30 million.

The Malaysian Indian community is a heterogeneous group drawing from various parts of India. The major Indian sub-ethnic group is the Tamils, who constitute approximately 80 percent of the total Indian population. In terms of the religious composition, Hindus consist of 81.2 percent of the Malaysian Indian population; Christians 8.4 percent; Muslims 6.7 percent; Sikhs 3.1 percent; Buddhists 0.5 percent. As the Tamils are the majority among the Indian ethnicities, 'Tamil-ness' is prominent in Malaysia's culture, religion, and political realms. In the jargon of Indian policymakers, the Malaysian Indian diaspora can be classified as the old Indian diaspora or people of Indian origin (PIO), the largest Indian ethnic minority living outside India.

The formation of the Indian diaspora is a legacy of British colonialism. Under the British regime, the race-based division of labour resulted in a reconfiguration of Indian socio-cultural norms in an alien land. Indian women, as a social category within the Indian community, faced several socio-economic and cultural issues and challenges.

Race and ethnicity-based economic and political models favouring native Malays, which have continued from colonial to contemporary times, have over the years, marginalized immigrant Malaysian Tamil/ Indian ethnic populations vis-a-vis immigrant minority Chinese and the majority Malays. As a result, the Indian community is reeling under socio-economic instability and is plagued with social problems. This essay seeks to explore the experiences and status of Indian women within the gendered, racialized, and ethnically embedded society of colonial and post-colonial Malaysia.

Existing literature provides a comprehensive approach to Indian migration and socio-economic conditions of the Indian community in Malaysia (Kaur, (2014), Arasaratnam, (1970), and Sandhu, (1969). There are numerous studies on the marginalization of the Malaysian Indian community (Mani and Sandhu, (1993), Nagarajan, (2000), and Anbalakan, (2003). However, studies dedicated to the position of Indian women in Malaysian society are scant. Very few studies focus on women's status and political participation in the plantations during the colonial period (Dancz, 1987), Oorjitham, (1993a), Krishnaswamy, (1992), Datta, (2015), and Syamala Nair Gopal and Mahani Musa, (2020).

This essay, based on socio-historical perspectives, attempts to fill the existing lacuna in studies on Malaysian Indian women by comparing the status and experiences of Indian women during the colonial and post-colonial periods. The study incorporates macro and microanalysis, case analysis, and qualitative data analysis.

Conceptualization and Theoretical Perspective of the Study

For analysing the status and experiences of Indian women in colonial and post-colonial Malaysia, the present study uses the concept of intersectionality as an analytical tool for a deeper analysis of the phenomenon under study. As a concept, intersectionality derives from the works of critical legal scholar Kimberley Crenshaw whose pioneering work has shown that African-American women's treatment within the law can be understood, analysed, and interpreted through the dual lenses of gender and race discrimination (Crenshaw, (1989).

According to the United Nations, intersectionality is a concept that captures 'the structural and dynamic consequences of the interaction between two or more forms of discrimination or systems of subordination.' Intersectionality specifically addresses how racism, patriarchy, economic disadvantages, and other discriminatory systems contribute to creating layers of inequality that structure the relative positions of women and men, races, and other groups (United Nations, (2000).

In social sciences, 'intersection' implies the crossing, juxtaposition, or meeting point of two or more social categories and axes, or systems of power, dominance, or oppression. The social categories and systems include social identities (e.g., woman, Pakistani), sociodemographic categories (e.g., gender, ethnocultural), social processes (e.g., gendering and racializing), and social systems (patriarchy and racism) (Dhamoon, (2011).

Else-Quest and Hyde,(2016) list three assumptions underlying most definitions of intersectionality: (1) a recognition of people's membership in different social categories (e.g., gender, ethnicity, religion, sexual orientation, able-bodied-ness, etc.), and being aware of the experience of one social category is linked to or intertwined with their membership of other categories; (2) embedded within each socially constructed category related to power and power interrelations; (3) social categories are intrinsically linked to personal identities, as well as to wider institutional processes/practices and structural systems.

Intersectionality is a conceptual tool and research paradigm to understand identity, power, interlocking oppression, multiple subordination, and dominance. It provides a critical framework for examining interconnections and interdependencies between social categories and systems.

Intersectionality acknowledges that power relations play an essential or fundamental role in the construction of thought, experience, and knowledge. It conceptualizes knowledge as situated, contextual, relational, and reflective of political and economic power. So, it closely aligns with social constructionist and feminist epistemologies (Else-Quest & Hyde, (2016). Hence, it avoids the risk of essentialism.

This concept is an appropriate tool to conceptualize the status and experiences of Indian women within the gendered, racialized, and ethnicity-embedded society of colonial and post-colonial Malaysia. In the ensuing discussion, we will look at the formation of the Indian diaspora community in Malaysia.

The Formation of the Indian Diaspora Community in Malaya/Malaysia

Given its geographical proximity, there have been symbiotic trade and cultural relationships between India and Southeast Asian regions since antiquity. The islands of the Malay Archipelago find mention in the Ramayana and the Mahabharata as 'Suvarna Dvipa' and 'Yavana Dvipa' (Krishnan, (1936). Moreover, Indianisation occurred following the spread of Indic religions, namely Hinduism and Buddhism (ibid). One can discern Indian influences in Southeast Asia's language, literature, manners, customs, folklore, and culture (ibid).

During the early seventh century, the advent of the Hindu Empire of Srivijaya in Sumatra (about 600-1000AD) reinforced trade, religious, and cultural influences from India (ibid). According to archaeological findings, the Chola kings of the Tamil region of southern India had conquered the kingdom of Kadaram in the northern part of the Malay Archipelago (ibid).

During the pre-colonial phase, Indians who arrived in Malaya were merchants, traders, missionaries, and adventurers.

The early Indian settlers before the colonial era were the following trading communities: Malacca Chetties, Chulias, and Jawi Pekan (Indian Muslim traders intermarried with locals). Intensification of trade relationships between the two areas began after the establishment of the Malay Kingdom during the fifteenth century (ibid).Trading activity between the two regions continued during the Portuguese and Dutch rule of Malacca during the sixteenth and seventeenth centuries.

After the establishment of the British government in the Malay Peninsula in the early nineteenth century, there was a paradigm shift in Indian migration to Malaya. In the beginning, Singapore, Malacca, and Penang—known as Straits Settlements—served as penal colonies for the British Empire. A small number of Indian convicts also arrived to toil in the construction of roads, buildings, and bridges (Dancz, (1987).

Later, since colonial activities in these parts pivoted around plantation agriculture, the colonial government started importing cheap labour force from its colonies (Sandhu, (1969) and (Arasaratnam, (1970). India became an indispensable destination, and south Indian labourers, especially unskilled Tamil labourers, were preferred as the British planters were familiar with the psyche and lifestyle of the Tamil labourers in Sri Lanka (ibid).

Initially, Indian migrant labours were engaged in the cultivation of tapioca, tea, coffee, and sugarcane, and the construction of railway and public works (ibid). Around 250,000 indentured Indian labourers arrived in Malaya between 1844 and 1910 (Sandhu, (1969). Moreover, there were free or independent migrants who came seeking trade and employment in private and government services.

There was a constant demand for unskilled labourers after introducing and expanding the rubber crop cultivation in the late nineteenth and early twentieth centuries. Assisted labour recruitment, the 'Kangany' system, was introduced in 1844, remaining in vogue till 1938. Kangany-assisted migration accounted for 62.2 percent of total Indian labour migration compared to 13 percent for indentured migration (Sandhu, (1969). The mass influx of unskilled Indian labourers led to monopolization of labour in the plantation sector.

Apart from labour immigrants, other skilled professionals and traders also immigrated voluntarily in large numbers to take up jobs in the colonial government. For instance, the recruitment of Sikhs as policemen, paramilitary forces, security guards, and caretakers became common. Immigrants from north India were primarily merchants, traders, shopkeepers, and peddlers. Gujarati traders were especially visible in the urban landscapes of Malaysia, selling silk and other textile goods in exchange for tin and other spices (Sandhu, (1969), (Arasaratnam, (1970). The Chettiars of the Tamil region of India played an essential role in the colonial economy of Malaya (Arasaratnam, (1970).

Locating Indian Women's Migration and Settlement

Indian women from different classes, regions, and caste backgrounds immigrated to Malaya. Since Singapore, Malacca, and Penang served as penal settlements for the British, the migration of Indian women to Malaya began as convicts. Based on available records, one female and seventy-three male convicts from Madras arrived in Singapore to serve life sentences on 18 April 1825 (Sandhu, (1969). One week later, it was reported that a hundred and twenty-two convicts, including one woman, arrived from Bengal to Singapore. The following year saw the arrival of another eighty men and three women.

The number of women convicts increased in pace with the surge in deported prisoners. These convicts assisted in the construction of the strait settlements, roads, buildings, and bridges. When en masse migration of Indian labourers to the Malayan plantations began during the nineteenth and twentieth centuries, Indian women were discouraged from following suit due to the transient nature of migration of their male counterparts.

The immigration was, therefore, primarily undertaken by men. Further, Indian patriarchy, culture, and tradition prevented women from emigrating (Dancz, (1987). Women were not allowed to leave independently, requiring them to be accompanied by either husbands or relatives. Safety concerns acted as a yet another deterrent against emigrating. Hence the number of women immigrants remained limited. Sandhu wrote that 'this predominantly male character of the Indian movement was because the majority of the Indian immigrants were simply 'birds of passage' or 'sojourners' in Malaya and preferred to leave their families in India (Sandhu, (1969).

Indian women, on account of their economic dependence, often accompanied their husbands who were hired as clerks, teachers, merchants, etc., from 1867-69 (ibid). Data about

Indian women immigrants to Malaya from 1867-1869, is shown in Table 3.1

S. No	Year	Indian Women Immigration	Total Indian Immigrants
01.	1867	264	8,697
02.	1868	225	10,268
03.	1869	188	10,268

Source: K.S. Sandhu. (1969). *Indians in Malaya, Immigration and Settlement 1786-1957*. Cambridge University Press. p. 311.

The 1891 census for British Malaya noted that the Indian female-to-male ratio was 18 per 1,000, while by 1901, this ratio had risen to 171 per 1,000 males (Arasaratnam, (1970). During the indenture period from the 1830s-1910s, women's migration was encouraged to meet growing demands of the labourers. As the rubber industry in the 1890s was expanding, it needed a cheap labour source. Sandhu adds that female immigrants accounted for 24 percent of the annual arrivals between 1901 and 1933. Most of these were probably wives travelling with or joining husbands already present in Malaya. Children, he noted, were seldom over 10 percent of the total number of immigrants (Sandhu, (1969).

In 1879, the sub-collector of Tanjore, Mr. Hathaway, observed that recruiting involved a regularly organized system of kidnapping. Further, female immigrants were destined to a life of prostitution (Kondapi, (1951). Hathaway's successor, Stokes, confirmed that the abduction of women and children did take place and that recruitment also occurred under duress (ibid). Sandhu also notes that 'women who have a passing quarrel with their husbands or parents are seduced away by females employed for the purpose, who bring them on board ship before they know what they have done' (Sandhu, (1969).

A second form of recruitment began in the last quarter of the nineteenth century. This was the 'Kangany' system of recruited labour. The Kangany system (1890s-1930s), which depended on kinship and village ties, perpetuated the South Indian connection and promoted female migration. Between 1891 and 1931, female to male ratio among Indian migrants jumped from 18 per 1000 in 1891 to 482 per 1000 by 1931. By this time, 20,2981 Indian women were present in Malaya (Vileland, (2014).

Though the number had improved, there was no slackening of traditional shackles away from the home shore. Concerns about their wives being enticed away to a foreign land generated considerable anxiety among the largely male labour force—there were higher incidences of promiscuity and certtu-k-kolu-tal (illegalunions) (Dancz, (1987). Colonial governments in India and Malaya took measures to increase the ratio of Indian women workers by reducing recruitment tax, introducing the Indian Immigration Act, 1922, and the Indian Immigration Regulations 1923, resolving to bring the ratio up to 1 woman per 1.5 men. (Sandhu, (1969).

Substantial numbers of Indian women came from South India. They were Tamil, Telugu, and Malayali. Other communities included the Sikhs, Punjabis, Bengalis, and Gujaratis. Almost 80 percent of the entire multitude of women was of Tamil descent (Annual Reports of Labour Department Malaya).

To encourage women's immigration, the Labour Department allocated extra allowances for married couples and a bonus to each child of a non-recruited immigrant (ibid). The Malayan Labour Ordinance of 1923 required that the estates provide paid maternity leave one month before and one month after delivery, and provide nursery crèches (ibid). The rubber industry offered more employment opportunities for women and children than the sugar and coffee industries. Yet, the sex ratio disparity always persisted in the plantations.

Socio-Cultural Life and Indian Women in Colonial Malaya

A usual cavalier attitude of the colonial administration towards labour welfare, as well as the factor of plantation work, was instrumental in the establishment of labour camps within these isolated spaces. Consequently, labourers in these plantations led a sequestered, segregated existence in a cocoon-like environment (Stenson, (1980).

Free from any substantive intervention or disruption in such isolated spaces, the continuation of traditional patriarchy remained unhindered among the Indian labour communities. Arranged marriage was the preferred choice. On the estates, the establishment of Hindu shrines facilitated the celebration of important festivals. Generally, existing in an unfamiliar space away from the homeland did not result in any significant disruption in traditional methods of control.

In Malaya, the plantations offered housing to enable the development of nuclear families, and it was easy for adult sons to set up separate households (Dancz (1987). Male authority was weakened to some extent as women often worked for wages (ibid). Importantly, divorcees and widows were able to remarry. Dissolution (of marriage) and divorce were possible for both, men and women although the scope was much narrower for the latter. It resulted in increasing instances of desertion by either partner. The subsequent growth of certtu-k-kolu-tal, or illegal unions, reflected higher incidences of broken marriages (ibid).

Thus, immigration to Malaya caused considerable disruption of the institution of marriage, causing plight, but also opening up avenues for immigrant Indian women to pursue their aspirations. Many women became wage labourers, which elevated their position within the family. Although such women were compelled to manage the dual role of employment and household, it could be asserted that migration indeed provided them with both control and agency in their own lives.

Devi Sarojini noted in her study of Indian women on a rubber plantation in 1970 that, Indian women remained subordinate to their husbands in almost all matters (Sarojini, (1971). These included the economy and politics of family life and the husband-wife relationship. The male dominance was noticeable in all external aspects of the family (ibid).

Status and Experience of Indian Women in the Plantation Economy of Colonial Malaya

As discussed above, Tamil/ Indian labourers monopolized the plantation sector of Malaya/Malaysia (Sandhu, (1969), and Arasartanam, (1970). The intake of female labour force was higher in rubber plantations than in coffee and sugar plantations (Dancz, (1987). With the expansion of rubber plantations during the nineteenth and twentieth centuries, female labour force participation in the plantation industry also increased.

The census conducted in 1921 listed 1,36,181 Indian women in Malaya, 73,084 among them working in agriculture and other economic sectors (Nathan, (1922). Indian women's employment in Malaya was largely concentrated in the agricultural sector (Dancz, (1987). Most such women lived in rural areas and earned low salaries (ibid).

Till the late nineteenth century, women comprised approximately 20-25 percent of the total immigrant labour force in Malaya (Sandhu, (1969). With the Indian Emigration Act of 1928, which was committed to increasing the female-to-male ratio on the plantations, these numbers started to increase consistently (Heyzer, (1986). Subsequently, female labour force participation in plantations increased to 35 percent by 1931 and later, to 43 percent of the total labour force in plantations (Vileland, (2014).

Management of rubber plantations preferred a female workforce for the following reasons: workload was not manageable with a male labour force alone; permanent labour force and labour control; payment of low wages to increase profitability (Dancz, (1987). Grinding poverty and an urgent need for supplementing the incomes earned by family men meant that Indian women were willing to work for low salaries.

Women workforce became a permanent feature of the rubber estates; women were employed in tapping, weeding, spraying, and rubber processing. They would be employed in similar capacities in palm oil plantations as well. However, they were never appointed to relatively higher positions such as field conductors or managerial staff, and would continue to toil at the lowest rung of the plantation system. Further, it was only in 1953 that equal pay between men and women was regularized (Dancz, (1987). For several years, wages of both, the wife and the husband, were paid directly to the latter (ibid).

Women routinely experienced verbal assault and sexual harassment by employers, supervisors, and male co-workers. Sexual assault was a common and frequent risk in the plantations. The Tambang rape case of 1925 is a classic example: a young Indian woman was held hostage and raped by the plantation manager of Tambang Estate in Johor (Amrith, (2010). They also suffered sexual abuse, divorce, adultery, desertion, and forced prostitution (Dancz, (1987). The kind of services that women mostly engaged in, such as weeding and spraying, resulted in the manifestation of several bodily effects such as peeling fingernails and respiratory infections. The lack of basic amenities and medical facilities on the plantation exacerbated these conditions further.

The women labour force was generally maintained as a reserve force. Any downsizing would, by default, sack women workers despite them contributing equal to their male counterparts. Indentured women had the burden of domestic household chores besides working on the plantations (Dancz, (1987). Mostly, women had to toggle between their domestic and occupational responsibilities. Young girls on the plantation were not encouraged to attend plantation school as they needed to mind the younger ones while their mothers were out for work. Only a few girls went to the plantation school which imparted Tamil medium education.

The schools were dilapidated and the teachers were underqualified. The education imparted had little to do with anything apart from essentially preparing future generations of labour forces. According to Coletta (1971), the plantation school was an instrument for the labouring class to push their children into the working class, instead of social mobility. The literacy level of Indian women was far behind that of Indian men. The productive and reproductive labour of Indian women facilitated capital accumulation, especially in the rubber business.

Experience of Indian Women under Japanese Occupation in Colonial Malaya

During the Japanese occupation of Malaya from 1941 to 1945, life became harder for the immigrant Indian community irrespective of class. The Indian labourers were the worst affected as the Japanese assumed ownership and administration of the plantations. The Syonan Rubber Syndicate was established by consolidating Japanese rubber companies, and aimed at assuming control of the rubber industry in Singapore and Malaya (Stenson, (1980).

As English men, including estate planters fled, the Japanese appointed Indian kiranis (clerical staff) as managers, and the kanganis (Tamil word referring to heads of coolie /labourer/ porter groups), as estate clerks and overseers to fill the vacuum of managerial staff on the estates (ibid). The Syndicate capped the maximum work ceiling for labourers between ten to fifteen days per month, and wages were paid daily, at rates 30 to 40 percent lesser than pre-war wages in British Malaya (ibid). Incentives of compliments and rewards from the Japanese overlords inspired the Indian kiranis to exert themselves with more authority and aggression (Jain, (1970). Often, citing meagre wages and the absence of adequate food, labourers struck work. But the kirani would raid the coolie lines to locate errant coolies and force them back to work.

The kirani would often force their way into coolie households, compelling coolie women to run out with nothing more than gunny bags to cover themselves (Jain, (1970). Without work, food, and medical care, mere survival became a constant challenge for the resident labourers. Michael Stenson notes that the Indian population of Malayan estates fell by 7 percent during the Japanese occupation (Stenson, (1980).

Plantation labourers were often forced by the Japanese to work on construction projects. Indian workers were forced to labour in various such projects including the infamous Thailand-Burma 'death railway' (Datta, (2015). Women were as well pressed into such forcefully extracted labour, although that was not always the case. While the men were hauled off by the Japanese military to work on these projects, the women were left alone on the plantations. Predictably, Japanese soldiers would often avail of such opportunities to enter the plantations and subject the women to sexual violence (Datta, (2015).

The shift from British to Japanese management following the invasion, made the excesses of British colonialism, particularly in context of plantation administration, stand in a much more favorable light than they deserved. Pachaimmal, wife of a plantation worker, Marimuthu Sabapathy, and an ex-plantation worker herself, communicated this sense in her narrative:

> We had a good life when the British were here; they treated us fine. They used to come regularly to the estates and send police to inspect the law and order in the estates—we were safe... During the Japanese, there was no plantation, no food and it was dangerous. Men were taken to the railway and we were taken to work on dockyards to bind fences... It was only after the British came back, that life went back to being normal again [Cited in Datta, (2015), p. 85].

Parents were often compelled to hide their daughters or send them away to some distant relative's place in order to protect them from being forced into sex slavery by the Japanese (Datta, (2015). A British Intelligence report from 1943 corroborated that women on the plantation were in constant fear of Japanese raids in the absence of their menfolk. In many instances, the kirani forcibly separated newly married coolie couples under Japanese supervision, sending the men off to work on the railway and forcing the wives to become their mistresses (Jain, (1970).

The scope of arbitrary and violent sexual intervention stood in full glare in one instance in Sivan, where a kirani 'advised' all women on the Pal Melayu Estate to consider him as their husband since their husbands were sent off to work on the 'death railway' (ibid)

Indian Nationalism and Experience of Indian Women in Colonial Malaya

Indian nationalism entered Malaya with the emergence of the Indian Independence League (IIL), a political organization formed in 1928 by Indian nationalists in the Southeast Asian region.

After assuming leadership of the IIL, Subhas Chandra Bose established the Rani of Jhansi Regiment (RJR), a women's infantry unit based in Malaya (and later in Singapore and Burma), in 1943 (Dancz, (1987), and Datta, (2015). Thousands of women responded to Bose's clarion call, swelling the ranks of the regiment. Though exact figures are unavailable, it is understood that a vast number of women joining the regiment were second-generation, illiterate coolie women of the Malaya plantations (Datta, (2015).

Following six months of intensive training, the first contingent consisting of five hundred women soldiers of the Rani of Jhansi Regiment left Singapore for Burma in 1943, reaching their destination by early January 1944. Dato Rasammah Bhupalan from Malaya was one of the youngest RJR recruits joining the force at the age of sixteen.

She described her excitement thus:

> The first all-women's regiment in the world was the Rani of Jhansi Regiment!... Come rain or storm you had to do your day and night marches, map readings... it was so exciting! We were no tin soldiers. We were real soldiers. We underwent all training of signals, map reading, shooting, charging, we shot 303 rifles and also machine guns among others... we were a part of such a great revolutionary army [Cited in Datta. (2015), p. 78].

There are conflicting views about the recruitment of women in the INA. On one hand, their joining the INA was perceived as an excellent opportunity to expand their life roles beyond motherhood and housework. On the other hand, though Bose personally believed in gender equality, he is believed to have had a political motive in engaging women in the RJR as a propaganda machine (Datta, (2015). Women on the battlefield were expected to rouse men into acknowledging their 'natural role' and responding to the call to arms. Despite its progressive outlook, in the field, women were entirely reduced to their stereotypical roles of caregiving consisting of nursing, cooking, and various logistical supports for the men. Despite his enormous stature and leadership capabilities, Bose was not impervious to the influence of tradition.

The typical mindset that permeated the INA and the RJR was reiterated in the recounting by Dr. Lakshmi Sahgal:

> The INA soldiers brought to the hospitals where the Ranis offered them care and support, were touched to the core to find a woman offering him a cool drink of water or sponging his feverish limbs. The wounded bit their lips and stifled their screams and curses when they found their most painful and foul-smelling dressings being changed by gentle hands and not the tough hands of the male orderlies [Cited in Datta, (2015), p. 95].

According to Menon, an ex-officer of the IIL, RJR was not a 'real fighting force'. Rather, it offered supplementary services to the real fighting force which was the INA. He said:

> It [the RJR] was a mere puppet show.——-. They are not going to fight, you know, but they are going to do another service for the army——the regular army... [Cited in Datta, (2015, p. 89)].

Further, according to Motiwalla, an Indian businessman who supplied stationery items to the INA, it was a propaganda force to inspire the Indian soldiers of the British Indian Army (BIA) to rebel against the British. To quote him,

> 'It [the RJR] was just propaganda. What Bose told us was, these were a handful of Indians [referring to RJR], which I have selected… [they] are not going to conquer India. And not only that, I don't trust each and everybody. Because once they cross the border, they might go home. Only some of them will stay. My purpose out of these recruits…is to transfer armour (sic) this British Indian Army in India to rebellion'. [Cited in Datta, (2015), p. 89].

Dato Bhupalan, the RJR veteran, echoed a similar sentiment, reiterating that RJR was used as a psychological force to influence the INA, as well as the BIA, to fight against the British (Datta, (2015), p. 90).

The RJR was also not impervious to class distinctions. Recruits from socially elite backgrounds discriminated against recruits from estate backgrounds (ibid). After INA's downfall at Imphal in 1945, the RJR recruits returned to Malaya.

Within the IIL, funds rotated only in the hands of the elites, bettering their conditions. These were never granted to recruits from the plantations (Datta 2015). On the whole, the ILI provided Indian women a platform to engage in anti-colonial politics.

Political Economy and Malaysian Indian Women in Post-Colonial Malaysia

Malaysia achieved its independence in 1957 from the British colonial yoke. An ethnicity-based political model, 'Consocial' or 'Consociational democracy' was adopted, and a ruling coalition, the Barisan Nasional (National Front), was formed, led by the United Malay National Organization (UMNO) and including immigrant-specific political parties like Malaysian Indian National Congress (MIC) and Malaysian Chinese Association (MCA). The coalition remained in power until recently.

While framing the Federal Constitution of Malaysia, as demanded by the Malay political elites, the doctrine of 'Ketuanan Melayu'(Malay Supremacy) was incorporated in Article 153, substantiating native Malay claims of the 'Bumiputera (Son of the soil). Hence, Malays are considered 'first among equals.'

Given its hegemonic political position, the United Malay National Organization (UMNO) has conveniently manipulated Article 153 to establish Malay ethnocracy and dominance over the years. As a result, the ethnic minorities of Chinese and Indian descent have been bearing the brunt of pro-majoritarian policy (Sandhu and Mani, (1993). Indians were especially crammed between economically strong Chinese and politically strong Malays. Subsequently, over the years, they were relegated to 'third race' or third-class citizens of the multi-racial Malaysian society (ibid).

In line with pro-Malay majoritarianism, the UMNO-led BN coalition government, by successive Prime Ministers, has implemented a slew of public policy measures to advance the economic interests of the majority Malay community. For instance, the social engineering policy or positive affirmative action policy, popularly known as the New Economic Policy (NEP), was an instrument of Malay economic nationalism. The extension of the policy as National Development Policy (NDP) and National Vision Policy (NVP) has reduced the economic equity and upward mobility of Malaysian Indians considerably over the years (Anbalakan, (2003).

It has led to diminishing employment opportunities for the Indian community in Malaysian public services. Therefore, the dismal participation of Indian women in Malaysian public services does not come as a surprise. However, given their cultural and social capital, Indian women from middle-class backgrounds could still join the private sector.

On account of crop diversification and fragmentation of plantations, retrenchment of the plantation labour force was once again on the rise. The Indian women workforce was first in this line of fire. Moreover, in the face of rapid urbanization and industrial development in recent decades, plantations are being sold off or promoted for property development, resulting in forced eviction and displacement of Indian plantation labourers from rural to urban areas, in search of employment opportunities (Nagarajan, (2000). The illiterate and unskilled Indian plantation labourers, including poor Indian women, added to the already bustling urban working classes, settling for lower wages and forced to live in squatter settlements on the urban fringes of important cities and towns.

Owing to pro-Malay policies in higher education, deserving Indian students cannot avail of scholarships and financial grants. Indian students could not avail of local and overseas JPA (Jabatan Perikhidmatan Awam or Public Service Department) scholarships, or secure matriculation seats and public university seats, despite having good grades. Par for the course, the situation affects the prospects of female students far more adversely.

Pro-Malay majoritarian public policies have substantially degraded the socio-economic position of the Malaysian Indian community over the years. Subsequently, the community has been rendered socio-economically disadvantaged. It is plagued with social ills like alcoholism, drug addiction, gang violence, domestic abuse, divorce, single motherhood, and suicide, (Krishnaswamy, (1992), Rajoo, (1993), and Oorjitham, (1993).

Socio-economic marginalization has taken a serious toll on the physical and mental well-being of Malaysian Indian women. According to a study by the Malaysian Mental Health Association, Malaysian Indian women are more prone to anxiety and depression, and more susceptible to diseases and suicide.

They therefore constitute a high-risk group (New Straits Times, 26 September, 2016). Social ills like domestic violence and child abuse were reported in the media. In 1994, one-fourth of 419 cases of wife-beating and 112 cases of child abuse were among Malaysian Indians (Far Eastern Economic Review, 19 October 1995).

Issues of Statelessness and Indian Women

In post-independence Malaysia, a large number of Indian plantation workers failed to register with the National Registration Department to obtain citizenship. This was due to a combination of ignorance and lack of accessibility from remotely located plantations. Combined with the fact that these workers were born and raised on Malaysian soil, it has rendered these generations of plantation workers stateless. Following is a case concerning this issue:

Case Study-Citra Dorai

Citra Dorai is fifteen years old. As she was born in Alor Setar prison, her parents did not register her birth. Her mother died, and her father deserted her. Along with her siblings, she stays with her aunt at present. The lack of a birth certificate has diminished her prospects of education in a society that is committed to a policy of universal education. For a similar reason, the girl could not obtain a national identity card.

Many poor children like her do not have birth certificates and national identity cards due to similar histories. Lack of such identification, more often than not, results in denial of fundamental rights and privileges.

Islamisation and Indian Women: Issues and Challenges

The Islamisation programme commenced during Prime Minister Mahathir Mohamad's rule and has been sustained by successive Prime Ministers. There are three stages of the Islamisation programme executed by the UMNO-led government to promote Malay Muslim religious nationalism. The first stage comprises initiatives in education, Islamising architectures of new government buildings, revising dietary and dress practices, and establishment of Suraus and Islamic townships.

The second stage saw the expansion and progressive establishment of Islamic institutions such as Islamic banks, universities, Islamic centres, and mosques. The Pusat Islam (Islamic Center) was established under the aegis of the Prime Minister's department to play a vital role in implementing government-led Islamisation projects (Mauzy and Milne, (1999). The third phase included the Islamisation of laws and the expansion of the jurisdiction of the Syariah court over the civil court. Article 121(1A) was incorporated through constitutional amendment. The Article prohibits civil courts from extending jurisdiction over matters under the jurisdiction of Syariah courts. Finally, the high point of Islamisation was marked by the declaration of Malaysia as an Islamic state in 2001, during Prime Minister Mahathir Mohammed's rule (Martinez, (2001).

Given the conspicuous backing of the state to the project of Islamisation, at least since the 1980s, conversion to Islam is carried out by certain Islamic groups hand in glove with the State Religious Department. Poor working-class Indians are most vulnerable to such actions. Often, families are kept in the dark about the conversion of a family member. Consequently, it affects inheritance, matrimonial rights, and the religious status of children. Moreover, it increases involuntary converts like Banggarma of Perak, Rani from Malacca, and Regina Mohd.

Zaini alias Krishnan, her sister, Rajiwah Krishnan alias Mohd. Zaini, and brother Rajeni Mohd. Zaini, of Johor Baru. They were either not aware of their conversion to Islam or were forced to convert in light of their parents' conversion

Case Study-1: Banggarma

Banggarma was born on 13 August 1982, at Keratong in Pahang, to plantation worker parents B. Subramaniam and Latchumy Ramadu. As a child, she was sent to a welfare home at Kepala Batas in Penang. She fled the home, along with some inmates, at the age of sixteen. Later, she married a fisherman, S. Socka Lingam in 2000 and lived at Tanjun Piandung in Perak thereafter. At present, she has two children: Kanagaraj, aged eight, and Hisyanthini, aged two. She became aware of her conversion while trying to register her marriage with Socka Lingam. She found that her Muslim name was Siti Hasnah Vangarama Abdullah. Following this discovery, she filed a petition at the Penang high court to change her name and nullify her conversion to Islam. She deposed that she was converted by the State Religious Islamic Affairs Department during her residence at the welfare home, at the age of 7, sans her knowledge and consent. The Penang high court turned down her petition on 4 August 2010, contending that Judicial Commissioner Yaacob Sam had declared the twenty-eight years old mother of two as a Muslim and therefore, she would have to take up her 'unwitting' conversion dispute with the Syariah court as the civil court has no jurisdiction to hear a case involving conversion to Islam. She called the verdict unfair and unrealistic. She said, 'I am always Hindu and I will die as a Hindu.' Her lawyer Gooi Hsiao Leung has prepared documents to file an appeal against Yaacob's decision.

Case Study-2: Indira Gandhi

Indira Gandhi is a kindergarten school teacher of Malaysian Indian descent. She married K. Pathmanathan through Hindu rites fourteen years ago. They have three children, Tevi Darsiny, thirteen years, Karan Dinish, twelve years, and Prasana Diksa, all of twenty-three months. In March 2009, Pathmanathan suggested that the family should embrace Islam for the sake of economic advantage. But, she refused and argued that she wanted to remain Hindu. Incensed by her denial, Pathmanthan took away their third child Prasana Diksa, who was then 11 months old, cut off ties with Indira, and started living in another state called Kelantan. Indira lodged a police complaint. The police told her that her husband embraced Islam in early March of 2009 and had changed his name to Mohd. Ridzuan Abduallah.

She further learnt that all three of her children were converted on 3 April 2009, without her consent or knowledge. Indira sought custody of the third child. Since her husband was now a Muslim, and so were her children, the Syariah court intervened and gave its judgement in favour of Pathmanathan who won custody of the children. But, she took her fight to the civil court to nullify the conversion of her children and gain their custody. The lawyer, Kulasegaran, represented her. Her case hearing took place on 11 March 2010.

The Perak high court ruled in favour of Indira by overruling the decision of the Syariah court. She could finally get the custody of her third child. The Religious Department objected to the civil court adjudicating over Islamic matters. Her husband applied for a stay of execution on the high court order since he has legal impunity being a Muslim. Indira's legal impasse is still not resolved, and her childrens' religious status remains to be determined.

The intrusion of Syariah law upon secular laws impinges upon the rights of Indian Hindu women. In the absence of legal rights, the legal impasse continues, with the religious status of Indian Hindu women hanging in limbo.

In Lieu of Conclusion

The migration of Indian women to Malaysia has emancipated them from some aspects of repressive Indian social and cultural traditions. At the same time, the ethnicity-based socio-economic and political systems of colonial and post-colonial Malaysia have impacted the status and experiences of the current generation of Indian women in Malaysia. Given the repressive socio-economic structures and gender stereotypes, there has been limited scope for them to use their agency.

Due to intersectional factors like class, gender, race, and ethnicity, women have experienced exploitation, discrimination, subordination, deprivation, alienation, and marginalization at various levels through colonial and post-colonial periods. As discussed above, the Malaysian Indian community is a marginalized group, or ethnic minority. Within this group, women experience a 'double marginalization' given their fundamental vulnerabilities. Despite such oppressive socio-economic marginalization, Indian women have managed to cope with the prevailing challenges through colonial and post-colonial times. Some of them have turned their adversity into advantage by inventing survival strategies in a coercive and oppressive socio-political milieu, and carving a niche for themselves in various walks of life.

Authors note: This essay is a humble tribute and a token of gratitude to Prof. Renuka Singh, who introduced me to the academic fields namely, gender, society, and youth and society, during my academic pursuits at the Centre for the Study of

Social Systems (CSSS) in Jawaharlal Nehru University (JNU). Further, she was my supervisor for the fulfilment of the award of M.Phil. and Ph.D. degrees.

References

Anbalakan. K. (2003). The New Economic Policy and further Marginalization of the Indians. *Kajian Malaysia,* 11(1&2), 379-399.

Amrith, Sunil S. (2010). Indians Overseas? Governing Tamil Migration to Malaya 1870–1941. Past & Present. 208,(1), 231–261,

Arasaratnam, Sinnaph. (1970). Indians in Malaysia and Singapore. Oxford University Press.

Crenshaw, K. (1989). Demarginalizing the intersection of race and sex. In A black Feminist Critique of Antidiscrimination doctrine, Feminist theory, and Antiracist politics. (pp.139–167). University of Chicago Legal Forum. (Reprinted from *The Politics of Law:* A Progressive Critique, pp.195–217 by David Kairys, Ed., 1990, Pantheon)

Colletta, N.J. (1971). Malaysia's Forgotten People: Education, Cultural Identity and Socio-Economic Mobility among South Indian Plantation Workers. *Contributions to Asian Studies,* 7, 87-112.

Datta, Arunima. (2015). Social Memory and Indian women from Malaya and Singapore in the Rani of Jhansi Regiment. *Journal of Malaysian Branch of Royal Asiatic Society.*88(2), 309, 77-103.

Dancz,Viginia. H. (1987). Women and Party Politics in Peninsular Malaysia. Oxford University Press.

Dhamoon, R.K. (2011). Considerations on mainstreaming intersectionality. *Political Research Quarterly, 64*(1), 230–243.

Else-Quest, N.M., & Hyde, J. S. (2016). Intersectionality in quantitative psychological research II. Methods and techniques. *Psychology of Women Quarterly, 40*(2), 155–170.

Janaki, Athi Nahappan. (1992). *The Rani of Jhansi Regiment in Netaji Subhas Chandra Bose: A Malaysian Perspective.* Netaji Centre.

Jain, Ravindra. (1970). South Indians on the Plantation Frontier in Malaya.Yale University Press.

Kaur, A. (2006). Indian Labor, Labor Standards, and Workers' Health in Burma and Malaya, 1900-1940, Modern Asian Studies, 40(2), 425-475. https://doi.org/10.1017/S0026749X06001788
Kaur, A. (2006). Indian Labor, Labor Standards, and Workers' Health in Burma and Malaya, 1900-1940, Modern Asian Studies, 40(2), 425-475. https://doi.org/10.1017/S0026749X06001788

Kaur, A. (2006). Indian Labor, Labor Standards, and Workers' Health in Burma and Malaya, 1900-1940, Modern Asian Studies, 40(2), 425-475. https://doi.org/10.1017/S0026749X06001788
Kaur, Amarjit. (2006). Indian Labour, Labour standards and Workers Health in Burma and Malaya, 1900-1940. *Modern Asian Studies,* 40(2), 425-475.

Krishanan, R.B. (1936). Indians in Malaya: A Pageant of Greater India: A rapid survey of over 2,000 years of maritime and colonising activities across the Bay of Bengal. Malayan Publishers.

Krishanswamy, Saroja. (1992). Alcoholism in Malaysia. In Cho Kah Sin and Ismail Mohd Salleh (Eds.), *Caring society.* ISIS Malaysia.

Kondapi, C. (1951). Indian Overseas 1838-1949. Oxford University Press.

Mauzy, D. K. and R.S. Milne. (1983-84). The Mahathir Administration in Malaysia: Discipline through Islam. *Pacific Affairs,* 56(4), 617-48.

Martinez, Patricia A. (2001). The Islamic State or the State of Islam in Malaysia. *Contemporary South East Asia,* 23(3), 474-503.

Nathan, J.E. (1922). The Census of British Malaya. Waterlow and Sons.

Nagarajan. S. (2000). Marginalization and Ethnic Relations: The Indian Malaysian Experience. In Lim Teck Ghee, Alberto Gomes and Azly Rahman(Eds.), *Multi-ethnic Malaysia: Past, Present and Future* (369-90). Strategic Information Research Development (SIRD).

Oorijitham, Susan K. S. (1993a). Urban Working-Class Indians in Malaysia. In A. Mani and K. S. Sandhu (Eds.), *Indian Communities in South East Asia.* Times Academic Press and ISEAS.

Rajoo.R. (1993). Indian Squatter Settlers- Indian Rural-Urban Migration in West Malaysia. In A. Mani and K.S. Sandhu (Eds.),

Indian Communities in South East Asia (484-503). Times Academic Press and ISEAS.

Sandhu, Kernial Singh. (1969). Indians in Malaya: Some Aspects of their Immigration and Settlement (1786-1957). Cambridge University Press.

___and A. Mani (eds.). (1993). *Indian Communities in Southeast Asia.* Times Academic Press and ISEAS.

Sarojini, D.A. (1971). Socio-Economic Aspects of Women Plantation Workers: A Case Study of the Indian Women workers of Ladang Tengah (Unpublished BA Graduation Exercise). University of Malaya.

Stenson, Michael. (1980). Class, Race and Colonialism in West Malaysia: The Indian Case. University of Queensland press.

Syamala Nair Gopal and Mahani Musa. (2020). Indian Women During the Japanese Occupation in Malaysia, 1941-1945. International Conference on Humanities, European Proceedings of Social and Behavioural Sciences, 531-539, DOI: 10.15405/epsbs.2020.10.02.48

United Nations. (2000). Gender and racial discrimination: Report of the Expert Group Meeting, November 21–24. Zagreb: Croatia.

Vileland, C.A.(2014). British Malaya: A Report on the 1931 Census(1932). In David Sunderland, (Ed), Economic Development in Southeast Asia, 1880-1939(Vol.3.)(pp. 246-51).Routledge.

Wiebe, P. and Mariappan. (1978). Indian Malaysian: The View from the Plantation. Manohar Publisher.

ACKNOWLEDGEMENTS

This volume was conceived in honour of our teacher, Professor Renuka Singh, who has significantly contributed to our academic journey. I am grateful to the contributors of this volume as without their efforts, this book would not have been a reality. I am also grateful to my teacher, Professor K.L. Sharma, for writing the foreword for this book. I would like to thank Mr Ravi Singh, Publisher and Co-Founder of Speaking Tiger, and his team, particularly Mr. Deep Narayan Chatterjee, for their support in making this volume possible. I would like to thank all my colleagues at CSSS, JNU for their constant support.

NOTES

Disciplined Body of Widows: A Sociological Analysis

1. The concept of the panopticon serves as a foundational framework for understanding the discipline and docility imposed upon the widow's body. Foucault explores the notion of discipline through societal rules and norms, elucidating how individuals conform to these standards within communities (Foucault, 1995). Central to his discourse is the panopticon, notably articulated by Jeremy Bentham, which consists of prison cells arranged around a central watchtower. Foucault illustrates how surveillance from this central watchtower exercises psychological control over individuals, fostering self-discipline and adherence to institutional parameters (Foucault, 1995; Dolezal, 2010:361). The panopticon operates on the principle of constant monitoring, instilling fears of judgment and punishment within subjects and concurrently cultivating self-restraint (Dolezal, 2010:362). In this context, physical coercion becomes unnecessary, as the mere awareness of being observed shapes behaviour and engenders a sense of internalized control (Foucault, 1995).

Death Rituals Among Odia Hindus: An Ethnographic Account

1. Preta rites
2. Karma theory
3. Salvation
4. Census, 2011, Government of India.

5. Riley, J.W.Jr. (1983). Dying and the Meanings of Death: Sociological Inquiries. *Annual Review of Sociology*, Vol. 9, 191-216
6. Tylor, Edward, B. (1981), *Anthropology: An Introduction to The Study of Man and Civilization*. London: Macmillan (p343-44)
7. Hertz, R. (2004). *Death and the Right Hand*. Oxon: Routledge Page (27-28)
8. Hertz, R. (2004). *Death and the Right Hand*. Oxon: Routledge Page (27-28)
9. Radcliffe-Brown, A.R. (1968) Taboo, on Studies in Social and Cultural Anthropology, *Ed.* John Middleton. New York: Thomas A. Crowell Co., pp. 175-195.
10. Swami, S. (1968), *The Bhagavad Gita*. Tehri-Garhwal:. Divine life society
11. Swami, S. (1968). *The Bhagavad-Gita*, Divine life Society. Tehri-Garhwal:. Divine life society .
12. Ibid p (346)
13. Blochm, M. & Parry, J.(ed). (1982). *Death and the regeneration of life*. London:Cambridge University Press.
14. Parry, J. (1982). Sacrificial death and the Necrophagous ascetic, Bloch, M and Parry, J (ed) *Death and regeneration of life*.New York: Cambridge University Press

Menstruation and Ritual Symbolism

1. Lee, Janet. (1994). Menarche and the (Hetero) Sexualizationof the Female Body. *Gender & Society* 8(3): 344
2. Seat of power
3. https://directortourism.assam.gov.in/frontimpotentdata/ambubachi-festival, accessed on 25-05-2021, time 9:00 hours
4. Vagina or Vulva
5. Sanctum sanctorum
6. This popular story takes us to the marriage union of Shiva and Sati and the disapproval of Sati's father, Daksha towards his son-in-law. So, when King Daksha organized a yagna inviting the lords and kings of the three worlds, he intentionally avoided inviting his daughter and her husband. This infuriated Sati that despite

being forbidden by her husband, she reached the Yagna spot where her father insults her presence as well as her husband. The hurl of abuse towards her husband enraged her who in a fit of anger committed suicide by throwing herself into the sacrificial fire. When the news of her self-immolation reached Shiva, his rage knew no bounds. He destroyed the yagna, beheaded Daksha (later replaced his head with the head of a goat) and threatened the existence of the entire universe with his destructive dance (*tandava*) carrying the corpse of his wife. To save the universe and its existence, Vishnu used his Sudarshan chakra and dismembered the body which was scattered in various parts of the world. Her Yoni is believed to have fallen in the place where the temple exists today.

7. Ten great Mother Goddesses of Wisdom
8. https://directortourism.assam.gov.in/portlet-sub-innerpage/temples-pilgrimages accessed on 22-10-2020 at 16:45 hours
9. A custom of ritual seclusion observed by Assamese Hindu households who believe in Sakti worship or Goddess worship, where they avoid any kind of religious events, have restrictions in diet, daily worships, and keeps a separate part of the household where one is not allowed to enter.
10. https://www.tourmyindia.com/blog/ambubachi-mela-kamakhya-temple/ assessed on 16-10-2022, time 20:00 hours
11. Yinger, J. (1958). The Influence of Anthropology on Sociological Theories of Religion. *American Anthropologist. 60*(3). New series, 488
12. Occurrence of the first menstrual period in a female adolescent
13. Buckley, T., & Gottlieb, A. (1988). *Blood magic: The Anthropology of Menstruation.* University of California Press: Berkeley, 3
14. Muthukumar S., David. (2019). *Goddess Spirituality in Feminism,* Pre-printed, 6
15. Eller, C. (2000). Divine Objectification: The Representation of Goddesses and Women in Feminist Spirituality. *Journal of Feminist Studies in Religion, 16*(1), 27

16. Earlier name of Assam
17. Festival means a recurring social occasion that happens periodically through various forms, where members of a society participate directly or indirectly united by linguistic, religious, ethnic, and a historical world-view.
18. Mela provides a competitive space for a periodic gathering where buyers and sellers meet at an appointed place.
19. Marglin, Frederique Apffel. (1985). Female Secuality in the Hindu World. *In Imaculate and Powerful: The Female Sacred Image and Social Reality*, eds., by Clarrisa W. Atkinson, Constance H. Buchanan and Margaret R. Miles. Beacon Press: Boston, 44
20. Summers-Effler, E. (2006). Ritual Theory. In: Stets, J.E., Turner, J.H. (eds) *Handbook of the Sociology of Emotions. Handbooks of Sociology and Social Research*. Springer, Boston, MA, 136

Building and Sustaining a Spiritual Organisation: A Case Study of Sri Aurobindo Society

1. Clarke, G. (2007). Agents of transformation? donors, faith-based organisations and international development. *Third World Quarterly*, *28*(1), 77–96. https://doi.org/10.1080/01436590601081880
2. Bradley, T. (2010). *Religion and Gender in the Developing World: Faith-Based organisations and Feminism in India (Library of Development Studies)*. Tauris Academic Studies.

Exploring the '*Other*' in Hindu Mytho-Epic Imagination: A Gendered Rereading

1. Here I am referring to the Jungian *shadow archetype*, the reason for this will be elaborated on in the following sections of the chapter.
2. As play on words go, the argument for it was persuasive.
3. This assumption is based on Levi-Strauss's approach to myths and mythological texts from a linguistic structural perspective. See: (Gras, 1981; Levi-Strauss, 1955)
4. Among Jung's most important work was his in-depth analysis of the psyche, which he explained as follows: 'By psyche I understand the

totality of all psychic processes, conscious as well as unconscious,' separating the concept from conventional concept of the mind, which is generally limited to the processes of the conscious brain alone. See: http://journalpsyche.org/tag/jung-and-collective-unconscious/

5. The theory of the collective unconscious is one of Jung's more unique theories: Jung believed, unlike many of his contemporaries, that all the elements of an individual's nature are present from birth, and that the environment of the person brings them out (rather than the environment creating them).
6. See: Janaky. (1992). On the Trail of the Mahabharata: A Response. Economic and Political Weekly. Vol. 27(37). pp. 1997-1999. https://www.jstor.org/stable/4398882
7. This paragraph is partly an unsophisticated rereading of the Ramayana and The Mahabharata, with elemental events as core story lines. Focusing more on the specific gendered aspects of events, decisions and histories.
8. Which is a quite Jungian notion, bearing conceptual bearings to his observations on human psyche, and especially to the shadow archetype.
9. Section 377 has since been turned over, and homosexuality in this country has been officially decriminalized. However, the reality of the prejudice and disinformation along with social isolation of sexual minorities is a much more insidious than accepted. See: https://economictimes.indiatimes.com/news/politics-and-nation/sc-delivers-historic-verdict-hereseverything-you-need-to-know-about-section-377/articleshow/65698429.cms
10. It is important to note that, the narratives used here have been recorded and translated from Bengali to English, often summarized, when the respondent would digress from topic, or deflect to avoid speaking painful truths. Some interviews were conducted over months, and had to be edited down to extract usable material. However, the core essence of each individual's story was maintained with utmost loyalty to the spoken word.
11. Important to note here that the narratives used in this work are

excerpts of longer discussions. I have only included introductory sections, and general information about the cases, without going into the indepth discussions on their experiences.

12. Though the narrator clarifies this, 'trans-sexuality' represents a part of the queer spectrum where the assigned gender-sexuality does not match their psychic association. In this case, the narrator is physiologically male, but internally they are a woman. Their gender association makes them transgender, but in their sexuality experience they are attracted to the same sex—so a lesbian in this case—hence a transsexual lesbian.
13. '*cis*' gender represents those who identify with their external/ physical gender at birth, or biological sex. See also: https:// theconversation.com/explainer-what-does-it-mean-to-be-cisgender-103159

Urban Women and Matters of Land: An Analysis of Land Politics in Urban India through Gendered Lens

1. Grown, Caren, et al., 'Taking Action: Achieving Gender Equality and Empowering Women,'2005.
2. Steinzor, Nadia. 'Women's Property and Inheritance Rights: Improving Lives in a Changing Time,'2003.
3. Ibid
4. See UN Habitat web page '*Making Urbanization Work Equally for Women and Men.*' http://www.unhabitat.org.
5. The Millennium Development Goals (MDGs) reflect the multiple dimensions of poverty. In establishing these goals, the development community also recognized the link between poverty and the situation of women by making the promotion of gender equality and empowerment of women one of the primary goals.
6. Food and Agriculture Organization of the United Nations (FAO). '*Women's Right to Land: A Human Right,*' 2002.
7. Section 3(2) of the Judicature Act. (Cap. 8 Laws of Kenya).
8. For example, in the Millennium Challenge Corporation (MCC) land tenure program in Mali, experts determined that joint titling would be far more difficult to achieve than allocating separate

market garden plots to women, even though the program promotes joint titling for commercial property. Women receive tenure rights to the garden plots through membership in a small association of women rather than directly since inheritance norms would have meant that the plots would revert to sons or husbands in the event of the woman's death.

9. Land reform is generally understood to mean the statutory division and re-allocation of large plots of land, usually owned by the government but sometimes by large private estates, to achieve more equitable distribution and greater productivity. While land reform is often thought of in a rural context, it could also take place in peri- urban or urban areas where large plots of land are often underutilized.
10. World Bank Group 'Jordan NOW: Building Confidence, Creating Job Opportunities, Changing Lives,' 2010.
11. The World Bank Group, 'Women, Business and the Law 2010,' 2010.
12. UNICEF. 'Gender Equality-the big picture,' 2004.
13. Chen, Martha Atler. 'Women and Informality: A Global Picture, the Global Movement.'
14. USAID. 'Women in the Economy: A Review of Recent Literature,' 2006.
15. World Bank Group, 'Why is women's economic empowerment important for development?' Available at http://siteresources.worldbank.org/INTGENDER/Resources/womens_economic_empowerment.pdf(undated).
16. USAID. 'Enhancing Women's Access to Markets: An Overview of Donor Programs and Best Practices,' 2007.
17. USAID. 2006.
18. USAID. 2005.

Women and Violence in the Workplace in India

1. UN (2021), Commission on Status of Women, Sixty-fifth session, 15-26 March 2021, Report of the Secretary General, Economic and Social Council, United Nations.

2. Please see https://www.undp.org/content/undp/en/home/sustainable-development-goals/goal-5-gender-equality.html
3. https://www.ilo.org/global/standards/introduction-to-international-labour-standards/lang--en/index.htm. The concept of decent work was coined by ILO in 1999 which comprises ensuring the workers employment, social protection, workers rights and social dialogue.
4. https://www.ilo.org/dyn/normlex/en/f?p=NORMLEXPUB:12100:0::NO::P12100_ILO_CODE:C190
5. https://www.ilo.org/dyn/normlex/en/f?p=NORMLEXPUB:12100:0::NO::P12100_ILO_CODE:C190
6. This is explained in the convention 190 2019 of the ILO.
7. https://www.ilo.org/dyn/normlex/en/f?p=NORMLEXPUB:12100:0::NO:12100:P12100_ILO_CODE:R206:NO
8. The international labour standards on Occupational safety and health includes the Occupational Safety and Health Convention, 1981 (No155) and the Promotional Framework for Occupational Safety and Health Convention, 2006 (No 187).
9. This judgement was passed in 1997 in the case of a social worker Bhanwari Devi who was employed with the government of Rajasthan in a rural development programme. She was also against child marriage and was attempting to stop such practices for which she was raped by the men of the village.A case was filed in the Rajasthan high court which later on led to the Vishaka guidelines.
10. Paper prepared for the ILO in 2019 on Overview of Laws, Policies and Practices on Sexual Harassment and Violence: Specific focus on India, Sri Lanka and Afghanistan, International Labour Organization, New Delhi.
11. The POSH Act 2013 in Gazette of India ,22 April 2013.
12. Ibid.
13. http://www.shebox.nic.in/user/about_shebox
14. https://indiankanoon.org/doc/87321004/
15. GSR 729E Draft Rules on OSH Code, 2020 notified on 19th November 2020, Ministry of Labour and Employment, Government of India. A Socio-Legal Perspective.

Marrying Out: Why Khasi Women Marry Non-Khasi Men?

1. Extract from the poem 'For Sale' by Lyngdoh, P. (2009). In R.S. Ngangom, & K.S. Nongkynrih, *Dancing Earth: An Anthology of Poetry from North-East India* (p. 171). New Delhi: Penguin Books.
2. Non-Khasi means a person not belonging to indigenous Khasi tribe classified as Scheduled Tribe under the Constitution (Scheduled Tribe) order, 1950 (Part III- Rules and Orders under the Constitution) Part XI-Meghalaya.
3. As per the then CEM of the Khasi Hills Autonomous District Council (KHADC), this bill was necessitated due to 'the repercussions of mix marriage and laws that are unable to protect the indigenous people vis-à-vis the immigration crisis which according to him pose an imminent danger for the minority Khasi community.' He termed this threat a 'silent invasion' (*Shillong Times*, 2018, July 25).

African Diaspora in India: Cultural Hybridity, Memory, and Human Ecology

1. Nizams were Muslim rulers in India.

Negotiating Masculinities: A Case of Male Sex Workers in Mumbai

1. I take my role as per the demands of others. Source: Extract of an interview with my respondent Sameer, this was in response to my question about how he identifies himself. on June 24th, 2016 at 4:30 pm at Gaurav office in Juhu Koliwada, Mumbai.

ABOUT THE AUTHORS

Anindita Tagore, a Ph.D. in Sociology from Jawaharlal Nehru University, New Delhi. Dr. Tagore, post her Ph.D joined Educational Initiatives, where she has developed workshops for government school educators, focusing on learning outcomes, assessment design, and social science education. She has collaborated with the Govt. of Nagaland, CISCE, and CBSE, focusing on improving Class 10th and 12th board examinations.

Elizabeth Imti, Ph.D from JNU, is the Program Officer for the Indigenous Women Program at AIPP, Thailand. With a robust background in the Civil Society sector, she has been a catalyst for change, advocating passionately for the rights and empowerment of indigenous women across Asia. She has accumulated rich experiences as an independent consultant for NGOs in India and as an Assistant Professor at Fazl Ali College, Nagaland, India. Dr.Imti stands as a noteworthy contributor, leaving an indelible mark on the landscape of indigenous rights and women's empowerment in Asia.

Ellina Samantroy is a Sociologist working as Fellow at the V.V. Giri National Labour Institute (VVGNLI). She has completed her Ph.D from the Centre for Study of Social Systems, School of Social Sciences, Jawaharlal Nehru University, New Delhi. Her research interests include unpaid work, time use studies, gender statistics, work and family life balance, gender and social protection, child labour, labour regulation and international labour standards. She has published extensively on gender issues in the form of books, research monographs, chapters in edited volumes papers and articles in peer-reviewed academic journals.

Geetanjali Atri is an Assistant Professor (Sociology) at Symbiosis Law School, Hyderabad, a constituent of Symbiosis International (Deemed) University, Pune. She has received her doctorate from Centre for the Study of Social Systems, Jawaharlal Nehru University. Her research interest lies at the intersection of religion, identity and politics. She has published in several peer reviewed journals and is also a regular contributor of course material at the Indira Gandhi National Open University.

Himashree Sarma is a passionate social development sector professional who has completed her graduation from Hindu College, Delhi University; post-graduation from Jamia Millia Islamia, and MPhil & PhD from Jawaharlal Nehru University, in the discipline of Sociology. Currently, she is working with World Resources Institute-India, which is an international research organization that turns ideas into action at the junction of environment, economic opportunity, and human well-being.

Ipsita Mitra is a Literacy and ELL Teacher with Jadis Blurton Family Development Center, Hong Kong. She obtained her doctorate in sociology, specialising in spirituality and social welfare from JNU in 2018. She has also worked with children on the learning spectrum as part of this assignment. She currently specialises in Orton-Gillingham and LBLP methods to support young learners in their literacy journey.

Kamalini Mukherjee is a faculty, Department of Sociology at the Bhawanipur Education Society College, Kolkata. She has completed her Ph.D from the Centre for the Study of Social Systems, JNU, New Delhi.

Koyal Verma is an Assistant Professor at School of Liberal Arts, Bennett University. She has been awarded her Ph.D. in Sociology from the Centre for the Study of Social Systems, School of Social Sciences, Jawaharlal Nehru University. She has recently published a book titled 'African Clusters in India'. She has an active record of publications in the area of African diaspora, gender, urban studies, migration, religion and identity. Her research interests lie in the areas of race and ethnicity, African studies, migration and gender.

M. Mahalingam is currently working as Associate Professor (Social Sciences) at the Faculty of Law of SGT University, Gurugram, Delhi-NCR, India. He has numerous research publications to his credit.

Nilanjana Goswami is an Assistant Professor in the Department of Humanities and Social Sciences, BITS Pilani, K.K. Birla Goa Campus. She has dedicated the past 6-7 years to conducting research at the dynamic intersection of ageing and gender. Her profound expertise in these fields is showcased in her recent accomplishment—an edited book titled 'Discourses on Ageing'.

Reenu Ram is Assistant Professor in the Department of Social Work, Delhi University. She has completed her Masters from University of Delhi and Ph.D from Centre for the Study of Social Systems, Jawaharlal Nehru University. Her interests include gender and sexuality, LGBTQI, HIV, sexual and reproductive health rights, ecology and sustainability and law and human rights.

Sarah Jayal Sawkmie is a civil servant. Her research interests include cross-cultural marriages, popular culture, youth and tribal sociology. She graduated in Sociology from Lady Shri Ram College, New Delhi and completed her Masters, M. Phil. and Ph.D. in Sociology from the Centre for the Study of Social Systems, Jawaharlal Nehru University.